WITH THE COMPLIMENTS
OF
THE INTERNATIONAL CULTURAL SOCIETY OF KOREA
C.P.O. BOX 2147 SEOUL, KOREA

Main Currents of Korean Thought

Main Currents of Korean Thought

Edited by
the Korean National Commission for
UNESCO

The Si-sa-yong-o-sa Publishers, Inc., Korea
Pace International Research, Inc., U.S.A.

Published simultaneously in KOREA and the UNITED STATES

KOREA EDITION
First printing 1983
The Si-sa-yong-o-sa Publishers, Inc.
5-3 Kwanchol-dong, Chongno-ku
Seoul 110, Korea

U.S. EDITION
First printing 1983
Pace International Research, Inc.
Tide Avenue, Falcon Cove
P.O. Box 51, Arch Cape
Oregon 97102, U.S.A.

ISBN: 0-89209-020-0

This book is a co-publication by The Si-sa-yong-o-sa Publishers, Inc.
and The International Communication Foundation.

Foreword

The Korean people are artistic, expressing their innermost being in pottery, painting, poetry, drama, music and dance. To most foreigners familiar with Chinese and Japanese art, Korean art comes as a profound revelation and a delightful experience. Korean art differs from the strong, bold aspects of continental Chinese art and from the dazzling colours of Japanese art. Its basic characteristic is simplicity, reinforced by the atmosphere of quiet and serenity which it creates.

Following the publication of *Modern Korean Short Stories*, the Korean National Commission for UNESCO embarked upon a new project, dedicated to seeking real character of Korean culture. This new series deals with various aspects of Korean culture—language, thought, fine arts, music, dance, theatre and cinema, etc. It concentrates on baring the roots of the Korean cultural tradition and demonstrating the process of its transformation. It is hoped in this way to reveal the framework of traditional thought which is fundamental to any understanding of Korea's past and present.

Profound thanks are due to the writers of the individual articles and to the generous sponsorship of the Si-sa-yong-o-sa Publishers, Inc., who once again have turned a dream into a reality. This series, edited by the Korean National Commission for UNESCO, is published by the Si-sa-yong-o-sa Publishers, Inc., in commemoration of the thirtieth anniversary of the Korean National Commission for UNESCO.

Bong Shik Park
Secretary-General
The Korean National Commission
for UNESCO

Contents

Contents

Introduction

A basic knowledge of religious and philosophical thought is fundamental to an understanding of the Korean mind. The introduction of Buddhism, Taoism and Confucianism has accompanied the historical development of the Korean people from ancient times through the Three Kingdoms period, the Silla era and the Yi dynasty and has been instrumental to the formation of the unique national thought patterns of the Korean people. These thought patterns achieve a sense of harmony stratified like layers within the thought pattern of the modern Korean of today. In order to understand the Korean perspective upon the world and humanity the meaning of the main currents of these thought patterns must be grasped.

This collection of seventeen essays, selected from among the writings of Korean scholars, should be of assistance to the understanding of the main currents of Korean thought.

Wŏnhyo, Wŏn'gwang and Hyujŏng were Korean priests and Yi T'oegye and Yi Yulgok were two great Confucian scholars who lived in the Yi dynasty. These theses on Korean Confucianism will provide an understanding of the social norms and the political obligations of Yi dynasty society as well as the basic cultural concepts. They will also assist in giving a grasp of the ethos of the classical scholars among the literati.

Included in this volume are two essays about Pak Che-ga and Chŏng Tasan who were advocates of *Pukhak*, or Northern Learning, as well as *Silhak*, or Practical Learning, a reform of Confucianism which was a reaction to the ancient doctrine of Chu-tsu. Our attention is also drawn to *Tonghak*, the popular uprising of the peasants and lower classes against the nobility and ruling classes which was at the same time an attempt to bring about an indigenous religion. This uprising culminated in the *Tonghak* rebellion of 1894.

The spirit of modern nationalism was born with the *Samil* Independence Movement. Already in 1907, with the organization of the *Sinmin-hoe* by An Ch'ang-ho, a process of enlightenment had begun whereby the Korean people were being educated as to the meaning of democracy for the masses. The *Samil* Movement of March 1, 1919 clearly demonstrated the desire of the Korean people to replace the ancient rule of the monarchs with a new democratic form of society. The seeds of the new modern nationalism of Korea today were already sprouting in the *Samil* Independence Movement.

Although works on this subject have been scarce up until the present time, it is hoped that this collection can serve as a mirror into the thought patterns of the Korean people.

Sin Il-ch'ŏl

Main Currents of Korean Thought

Main Currents of Korean Thought

PAK CHONG-HONG

Korea is a peninsular country. In terms of natural conditions, she shares many similarities with Greece or Italy. Her people, since time immemorial, had held light in reverence. Her beautiful landscape spreading out under the exceptionally clear sky was suitable for cultivating in the minds of her people a strong inclination to peace.

Early Koreans were a clear-headed people and often displayed their unique originality, which frequent foreign invasions unfortunately prevented from being handed down to posterity for further development. A proper example might be found in the language, together with its written symbols (*Han'gŭl*)—the two being eloquent symbols of the characteristics of Koreans' spiritual culture which was faced with near elimination under the Japanese occupation (1910-1945).

It is doubtful that the Japanese ever correctly represented Korea to the world, especially her spiritual heritage of culture. And Koreans, being situated in such circumstances, hardly had any opportunity to reveal what had been inherent in themselves. This being the situation, it might be extremely hard for foreigners—now especially westerners—to gain a correct understanding of Korea's spiritual culture.

The liberation of the nation on August 15, 1945, could have somewhat changed the situation. But Korean intellectuals were suddenly confronted with instability in their daily lives which hindered them from studying their own spiritual culture. Nevertheless, it remains an undeniable fact that groups of promising young students, through hard work, have in the past reaped good results in their studies. They will continue to do so in the future.

Any outline of Korean cultural history is bound to be a record of the overcoming of successive adversities. Nevertheless, despite incessant struggles the people have always sought hope for tomorrow on earth rather than harbored a desire for eternal life after death. It has always been more urgent for them to get immediate relief rather than promises of a better life after death.

Koreans are often referred to as a people who are fond of making a plaything of an empty argument in the abstract. But they are by nature not so. Their rambling about scenic places by no means indicated an attempt to escape from reality. It was to nourish in their souls a noble character and a magnanimous disposition so that they could in the future make a greater contribution to their nation and society.

No doubt the *Hwarang* (Flower-boy) spirit which had so high a regard for external appearances must have been the manifestation of their morality that mind and body, word and deed should be consistent. The Koreans successfully accepted and assimilated foreign ideas through believing in Buddhism or by expounding the principle of Confucianism, and moving forward, exploited new areas and exercised an influence upon foreign nations.

Priest Nang was a Korean (of Koguryŏ) by birth. At an early age he went to the Chi Kingdom in China. During the Chenwoo Years (494-497) he toured the southern part of China and later settled on Mt. Shi-shan. At that time the Coonwin thought centered around the theory of entity prevailing in the northern part of China, while the Chengshih Lun thought dealing with non-entity was widely spread in the southern part. Upon proceeding southward, Priest Nang, who was called the High Priest of Chengshih, rooted out the extremities of the two theories and combined them into a coherent whole.

No advocates of the Chengshih Lun, it is recorded, could match Priest Nang in arguments. Thus he laid the foundation for the emergence of the Sanlun Sect. King Wooti of the Ryang dynasty selected 10 priests to learn from Nang; and later the king himself was converted to Nang's theory after abandoning his belief in the Chengshih Lun.

Wŏnch'ŭk (613-699) of Silla gained fame for his activities in China during the reign of Empress Chitien Wuhu of the T'ang dynasty. In his childhood, Wŏnch'ŭk was noted for being bright. As he matured, he became very wise, shrewd and well versed in both classical and contemporary Buddhist scriptures. He was especially excellent in mastering foreign languages, and commanded six languages at will. Highly respected by Empress Chitien Wuhu, he was assigned to a leading role in debates with high Indian priests who visited China.

In lecturing on or translating Buddhist scriptures he was always named a senior representative. Especially in study on the doctrine of the Wei-shik School, he excelled others. His study was profound and original, his analysis precise. His theory on the Wei-shik doctrine, however, was incompatible with that of Wei-shik School authorities of the T'ang Empire, such as Shien Chuang and his disciple, Kwei Chi; and hot debates ensued between the two opposing groups.

The dispute gave rise to the creation of different schools in the ages that followed. The followers of Kwei Chi, whenever they wrote new publications, used to dispute Wŏnch'ŭk's views. The fact, that his theory was the target of serious criticisms, should be understood as a proof of his eminence.

Upon his death, Wŏnch'ŭk was buried in the Shingchao Temple. A tower as large as those in memory of Shien Chuang and Kwei Chi was erected in the temple precinct to honor the Korean priest, who was highly revered by the Chinese people.

Priest Wŏnhyo (617-686) of Silla wrote as many as 92 volumes containing more than 230 books. In his numerous books, he combined and further elucidated the fundamental tenet of Mahayana, or Large Vehicle, Buddhism.

Among his books, the *Kŭmgang Sammaegyŏng Ryakso* (Commentary on the Book of Diamond Meditation—Vajra Samadhi Sūtra Satra) consisting of three volumes and the two-volume *Taesŭng Kisinnon So* (Commentary on the Origin of Mahayana Buddhism) were widely read in China. The founder of the Huayen School (Avatamsaka) in China, Priest Fa-tsang made frequent references to Wŏnhyo's books when he wrote his own. Handed down to his disciple, Teng Kwan, Wŏnhyo's works were frequently referred to when he proved the validity of his own theory.

These are clear indications of how great Wŏnhyo's influence on Chinese Buddhism was. His book, *Taesŭng Kisinnon So*, was known through the ages as *Haedong So* (Book of the East) which no Buddhist scholars in the Orient had ever read. His *Simmun Hwajaeng Non* among others, marked a new era in Korea's Buddhist development, for it contained no imitation of Chinese thought. He never was an ordinary priest-scholar, but his thought was supported by a ceaseless stream of profound experiences.

It was Chi Nul (1158-1210) of the Koryŏ dynasty who deepened a theory designed to unify the doctrines of the Zen (*Sŏn*) and the Doctrine (*Kyo*) schools. According to him, the *Kyo* sect was apt to glorify the ability of discernment alone, for its business was to clarify words, and could never reach the stage of enlightenment. The Zen sect, on the contrary, was likely to lose itself in worthless napping under the pretext of initiating mysteries.

In his famous works, the *Chinsim Chiksŏl* (Explanation of the True Mind) and *Susim Kyŏl* (Key to Self-culture), Chi Nul developed his theories in a clear and forcible manner. With his *Chŏlyo Sagi* he thoroughly analyzed and strictly criticized the substance of each sect and glorified the existence of Korea's *Chokye* School. His books were translated into Japanese and widely read by Japanese scholars.

Sŏ Kyŏng-dŏk (Hwadam) (1489-1546) is usually known as one of the most original Confucian scholars of Korea. This is because he advocated the monism of *Chi* (Element) for the first time in Korea when the dualism of *Chi* (Element) and *Li* (Principle or Reason), as founded by Cheng Tze and Chu Hsi, prevailed among Confucian circles. Sŏ Hwadam developed in this a unique natural philosophy.

According to him, there is in the universe only on *Chi* (Element) which has neither beginning nor ending but is everlasting and omnipresent. This *Chi* (Element) has no definite form and is called *T'aehŏ*, or the Great and Original Void. The Void cannot be grasped like non-entity, but it fills the universe, and therefore, is not non-entity. Reason never resides outside Element. Principle (or Reason) is the commanding force of *Chi* (Element). The former enters into the latter from without to command it. In other words, *Chi* (Element), in its movement, never deviates from its right course, which means its commanding force. Therefore, Principle (or Reason) never precedes *Chi* (Element). Should the former precede the latter, it would exist outside *Chi* (Element) and the conclusion would be that there is no *Chi* (Element) with no beginning. His works are contained in *The Complete Writings in the Four Divisions* (Ssu-k'u Ch'uan-shu) during the Ch'ing dynasty.

It was Yi Hwang (T'oegye) (1501-1570) who deepened Confucianism with his subjective thinking. He was Korea's representative Confucian scholar. He was clear-minded, pure, tender, and noble and upheld an extremely precise and critical attitude. According to him, man should realize that there is equality among things different and that there is difference among things equal. Even though a thing can be divided into two, its inseparability should be kept. When two things are combined into one, they should avoid confusion. Man should do his best not to run to an extreme. It is not recommendable, he said, to accept what accords with one's opinion or to try to adapt other's logic to one's purpose or to repudiate one's thinking.

Most outstanding among his theories is his *Four Beginnings and Seven Emotions.* By Four Beginnings, he meant sympathy, shame, concession, and reason, which originated from Mencius. His Seven Emotions: pleasure, anger, sadness, fear, love, hate, and desire originated from *Li Chi* (Book of Rites). According to him, the Four Beginnings emanate from Principle (or Reason), and the Seven Emotions from Element. As a result of an eight-year dispute with Ki Daesŭng (Kobong), his disciple, he later eased to a degree his dualistic theory by amending that the Four Beginnings originate in Principle (or Reason) but are followed by Element and that the Seven Emotions come from Element but are participated in by Principle (or Reason). His theory of the Four Beginnings and Seven Emotions was highly admired by Japanese Confucian scholars as being intrinsically his own. The theory remained to be the central subject of dispute among virtually all Korean Confucian followers and was recognized to be the most significant point of argument. The theory eventually was connected with party strife.

T'oegye's basic attitude was that the truth should not be sought in theories. He believed that the truth could be found in ordinary daily life. Man should partake both of knowledge and of its practice, he thought.

It is sincerity that penetrates into man's every deed. To attain that goal, man should possess reverence. The fundamental fruit of his academic achievements and his view of life could be found in his emphasis on reverence. T'oegye's put this belief into practice throughout his seventy years of life. There are numerous examples of how greatly Japanese Confucian scholars were encouraged by the influence of T'oegye. His academic tradition inherited by Japanese scholars is well known to have formed the basic educational principle of Japan in the Meiji era.

One of the two greatest authorities on Confucianism throughout the history of Korea, together with T'oegye, is Yi

I (Yulgok) (1536-1584). It did not suit Yulgok's taste to engage in analytic explanations of words or phrases. According to him Principle does not issue forth from any thing. What emits is Element which is sensible to outside stimuli. Element is only the vehicle of Principle. Since what emits is not Principle, there is no precedent for Principle to emit itself and Element follows Principle. Only Element emits. This principle, according to him, is not limited to the mind but can be applied to nature.

At the early age of 23, Yulgok passed the civil service examinations with the highest score with his *Ch'ŏndoch'aek* (Measures for the Way of Heaven). This treatise, which, for its remarkable quality, put examination officials to great astonishment, contained the seed of his Principle-Element theory which he later developed.

According to him, everything which moves or ceases to move is Element and Element moves or ceases to move because of reason. His *Ch'ŏndoch'aek* was widely read and circulated as far as to China. Late in his life when he received a Chinese delegation as a member of a reception group, the Chinese inquired after the author of the *Ch'ŏndoch'aek*. Knowing that Yulgok was the author, they mentioned him only with an honorific title.

According to Yulgok, Principle in itself does not possess any form and is voiceless and odorless. Although it exists throughout the universe, it can take definite shape only when it rides on Element. This resembles water conforming to the roundness or angularity of its container or the air yielding to the size of a bottle. While Principle is limitless, Element is endowed with limited one-sidedness. Principle can take many forms, such as omnipresence, purity or turbidity. There is only one and limited Element, which can be joined by the Principle. Principle can assume an innumerable number of different shapes because of the limitation of Element. The term, "the Principle's communication and the Element's limitation," was Yulgok's own invention.

Yulgok refused to accept the theories of foregoing scholars without criticism. Instead he sought for the truth from a free standpoint. His firm conviction, acquired through deep thinking and personal experiences, "cannot be subject to revision, even though a sage emerges again," he states. This saying unmistakably reveals a solemn aspect of Yulgok, the philosopher, who never ceased in his search for the truth.

A group of Confucian scholars in Korea had long before pointed to the necessity of developing practical learning with emphasis on moral practice rather than empty arguments. Thus, new academic traditions were established with a view to grasping realities more concretely. The new learning was called *Silhak* or Real Learning, devoted to introducing new institutions from advanced nations to keep the destiny of the nation from stagnation and decline.

Yi Su-kwang (Chibong) (1563-1628), during the reign of King Sŏnjo of the Yi dynasty, wrote the *Chibong Yusŏl* (Essays of Chibong) in which he touched on the situation in the outside world and Southeast Asia together with the new science of Europe. Besides him there were other scholars who imported and studied books on science from China during the latter part of the Ming dynasty and the early part of the Ch'ing dynasty.

It was, however, with Yu Hyŏng-wŏn (Pan'gye) (1622-1672) and Yi Ik (Sŏngho) (1682-1764) that the School of Real Learning was established. The *Pan'gye Surok* (Essays of Pan'gye), was also precise in dealing with such versatile subjects as the farm system, irrigation, mintage, the military system, road construction, vehicle utilization, etc. It contained the author's researches into fields which his predecessors had missed.

The *Sŏngho Sasŏl* (Writings of Sŏngho) was the summation and systematization of the theories and views of the author who had read a great deal of scientific books on Europe's astronomy, geography and arithmetic.

Sŏngho condemned absolute monarchism and aristocracy.

He also denounced the ill effects of civil service examinations based on literary writing.

The following period saw the *Silhak* ideas permeating into every field of learning, including history, geography, and philosophy. A number of outstanding scholars emerged in succession leaving behind them great new achievements. Among these scholars was Chŏng Yak-yong (Tasan) (1762-1836) who discussed in detail his social reform policies in his books entitled *Kyŏngse Yup'yo* and *Mokmin Simsŏ*. He asserted that reform should be carried out in conformity with the changes of the times.

These new trends of thought were brought to ever-increasing intensity especially after the visit to Peiping by a group of young scholars—such as Hong Dae-yong, Pak Chi-wŏn, Pak Che-ga, Yi Dŏk-mu, and Yu Dŭk-kong—as members of the Korean delegation to the Ch'ing dynasty. Pak Chi-wŏn (1735-1805), one of the group, asserted that people should strive to elevate their welfare in agriculture, commerce and industry by improving their familiar daily living modes.

He rejected mere reading on grounds that it could hardly contribute anything worthwhile to academic research. From this standpoint he promoted economic thought and tried to break down the caste system and love of fame and gain.

The *Silhak* was not designed to perfunctorily imitate the institutions of the Ch'ing dynasty as they appeared above the surface. The new school should be recognized as a product of the scholars' zeal to find a way out of the misery in which the common people had been situated. It was necessary to remodel their living modes and introduce a reform into the social structure, while discarding empty abstract arguments, and to help the nation keep itself abreast of the times. The *Silhak* thought, because it was aimed at introducing the scientific civilization of the western world, cannot be understood completely without considering its relations with Catholicism which at that time was being introduced into Korea. Naturally many of the *Silhak* scholars were greatly interested in Catholicism. The tight suppression of Catholicism in the latter part of the Yi dynasty resulted in the decline of the *Silhak* movement. If the *Silhak* School had been permitted to attain desired development, Korea's modern history might have taken a different course.

Anyhow, the characteristics of Korea's *Silhak* thought can be found in its emphasis, inwardly, on moral practice with sincerity and, outwardly, on reshaping of man by best utilizing new scientific techniques for advancement of the people's welfare. This task even today faces not only Koreans but everyone in the world.

Yi Wŏn-ku, during the reign of King Sunjo of the Yi dynasty, once said, "To honor morality alone and ignore one's occupation is equal to a widower, and to stress one's economy and take no notice of morality is equivalent to a widow." This saying may be taken as a frank expression of the gist of *Silhak* thought.

The *Silhak* ideas were largely the outcome of stimuli from the Ch'ing civilization. The *Silhak* School was devoted to accepting new scientific trends of western civilization to further national awakening. In the meantime, there developed a new academic trend known as the *Tonghak* Movement (Eastern Learning opposed to the Catholicism of the West), which endeavored to create a set of new ideas with original Oriental thought as the basis rather than mere acceptance of foreign ideas.

The advocate of the *Tonghak* Movement was Ch'oe Je-u (Su-un) (1824-1864). Reaching the stage of "enlightenment" at the age of 37, he died a martyr for his faith at 41. In his work, *Tongkyŏng Daejŏn* (Bible of Eastern Learnings) he introduced the name *Tonghak* (Eastern Learning) for which he was martyred by declaring, "I was born in the Orient and given the doctrine in the Orient. Although the doctrine is Heaven's way, it should be called *Tonghak*."

According to him, the permanency and immutability of the Heavenly Way were well understood in the Orient and every movement and success in human life, from time immemorial, was comprehended as Heaven's Providence. People admired Providence and followed nature's way. The fundamental principles of *Tonghak* thought, however, lie in the theory that Heaven should not be sought outside man but within him. The Heavenly mind is man's mind. One should master the doctrine by improving one's mind but not rely upon salvation from without. He should believe in God who resides in his mind but not worship Su-un the founder, he taught.

It should be avoided to long for Providence in reliance upon others without doing one's best. It was repeatedly emphasized that one should defend one's mind and correct one's energy. Su-un admitted that the theory of the defense of mind and correction of energy was his own invention. He stressed sincerity and the importance of respectfulness and fidelity.

His thought took concrete shape and was further developed by his followers. Ch'oe Si-hyŏng (Haewŏl) (1829-1898), the second leader of the *Tonghak* religion, taught that for one to comprehend the truth is nothing but to know oneself, that is, the Heaven is one's self and one is the Heaven. To serve God is to look into the way of God. Man's self-awakening was stressed by the leader. Since each man is a god, there should be no classes among them. Disdaining people is equivalent to offending Heaven. "Treat people as you, attend upon the Heaven." With this teaching, he emphasized respect for others. He further developed the *Tonghak* doctrine into the theory that there is nothing in daily occasions in human life that is against the will of Heaven and that everything in the universe is the copy of Heaven. With Haewŏl the thought on Heaven came to possess a more thorough meaning. By reading him, one can understand that reverence to Heaven, to man, and to things is basically of the same origin.

With Son Byŏng-hŭi (Ŭiam) (1861-1919), the third *Tonghak*

leader, the *Tonghak* Movement was elevated to a religion, called *Ch'ŏndo-kyo*, whose doctrine was that "Man is equivalent to Heaven."

Ch'ŏndo-kyo teaches neither after-death salvation nor eternal life. Its ideal is to realize a paradise on earth. To reach the goal, it upholds the ideas of peace, promotion of virtuous conduct, and prosperity to all. For reform, it was needed, first of all, to abandon old customs and start afresh with national self-awakening. Secondly, it was urged by the religion to enhance and purify the national spirit through propagation and enlightenment of the masses. Thirdly, an ideal world would be established where mankind would help each other for everlasting peace.

The *Tonghak* Revolution in 1894 was pointed at the corrupt feudalistic system. The *Tonghak* believers staged a series of demonstrations in the 1904 enlightenment movement taking the van in awakening the people to the necessity of improving their living. It is still fresh in the memory of Koreans that Ŭiam and his followers made an outstanding contribution in the nationwide move to regain Korean sovereignty during the *Samil* Independence Movement of 1919.

GLOSSARY OF CHINESE CHARACTERS

Hwarang (花郎)
Priest Nang (僧朗)
Wŏnch'ŭk (圓測)
Wŏnhyo (元曉)
Kŭmgang Sammaegyŏng Ryakso (金剛三昧經略疏)
Taesŭng Kisinnon So (大乘起信論疏)
Haedong So (海東疏)
Simmun Hwajaeng Non (十門和諍論)
Chi Nul (知訥)

Chinsim Chiksŏl (眞心直説)
Susim Kyŏl (修心訣)
Chŏlyo Saki (節要私記)
Chokye School (曹溪宗)
Sŏ Kyŏng-dŏk (Hwadam) (徐敬德－花潭)
The Complete Writings in the Four Divisions (四庫全書)
Yi Hwang (T'oegye) (李滉－退溪)
Four Beginnings and Seven Emotions (四端七情)

Ki Dae-sŭng (Kobong) (寄大升－高峯)

Yi I (Yulgok) (李珥－栗谷)

Ch'ŏndoch'aek (天道策)

Silhak (實學)

Yi Su-kwang (Chibong) (李睟光－芝峰)

Chibong Yusŏl (芝峯類説)

Yu Hyŏng-wŏn (Pan'gye) (柳馨遠－磻溪)

Yi Ik (Sŏngho) (李翼－星湖)

Pan'gye Surok (磻溪隨録)

Sŏngho Sasŏl (星湖私説)

Chŏng Yak-yong (Tasan) (丁若鏞－茶山)

Kyŏngse Yup'yo (經世遺表)

Mokmin Simsŏ (牧民心書)

Hong Dae-yong (洪大容)

Pak Chi-wŏn (朴趾源)

Pak Che-ka (朴齊家)

Yi Dŏk-mu (李德懋)

Yu Dŭk-kong (柳得恭)

Yi Wŏn-ku (李元龜)

Tonghak Movement (東學運動)

Ch'oe Je-u (Su-un) (崔濟愚－水雲)

Tongkyŏng Daejŏn (東經大全)

Ch'oe Hae-wŏl (崔海月)

Son Byŏng-hŭi (Ŭiam) (孫秉熙－義庵)

Ch'ŏndo-kyo (天道教)

Samil Movement (三一運動)

Wŏnhyo and His Thought

YI KI-YŎNG

Wŏnhyo's position in the history of Korean Buddhism is unique. Since the advent of Buddhism in Silla, the names of many Buddhist monks appear in history, but the character and thought of Wŏnhyo are revealed at once most clearly through his own extant works.

He lived in the period of Silla's unification of the peninsula, influencing the young men of this time deeply. His personality and thought are most original and very Korean.

His Time and Personality

Tradition says that Wŏnhyo, the holy monk, had the family name "Sŏl" and was born in the 39th year of King Chinp'yŏng of Silla (617 A.D.), at the village of Pulchi, south of what was then Amnyang-kun or presently Zain-myŏn in Kyŏngsang Province. A Sala tree stood in this village. Wŏnhyo's mother, with child, was passing there when suddenly she felt birth pangs and gave birth to Wŏnhyo under the tree, having had no time to reach home. A cloud of five colors hung in the sky at that time. This legend expresses the feeling of reverence succeeding generations have felt for the outstanding personality of Wŏnhyo. His child name was So-dong or Sin-dong, which was read in the current dialect, but the pronunciation of which is not known now.

The time was just 90 years after Buddhism was imported

14

into Silla. In China the Sui dynasty was just about to be replaced by the T'ang dynasty. Within the country of Silla, the aged Wŏn'gwang and Chimyŏng were reshaping national policy and social morals in line with Buddhism. Chajang, another famous monk of Silla, was born shortly before Wŏnhyo. Wŏnhyo's friend Ŭisang, another great monk, was born 16 years after him.

A long period of construction, called Kŏnbok began from Queen Sŏndŏk's time (632-647), just preceding the unification of the three kingdoms. This was also a time when groups opposing the queen's continued reign got together to plot. Buddhism more and more was coming into its own as a national protective cult. A Chinese apocryphal Buddhist scripture, called *Inwang Hoguk Panya-gyŏng* or *Scripture for Wise Royalty and National Protection*, was frequently preached, and the pagoda at the Hwangryong Temple was built in order to invoke the aid of the spirits to bring neighboring countries to their knees, "to open wide heaven and earth and unify the three kingdoms." In T'ang, Hiuan Tchang, a Chinese, had a high reputation for his theory related to the school of Vijnanavada which he had brought to China after his long stay in India. Hiuan Tchang's return took place in the 15th year of Queen Sŏndŏk, 648 A.D., when Wŏnhyo was 24.

Wŏnhyo and Ŭisang left for T'ang together, but became stranded on the way to Liaotung whereupon Wŏnhyo returned home with great difficulty, giving up his dream of education in China. It was in 650 A.D., when Wŏnhyo was 33 and Ŭisang 25. Shortly afterwards, King Muyŏl unified the peninsula. Before this, in 649, the Silla court was compelled under the pressure of T'ang to renounce her independent chronology and to adopt the costumes and chronology of T'ang. The joint forces of Koguryŏ, Paekche and Malgal invaded the northern frontier of Silla, and at the request of Silla the troops of T'ang attacked Koguryŏ.

A number of complicating changes took place, it seems, at

this time in the personal life of Wŏnhyo. Being open-natured, free, democratic and loving music and arts, Wŏnhyo fell in love with the Princess of the Yosŏk Palace who bore him a son, the celebrated scholar Ch'ong in the reign of King Muyŏl (654-661), when circumstances both at home and abroad were extremely complicated. His friend Ūisang went to T'ang by sea in 661 and, after staying near the Unje Temple on Mt. Chongnam in China for nine years, returned with the Avatamsaka Sūtra which he learned from Chiyuan.

The conduct of Wŏnhyo, who had given up his ambition to study in T'ang and had tasted the pains of breaking the commandments, looked outrageous and degraded to the so-called regulars, who insisted on form and norm. Consequently, he seems to have been censured and derided. He never presumed himself to be a monk who renounced all ties of the world and joined the order, but called himself simply "*Sosŏng Kŏsa*," or a small layman. To him, orthodoxy seemed filled with numerous inhibitions and commandments, and was not the end and goal of life. The "small layman" Wŏnhyo frequented all houses and fearlessly played the zither at shrines, felt no scruples in sleeping and eating with both the noble and the lowly, and often went to majestic mountains and streams to meditate. He used to drum on an empty gourd shell and sing, "Only a man with no worries and fears can go straight and overcome life and death or transmigration." Thus he popularized to pedestrians of the capital and outlying areas the meaning of worship of Buddha.

An old legend also says that he put his ink slab on top of the horns of an ox and wrote when he composed a commentary on *Kŭmgang Sammaegyŏng* (Vajrasamadhi-Sūtra or the Sūtra of Diamond Concentration). Hence his thought is called "*Kaksŭng*," the Vehicle of Horns, an indication of the depth of his personality and thought as a man liberated and unbound.

In his prime, Silla unified the three kingdoms, and Silla

Buddhism displayed its true worth. Although he did not take part in statecraft directly, as Ŭisang did, Wŏnhyo indeed exceeded in scholarship all the many learned men at that time. An ascetic, at the same time he revealed to all the world the spirit of Silla, the greatest first monk of Korea.

According to tradition he died in 686, the 7th year of King Sinmun.

His Works

The writings of Silla monks before Wŏnhyo were negligible. According to records, the first work ever done by a Silla monk was *Sabunnyul Galmagi*, a commentary on Dharmaguptabhiksukarman, a text of Monastic Rules by Chimyŏng, early in the 7th century, but this book is not extant. Ŭisang seems to have written a few notations, but the only one remaining is *Hwaŏm Ilsūng Pŏpkyedo*, Illustration of Dharmadhatu, the Domain of Truth, according to the Unique Vehicle of Avatamsaka, Vol. 2.

Extant records list 70 books, in 140 volumes, both commentary notes and doctrinal resumes edited by Wŏnhyo, covering all departments. A person who seeks to analyze superficially the thought and religion of Wŏnhyo by the type of work he did would be totally lost due to the variety of subjects he dealt in.

Most of these works do not exist now. Furthermore, research in old documents had revealed recently that some errors were involved in editing these records catalogues. It is confirmed that succeeding generations have added a few things to the list, so that the list of genuine works of Wŏnhyo must be trimmed down considerably. But it is undeniable that Wŏnhyo was interested in all of the scriptures, such as *Samnon* (Madhyamaka), *Sŏngsil* (Vijnanavada), *Hwaŏm* (Avatamska), *Pŏphwa* (Saddharmapundarika), *Chŏngt'o* (Pure Land), *Ch'ŏnt'ae* (Tien T'ai), *Sŏn* (Tch'an or Zen),

Samnon (Mahayanasamgrach), *Chiron* (Bhumaka), *Pŏpsang* (Dharmalaksana), *Yul* (Vinaya), etc., which formed the centers of argument at that time. The remarkable thing is that Wŏnhyo expostulated his own creative views in treating them. The extant works of Wŏnhyo are recorded in the ten volumes of the *Collection of Wŏnhyo's Works* published by Tongguk University, and a dozen books are also included in the Taisho Tripitaka. The following is a briefly listing of his extant works:

Volume I   *Essentials of Pŏphwa, Saddharmapundarika-Sūtra* (Lotus of True Law) *T. 1725* (T. for Taisho Tripitaka)
Essentials of Mahaparinirvana-Sūtra I (Great Nirvana) *T. 1769*
Essentials of Taehedogyŏng, Mahaprajnaparamita-Sūtra I (Perfection of Great Wisdom) *T. 1697*

Volume II   *Essentials of Muryang Sugyŏng, Amitayus-Sūtra* (Infinite Life) *T. 1747*
Notes on Amitagyŏng, Sukhavativyuha (Pure Land) *I T. 1759*
Essentials of Mirŭk Sangsaengyŏng (Ascension of Maitreya in Tusita Heaven) *T. 1773*

Volume III   *Essay on Kŭmgang Sammaegyŏng* (Scripture of Diamond Concentration) *III T. 1730*

Volume IV   *Notes on Posal Yŏngnak Ponŏpkyŏng* (Fundamental Acts which are Fineries of Bodhisattva) *II*

Volume V   *Posal Kyeponchipŏmyogi* (Essential Remarks on the Observation of Bodhisattva Morality) *I T. 1907*
Pŏmmanggyŏng Posal Kyeponyogi I (Notes on the Text of Bodhisattva Morality according to the Net of Brahma)

Volume VI   *Notes on Taesŭng Kisinnon* (The Awakening of

Faith in Mahayana) *II T. 1844*
Volume VII   *Second Notes on Taesŭng Kisinnon I T. 1845*
Volume VIII   *Punbyŏl III* (Essays on Madhamika Argument)
Volume IX   *Ichangŭi I* (Two Kinds of Obstacles)
Volume X   *Palsim Suhaengchang* (For Beginners in Spiritual Experience)
Yusim Allakto (The Way of Peace and Beatitude in a Delivered Mind) *I T. 1965*
Taesŭng Yukchŏng Ch'amhoe (Mahayanic Confession of Sins with Regard to Six Sense) *I T. 1908*
Simmun Hwajaengnon
Notes on Chinyok Hwaŏmgyŏng (Avatamsaka-Sūtra in Chinese, translated by Buddhabhadra)
Notes on Haesim Milgyŏngso (Sandhinirmocana-Sūtra) (Introduction only) *Inmyong P'anpiryangnon Palmun*

His Thought

Wŏnhyo's thought reflects his firm convictions based entirely on his own observations and personal experience. At the beginning of the Notes on *Kisinnon*, he writes as follows, dissatisfied with the current trend among contemporary Buddhist scholars:

Only a few of those who presume to interpret the deep meaning of this theory understand all the essential points. Most of them are busy with preserving what they have learned and quoting phrases, not prepared to explore the main core openly and freely. Without attaining to the intentions of the theoretician, they stray near tributaries, although the source is nearby, or let go the trunk holding onto leaves, or sewed the sleeves with cloth cut from the collar.

What mattered most to Wŏnhyo was not the interpretation of words and sentences or the demonstration of wide learning, but the comprehension of the central, basic spirit of various scriptures. We can therefore fully understand his feelings when he added to the name of the scripture the word *Chongyo*, which means essentials, for that was what he looked for. Human words are essentially imperfect and their logic can often be erroneous. Scholars who set out to explain in words the realm of awakening were led into frequent errors because of the trickiness of words and memory. That is why Che-yi, a Chinese monk of the Tien T'ai sect, lamenting the Buddhist world of the two dynasties of China (316-589), when learning and practice did not correspond with one another, ridiculed the monks as "masters of concentration who think they know something about reality, although knowing nothing" or "commentators and preachers who only memorize scriptures and can do nothing."

Wŏnhyo lamented most the tendency towards pendantry. To him Buddhism was no longer Indian or Chinese. It was his, the religion of a Silla subject. There was no time for the Silla people of the 7th century, rising healthily in a corner of the peninsula, to be occupied leisurely with the interpretation of phrases. It was painful for him to see, a hundred years after the transplantation of Buddhism in the country, the triumph of false truth clad in dignity and prestige.

All of his essays were his confessions, confessions of his own ethical sins, and furthermore confessions of the advanced meditations on the reality of things, or in other words confessions of his deep joy arising from the realization of reality. We can clearly distinguish these personal confessions in the synopses of the prologues to the essays, written in simple but elegant style. For instance: "One, having committed great treachery and sin, may *believe* in this scripture and can destroy the flame that leaps up." Here *believing* is the most important, most ultimate condition for salvation. The climax of belief is none other than "the meditation of reality and its confession."

The reality of things signifies the reality of the Buddhas, "where one is all and all is one, where nothing stays but nothing does not stay, where nothing is done but nothing is undone."

Wŏnhyo, commenting on the *Kŭmgang Sammaegyŏng,* says:

> The world itself is, essentially speaking, in everlasting Enlightenment. In other words, the essential base upon which the whole complex of relationships among the different living beings is standing, is the ultimate eternal reality which is beyond of time and space, and which is the source of life and light, completely different life and light, which make it possible for our life to be truly human, to be enlightened.

This reality is called in the *Kisinnon* the Original Enlightenment, Fundamental Enlightenment or Enlightenment *a priori,* in Korean *Pongak.* According to Wŏnhyo's understanding, *Pongak* is nothing but the *Pŏpsin* (Dharmakaya), Essential Body of Buddha, eternal Being beyond the whole relative restriction, the Father of every being. This is the Body which is exempt from various common needs of complementarity, the Asamskrita—Being beyond the necessities: the Absolute. Here the word body has only an analogical meaning, corresponding to substance, base, or foundation. This Absolute Being is, however, never excluded from the common people's reach: it is attainable, knowable, visible and is able to be in perfect communion with the common people, through the purification of their minds, a kind of participation, discovering and cultivating of its seed (Tathagatagarbha) in the depth of the minds of the common people. It might be said that the *Pŏpsin* (Dharmakaya) is recognizable only when men become aware of it. So the seed should not be understood as a material reality or any such conception. That is the seed because that is a beginning of growth, of a magnificent tree. Here the expression "seed" is only a metaphor. Since, in Buddhism, any reality as a matter is never conceivable as an eternal Being, Wŏnhyo does not identity this seed in the depth of the human mind with the *Pŏpsin*, which is at the same time seed and fruit, so to speak beyond the realistic qualifications. Wŏnhyo says that the *Pŏpsin* is not in our mind, when we reach truly for it. Only death can bring us that reality. This is the reason why death becomes a crucial key to the true life. The distance which separates the banal minds of common people from the Ultimate Mind (Original Enlightenment) depends upon the degree of ego-consciousness of the common minds. We can find for the first time clearly in the history of Buddhism this most characteristic point of view, a meritorious remark, in the writings of Wŏnhyo.

The other particularity which we discover in Wŏnhyo's understanding of the *Bodhi* is his keen interest in the so-called Enlightenment *a posteriori*; *Chigak* in Korean. This is the Enlightenment in its realization; this is the *Pŏpsin* in its active aspects as a seed becoming a tree which begins across the ocean of suffering to arrive at the final goal: the Fruit. Enlightenment *a posteriori* is on the way to that final end above mentioned, which is the Alpha of every being, the source of every thing (either conceiving subjects or conceived objects). Enlightenment *a posteriori*, the *Chigak* is, then, in the realm of imperfection except for the final achievement. This is the operation of the Unconsciousness.

The *Pŏpsin* or *Pongak* (Enlightenment *a priori*) as the final goal corresponds to the biblical Omega. Here Teillhardde Chardin comes close to our point. Wŏnhyo designates this Omega as the Ultimate Enlightenment (in Korean *Kugyŏng-gak*), which is nothing but the *Pongak* (Enlightenment *a priori*, Enlightenment for Eternity, the Alpha). The mystery of this reality (the Ultimate Enlightenment) rests in its character: being at the same time the beginning and the end, and being at the same time in our mind and outside own mind. Essentially speaking, this spiritual reality is beyond our consciousness, nevertheless, we can reach it through our minds.

In Wŏnhyo's understanding, this Ultimate, this Original Enlightenment could never have shape, form, sensation, imagination, impulsive activity or colored consciousness. Similarly, this Ultimate or Original Enlightenment was never considered as an abstract or neutral principle. Wŏnhyo says it is the Spirit, the Compassion, the True Life and Light. Karl Jaspers' *das Umgreifende* (the Comprehensive), *die Ursprung und die Ziel*; C.G. Jung's *kollektive Umbewusste* (Collective Unconsciousness), these are all merely different fingers pointing to the same moon id est. the Life, the Light and the Spirit which we, ignorant, mortal, blind, strayed sons of this country can recognize only vaguely.

Wŏnhyo, according to the *Kisinnon*, shows how common people can attain Enlightenment, crossing the different stages of awakening. The four stages of the Enlightenment *a posteriori* assure us the possibility of gradual awakening, gradual achievement of *Bodhi* in this world.

First Stage of Awakening: Non-Enlightenment

This is the stage in which a man becomes aware of his sinful state, repents and decides to correct his own misbehavior. But he is still not free from these misdeed, sinking again and again into the same faults in action. This is the stage in which common people, regardless of religious denomination, usually remain. This awareness is the only positive light they have in their minds. This is not an authentic Enlightenment, but it is the first crucial step to the Enlightenment.

Second Stage of Awakening: Apparent Enlightenment

This is the stage in which people such as Hinayanists, who

are blind religious believers without any personal reflection
on their duty toward others, can abstain at least from such
misdeeds as ailling, stealing, lying, committing adultery etc.,
thanks to their efforts, thanks also to their faithfulness, even
though they still have contaminating elements in their minds.
Legally speaking, they are not criminals, but they are never
able to defend successfully the accusation from others of their
sinful state of mind. People who do good deeds but still have
contaminated minds, such as obscurity or vagueness of judgment, craving, jealousy, hatred, etc. Stay in this stage; but
those who overcome such obstacles achieve the Third Stage
of awakening.

Third Stage of Awakening: Advanced Enlightenment

This is the stage of advanced Bodhisattva; they are free of
serious misdeeds and serious mental faults. They serve
society. They never forget this altruistic service for others.
What differentiates the Bodhisattva from the Buddha is that
they retain consciousness of ego, ego as a subject of good
deeds. This consciousness of ego we may call, with Reinhold
Niehbur, the narcotic reminiscences of man within his soul:
the trace of Original Sin. According to Wŏnhyo, this ego-
consciousness consists of the following: a) ignorance of self,
b) self-arrogance, c) self-indulgence, d) a general selfish attitude about everything. Unless a Bodhisattva eliminates this
ego-consciousness from his mind, even apparent good deeds
will not help him reach the goal.

The Ultimate Enlightenment

This consists of overcoming in the depth of our minds the
casual process of ego-consciousness. The prevailing ego-
consciousness has three causes: ignorant impulse (the hidden

drive to act), subjective activity, and the appearance of passive objectivity. The last two may be formulated as the subject-object dichotomy. What a remarkable coincidence in language with Jaspers' formula *Subjekt-Objekt Spaltung.* The assertion of "me," "myself" go to the necessary creation of the opposite of "mine" the object. Wŏnhyo says that Full Enlightenment is possible only by elimination of this dichotomy, this opposition, without doubt, through the death of this worldly life at last, through the entire conversion of meaning and value of this life.

Wŏnhyo says human life has become scattered because of those sensorial agents which are so crazy to possess their objects that they finally deny their essential ground of existence. Revolt against the Source, that is the origin of sufferings, disasters, sadness, in short, of human history. Return to this very Source, this is the way of religion. The meaning of triple refuge remains here. He says: I am listening to voices which come from the depth of this Source, that voice is the Perfect Voice—Wŏn-ŭm and it is calling to me to take the way of return to the origin in this world. Here the Paramita Virtues are to be practiced sincerely. Here the value of rites, of religious ceremony, are reaffirmed. He says: those things do not have ultimate importance, but should not be denied, for it has tremendous value for those who are still weak. The components of this rite enumerated by Wŏnhyo are in number five: Praise of the Perfect One (Bhagavat), Act of Contrition with deep repentance, Receiving the Instruction of Buddha, Manifesting the Joy to be with him, and Firm Decision to follow his way. These are, Wŏnhyo says, not the end but the necessary means to arrive at the end.

Wŏn'gwang and His Thought

YI KI-BAEK

His Age

Wŏn'gwang was born in the 14th year of Silla King Chin-hŭng's reign (533 A.D.). The monarch's reign corresponded to the period of Silla's peak prosperity. Before him King Pŏp-hŭng (r. 514-540) promulgated a set of laws to finalize the government system as a state. By introducing Buddhism, he established a spiritual basis. Following him, King Chinhŭng (r. 540-576) achieved exterior development, expanding his king's territory to the western bank of the Naktong River and to the northern bank of the Han River, his expeditionary forces advancing northward even to the Hamhŭng plain. Supporting the ambitious expansion policy was the *Hwarang* (Flower boy) corps founded during his reign. The king's reign witnessed the most active age in the Silla dynasty, and Wŏn'-gwang grew up in this atmosphere.

Wŏn'gwang's secular surname was Sŏl. *Sok Kosŭng-jŏn* (A Supplement to Biographies of Eminent Priests), a Chinese record, says that his surname was Pak, but is seems proper to follow his biography contained in *Samguk Yusa*, which says it was Sŏl. By Sŏl one is naturally reminded of Wŏnhyo and his son, Sŏl Ch'ong, who were truly great thinkers representing Silla. Sŏl must have come from the same clan as these two. There were six social classes in Silla, and the family Sŏl belonged to the middle class which, compared with the *Chin'gol* nobility, was subject to many restrictions. This fact is helpful

26

in understanding the life and thought of Wŏn'gwang.

Wŏn'gwang was brought up in Kyŏngju, the capital. The capital was very active in his day as a symbol of expanding Silla. The Wŏlsŏng palace and such magnificent temples as Hŭngnyun-sa and Hwangnyong-sa boasted great splendor. New Chinese architecture and sculpture were introduced, and Kyŏngju was rapidly transforming its features for added grandeur.

Parting from Shamanism

It is said that Wŏn'gwang entered the priesthood at the age of 13. Another theory has it that he became a monk during his visit to China. The two different accounts seem to be contradictory, but they have a significance of their own, the former being a Korean account and the latter a Chinese view. Wŏn'gwang probably learned Buddhism and trained himself as a monk even before his departure for China. What was the motive or his intention to enter the priesthood at such a young age?

It is recorded that Buddhism was officially accepted in the 22nd year of King Pŏphŭng's reign (535). Prior to the official sanction of Buddhism, Yi Ch'a-don died a martyr in the 14th year of the king's reign. This shows that a long period of strife preceded the acceptance of Buddhism. The trials Buddhist pioneers had to suffer were apparently due to a confrontation with the traditional shamanist faith. Even after its official recognition, Buddhism had to endure continued confrontation with the shamanist faith.

This shows that Wŏn'gwang lived in a period when shamanism was being superseded by Buddhism. It can be assumed that Wŏn'gwang underwent an ideological trial before he decided to enter the priesthood. *Kobon Sui-jŏn*, referred to in *Samguk Yusa*, offers the following legend told of Wŏn'gwang's religious self-training:

Wŏn'gwang was training himself on a mountain.
Four years passed, and a celibate monk built a hermitage not far from his place, a fierce man proficient in
magic. One day God appeared before Wŏn'gwang and
asked him to have the celibate monk remove to another
place because he would achieve nothing significant with
his enchantment, but only confuse the minds of others.
On the following day Wŏn'gwang went to him and
asked him to remove to another place. But his request
was rejected. That night God broke down the mountain
to destroy the hermitage. God recommended him to
make advanced study in China, and he followed the
advice.

Comparing Wŏn'gwang with the trivial celibate monk, we
may understand one aspect of the legend. As he was said to be
proficient in enchantment, he must have been a shaman.
There was no clear distinction in name between Buddhist
priests and shamans at that time. The confrontation between
the Buddhist priest and a shaman on the mountain ended in
the former's victory. His victory suggests criticism of
shamanist faith and conquest of it. Opposition to shamanist
faith meant opposition to the *Chin'gol* aristocracy. His decision to enter the priesthood may be understood as his revolt
against various social restrictions imposed on his social class.
We have some doubt about the thoroughness of
Wŏn'gwang's conquest of the shamanist faith. The appearance of God in the legend seems to offer some suggestion.
God is not a Buddhist deity such as Buddha or a Bodhisattva;
he is, in this case, a god conceived in the traditional faith. It is
also said in the legend that the god was transformed into an
old fox at the moment of his death. It was under his advice
that Wŏn'gwang went to China for advanced study, as well as
receiving his protection. This shows a conservative aspect of
Wŏn'gwang.
That he was not completely free from the shamanist world

is indicated by the fact that he set up *Chōmch'albo* (a method of leading Buddhist followers to confession by a means as simple as divination) in Kasūl-sa Temple in later years. The confession was aimed at promoting good and destroying evil by awakening to Buddhist truth, firming up national security, defending people from disaster, and extending their life span. The confession, in this manner, was devoted to pursuit of actual gains in reality; herein we find shamanistic elements. Even though a bridge was constructed to span Silla with Buddhism in the wake of its official recognition by King Pōphūng, a prayer hall was yet to be built to absorb it in depth. In this transitional period, Wōn'gwang may have thought it convenient for awakening the ignorant mass of people to compromise with the traditional faith.

In Wōn'gwang we find an admixture of Buddhism and shamanism. Nevertheless, Wōn'gwang showed a strong will to shake off the long tradition and advance toward a new world. While young men from the noble class usually entered the *Hwarang* corps, Wōn'gwang chose the priesthood.

Study in China

It was said in the legend that Wōn'gwang undertook study in China at the recommendation of God. It was in the 11th year of King Chinp'yōng's reign (589), and Wōn'gwang was 37 years of age.

Study in China was called *Sōhak* (Learning in the West) at his time. Before him such Silla priests as Kaktōk and Chimyōng studied in China. To learn in the "West" was beginning to come into vogue in Silla.

What motived Wōn'gwang to undertake study in China is explained in the legend mentioned earlier. God told him to study in China.

"I know all future events, as well as being well versed in all things in the world. If you remain in this place alone, it will benefit you but you cannot benefit others. If you do not make your name known to all, you will be unable to accomplish anything significant in the future. Why don't you learn the Buddhist doctrine in China and save the ignorant masses in Korea?"

Wŏn'gwang told the god that to learn in China had long been his cherished desire, but he could not find an opportunity to undertake it because China was far away beyond the land and the sea. The god, the legend continues, taught him a minute plan for learning in China, and Wŏn'gwang gained enough strength to undertake it.

The godly recommendation must have been Wŏn'gwang's own voice. He may have chosen to study in China as a means of rising in the Silla society which was bound up with the caste system. He wanted to make himself able to bring benefits to others and save his ignorant compatriots from illusion.

What did Wŏn'gwang learn in China? It was, of course, Buddhism. To say that he became a monk in China has some reasonableness, because he could grow into a real monk in China. It can be pointed out that even though Buddhism was officially recognized and basked in royal patronage in Silla by that time, there were still many shortcomings, especially in formalities. Wŏn'gwang wanted to be ordained in accord with Chinese formalities. With imperial sanction, he could finally be admitted to the Chinese priesthood.

There are many sutras, discourses, and schools in Buddhism. It is said that Wŏn'gwang knew all the "three basketfuls of" Buddhist scriptures and grew especially devoted to the Nirvana-Sūtra and Sŏngsillon. The Nirvana-Sūtra emphasizes that it does not mean death that one entered the Nirvana but rebirth with immortality. The Sŏngsillon asserts that man should liberate himself from all worries and pains, and bid farewell to the world of phenomena by entering the void.

At the request of his followers he lectured on Buddhist sutras in China, and his reputation began to spread in that country. When the Sui empire was at war with Chin to destroy it,

Wŏn'gwang was in danger of his life in the confusion, but his virtuous personality led him to safety. When Sui unified the Chinese continent, Wŏn'gwang went to its capital, where he converted to a new sect which grew rapidly dominant, called Sŏpnonjong. Wŏn'gwang's reputation was so high that he was included in *Sok Kosŭng-jŏn* (A Supplement to Biographies of Eminent Priests) compiled in China. He is one of the few Silla priests mentioned in the biographies.

Wŏn'gwang's reputation in China was spread even to his country of Silla, and the Silla government, having an interest in his high reputation in the Sui dynasty of China, requested the Sui government to send him back home. Accordingly, he embarked on travel home in the 22nd year of Silla King Chinp'yŏng's reign, 600 years after Christ, winding up his 11-year stay in Sui China.

Whether it was the change in himself or in Silla society that caused his homecoming is not known. He had once decided to live in Sui and not return to Silla. Whether the Silla government promised him a promotion in social status in Silla, finding the value of use in him, is also not known. However, the historical records of his life in Silla after his return give the impression that he did not suffer any social restriction in his Buddhist activities, and this must have been because of his status as a monk. He must have considered his homecoming trip as an adventure, removing a barrier which he never thought was possible.

Before he left for Sui China, a god appeared before him and advised him to go westward for study, saying, "Unless you win fame now, you will not bring about fruition in the future." This god can be considered as his secret desire to come to fame in Silla. In this connection, it is interesting to note that *Kobon Sui-jŏn* described in a part dealing with the life of Priest Wŏn'gwang that he met the god again after his return.

Truth and Reality

Wŏn'gwang was enthusiastically welcomed in Silla upon his return. The royal family and ranking government officials respected him as their mentor, and especially the king regarded him as a sage, according to historical records. In spite of such an enthusiastic welcome, he preferred a hermitic life and settled in Kasūl-sa Temple on Mt. Unmun, devoting himself to Buddhism. He was full of love for all, and smiled in preaching. He taught the way of Buddha to all people, irrespective of their social status. He preached the Mahayana Sūtra. In China he learned and preached the Discourse on Perfect Illumination, the Nirvana Sūtra, the Prajna Sūtra and the Mahayana Sūtra. He must have also preached all these sutras in Silla, raising his voice when he said that all people can attain the way of Buddha.

In spite of his enthusiasm for the preaching Buddhism, it is doubted that the Silla people at his time positively believed in Buddhism, because they were more attracted by shamanism and witchcraft. Moreover, his preaching must not have been welcomed by the royal family and the aristocrats, because they had no complaints about their present life of affluence. What they wanted was worldly fame and happiness, and they had these. So they must have prayed for the development of a government which guaranteed their fame and happiness. They had no ear to listen to Wŏn'gwang.

Without understanding him, they respected Wŏn'gwang as a great wizard. According to historical records, King Chinp'yŏng got over his illness after seeing a bright nimbus around Wŏn'gwang's head, and Queen Sŏndŏk personally gave food and clothes to him without help of others in order to monopolize his blessing, and allowed him to visit the court by cart when he was advanced in age.

Wŏn'gwang had to adapt himself to the life of Silla feeling as if he were in a strange land. In other words, he had to preach Buddhism in a manner suitable to the social realities of

Silla at the time. In this course of adaptation, he developed the divination-observation method in order to enlighten the people about Buddhism. He also preached the depth law of Buddhism to cure the king's illness, though the king did not understand it. By the depth law is meant the discourses on Nirvana, Prajna and Buddhist intellectualism. But it is more interesting to note that he made miracles by curing diseases by preaching.

The most serious problem to Wŏn'gwang must have been the relationship between the state and his Buddhism. Historical records say that the Silla dynasty relied on his for the methodology of government, and that he was at the head of a hundred priests when they held a prayer meeting in the prayer hall of Hwangnyong-sa Temple. The prayer meeting was called a Vajra meeting in which a hundred monks prayed for peace of the country and people and a bumper crop, chanting the Vajra Sūtra. Set up in the prayer hall were a hundred images each of Buddha, Bodhisattva and lions. But these—the presentation of an opinion on how to govern the country and the prayer meeting—were not problems to him.

What was a problem to him was the king's request that he write a letter to the Sui dynasty asking for its cooperation in Silla's scheme to destroy Koguryŏ. Historical records say that Wŏn'gwang replied to the King. "It is not the way for a monk to follow to destroy others for the sake of his own life. However, since I am a poor monk under Your Majesty and since I live on You Majesty's water and food, how can I object to Your Majesty's order?"

He had once forgotten the existence of Silla to pursue truth. But now he threw away the truth he believed in, in order to be faithful to Silla. Wŏn'gwang did not try to justify this contradiction himself. Instead he admitted that his letter to the Sui dynasty was against the teaching of Buddha. This suggests that he still had reason. However, he was no longer as enthusiastic and courageous in the quest for truth as he was when he left for China.

Wōn'gwang made a compromise between truth and reality. He thus became a weak-minded monk. But his compromise with reality was not on the basis of a base excuse, but was forced by the need to conform to the reality of Silla society at the time.

It must be noted that his compromise with social reality was in the direction of collaboration with the monarchy of Silla for political and social reforms. He shaved his head to become a monk and left for China to study Buddhism because he was disillusioned by the aristocratic society of Silla, and this suggests that he had in mind the possibility of collaboration with the monarchy due to his hatred for the aristocrats even before his departure for Sui China.

Silla noblemen called *Chin'gol* held in check the monarchial power by means of their institution called *Hwabaek* conference, while increasing their authority. The debate over the introduction of Buddhism was due to a power struggle between the monarch and the aristocrats. As a result, the adoption of Buddhism as national religion meant the victory of the monarch in this struggle. The monarchial law was made to agree with the Buddhist precept, and the country was called a Buddhist land. The people were the subjects of a king and at the same time the followers of Buddha. The monarch felt the need to reduce the power of *Chin'gol* noblemen who maintained their aristocratic tradition by means of shamanism. Wōn'gwang's collaboration with the monarchy also meant his collaboration with low-class noblemen, and he achieved, in fact, political collaboration between the monarch and low-class aristocrats.

The depth law of Buddhism which Wōn'gwang preached before the king must have had something to do with his collaboration with the monarchy. His preaching that all people can attain the way of Buddha can be regarded as his advice to the king that he appoint low-class aristocrats to important government posts. He had no eye to see the importance of commoners to government, but he apparently had an eye to see the importance of low-class aristocrats to government, especially the importance of their participation in the government. The fact that the king relied on him for the methodology of government can also be regarded as the king's approval of his political recommendations. Thus viewed, Wŏn'gwang was a pioneer of political and social reforms of the Silla society.

Faith and Morality

Two boys named Kwisan and Ch'uhang called on Wŏn'-gwang at Kasŭl-sa Temple and asked him to give the commandments they must follow until they die. Wŏn'gwang replied:

"There are ten Bodhisattva precepts in the Buddhist law, but I don't think you can follow them all because you are subjects of the king. So I give you the five mundane commandments—loyalty to the king, piety to parents, faith in friends, no retreat on the battleground, and selection in the killing of living things. Don't belittle them, but faithfully abide by them."

When the two boys asked for an explanation about the need for selection in the killing of living things, Wŏn'gwang said:

"Don't kill living things on the six purification days and in spring and summer. This means that when you must kill an animal, kill it on a selected day. Don't kill domestic animals such as cattle, horses and chickens, and small animals. This means that when you must kill an animals, kill the selected one. If you kill only what must be killed, and if you don't kill many animals, you will then follow one of the five mundane commandments."

Wŏn'gwang's five mundane commandments are well-known in Korean history. Legends have it that Kwisan and Ch'uhang strictly followed Wŏn'gwang's instructions, and that they were killed in action on the battleground observing the priest's commandment not to retreat before the enemy.

It is interesting to note that Wŏn'gwang separated the Bodhisattva precepts for monks from the law of morality for mundane people. This means that he did not forced all people to follow him. He followed the Bodhisattva precepts, but he did not impose them on ordinary people. Instead he presented them with a code of conduct suitable to them. This means that his understanding of society and life was deep and broad.

What relationship was there between his five commandments and the *Hwarang*, then? Although Wŏn'gwang's five mundane commandments are generally known as the code of conduct observed by *Hwarang* boys, there is no historical record supporting it. Kwisan and Ch'uhang were not members of the *Hwarang*, according to historical records. It is therefore considered that Wŏn'gwang must have given the commandments as a code of conduct not for the *Hwarang* only but for all youths of Silla. But considering the fact that the *Hwarang* were representative of Silla youths, and that monks played a role in the moral education of *Hwarang* boys, Wŏn'gwang's five mundane commandments can be regarded as the moral principles of the *Hwarang*.

Where did these five commandments come from? It appears that the first three commandments of loyalty, piety and faith came from Confucianism, and the fourth one of selection in the killing of animals from Buddhism. But they are all both Confucian and Buddhist morals in the broad sense of the two religions. Since Wŏn'gwang read many Confucian books his status as a Buddhist monk alone provides no basis for giving a definite answer to the question of the sources of these commandments. But this is not an important question, because all records of the time are in Chinese characters, though what they refer to are Sillan things. In other words, the records in Chinese characters tend to be modified by the Chinese way of thinking. What is important is that the five commandments were given as the code of conduct to Silla youths. Were the commandments suitable to the Silla society at Wŏn'gwang's time?

Of the five commandments, loyalty to the king is what must be kept by subjects in the expansion of the monarchial power. Piety is the standard of family morality and conforms to the patriarchal family system. The faith in friends is needed in group life such as the *Hwarang*. The item of no retreat before the enemy is a war rule required by a country rising by means of conquering others. Selection in the killing of animals places emphasis on domestic animals, as seen in Wŏn'gwang's addition explanation. Domestic animals were important property of Silla and one of the first prizes Silla soldiers took in war. This item is related to the development of a private ownership system in Silla, and also considered to show Wŏn'gwang's interest in the accumulation of national wealth.

Thus viewed, it can be said that Wŏn'gwang had a deep insight into the reality of Silla society and deep understanding of it. He fully deserved the name of a great spiritual leader of Silla. Correctly grasping Silla's potentiality of growth as a big power, he exerted himself toward the exploitation and development of it this growth potential of Silla. But we should not forget that he had a cold reason to separate strictly the religious life from the mundane life.

Epilogue

Wŏn'gwang died at 84, probably in the fifth year of Queen Sŏndŏk's rule, 636 years after Christ. He had left for China in the 11th year of King Chinp'yŏng's reign, 589 years after Christ, according to the Life of Priest Wŏn'gwang in *Kobon Sui-jŏn*. But some historical records say he died at 89 in the ninth year of Queen Sŏndŏk's rule.

He stayed long in Kasŭl-sa Temple, but he was in Hwang-nyong-sa Temple in the capital of Silla when he died. He must have spent the latter part of his life at Hwangnyong-sa Temple. Since this temple was considered as the shrine of the guardian spirit of Silla, it was a great honor for Silla monks to serve in this temple. Since historical records say that Queen Sŏndŏk personally gave food and clothes to him, she must have bowed first to him when she met him.

After his return from Sui China, the class system of Silla was no longer a problem to him. He must have thought that Silla was a Buddhist land, as Chajang did. But he always considered Silla as a Buddhist land as one thing, and Silla as a state another. He declared that killing the enemy for the sake of the country was against the teaching of Buddha. He separated the precepts for monks from the moral principles of mundane people. His goal was to propagate Buddhism and destroy the class system, called *Kolp'um*. Although his recommendations were accepted by the king on many occasions, and he had such a great disciple as Wŏnan, it is doubted that the Silla people at his time deeply understood him. Under the circumstances, he must have felt spiritual solitude.

High Priest Hyujŏng

—*Unity of Zen and Doctrinal Buddhism*—

U CHŎNG-SANG

Hyujŏng's real name was Ch'oe Yŏ-sin and later he made many pen names for himself such as Sōsan, another name for Mt: Myohyang in North P'yŏngan Province in which he lived long and to which he frequently retired.

As was usual in his time, there is an anecdote concerning his birth. His parent were in their fifties and without children. On a summer day his mother was dozing perched on the edge of the *maru*, or wooden floor, and met in her brief dream a hoary woman who told her: "Do not be surprised. I came to inform you of your impending pregnancy, a child destined to become a hero." When she awakened, the old woman was nowhere to be seen. It was a dream.

"What an absurd dream!" she said to herself. "To an old woman over fifty. . . ." So saying she blushed with shame on the one hand and on the other with secret joy. She had a secret longing for an heir.

The next spring, the 15th year of King Chungjong's reign (1520), she gave birth to a son. Nothing had given so much delight to her husband, Ch'oe Se-ch'ang. During the reign of King Yŏnsan when Se-ch'ang's father-in-law was implicated in a court plot and exiled, Se-ch'ang's father was also implicated and was stricken out of the *yangban* registry. The family recovered their honor eight years later, but Se-ch'ang was living late life in his native town, Anju, as a local government of-

39

ficial.

He named his only son Yŏ-sin, meaning "trust yourself.'
He so named his son because he was at the time so old that he
could no longer prepare the way to success for him and did not
expect to rely on him. Three years later, Se-ch'ang also had a
revealing dream, in which an old man appeared and said: "I
came to pay my respect to 'the child priest.' Please christen
him 'Cloud and Stork.'" He asked the meaning and was told:
"He is destined to wander about without settling in any one
place, like cloud or like a stork." He did not expect the prophesy
to prove right. But he sometimes called his son Unhak, Cloud
and Stork, and at other times teased his cute baby as "the child
priest." As he was growing up, his habit of play was different
from others; he piled up stones and called them Buddha and
built sand hills and called them pagodas.

As prophesied he became a Buddhist priest, but it was more
due to the unfortunate circumstances in which he grew up
than to the prediction that he became a priest. He was born
and grew up in a family not well-to-do but with the loving
care of his parents. However from his ninth year, family mis-
fortunes ensued one after another. He was bereaved of his
mother at the age of nine, and of his father the following year.
Later he wrote the following in his memorial ode to his parents:

> *"In the morning when my mother died when I was nine*
> *years of age, she called my name three times and I cried*
> *bitterly. I recall the day my father passed away, the even-*
> *ing my father embraced me tightly in his bosom under*
> *the bedding and passed away before I realized it."*

Thus he became an orphan in a year. It may be that from
this time on he might have felt the emptiness of life and the
longing for eternal life. At the time the magistrate of Anju, Yi
Sa-jung heard the sorry fate of this orphan and sent for him.
The boy composed and presented the following poem to the

magistrate:

> *"The sun began to decline over the tall pavilion congealed*
> *in perfume.*
> *And the snow that blankets the world looks like flowers."*

This impressed him as much as rumor had led him to believe. He adopted him as his son. Shortly afterward, he came up to Seoul when his foster father was reassigned to the central government in Seoul. Thus he was able to enroll in the *Sŏng-gyun'gwan*, the state college.

At the age of 15, he applied for the civil service examination for the first degree licentiate (*Chinsa*) but failed. Roused at the failure, along with a few of his unsuccessful colleagues, he left for the Honam area to meet Pak Sang, his teacher, who was on an official tour of the area. When he arrived there, Pak Sang had already left for Seoul. Dismayed at the news, the boys decided to have a sightseeing tour of the places of natural and historic interest in the province.

If Hyujŏng successfully passed the civil service examination, he might have become a priest considerably later or not at all. This trip to the southwestern province with his ill-starred friends became a decisive impetus for him to become a follower of Buddha.

The boys wandered around the large and small Buddhist temples scattered in and around Mt. Chiri and met an old priest, Sungin, in a small hermitage. He at once recognized the unusual features of Sōsan and said the following, more to himself than to anyone in particular: "You have an unusual body and spirit. If you change your mind and study Buddhism you may forget eternally the worldly gains and be free from pain. However hard you try in your life, the reward for travail is but an empty name. What a pity for you, Confucian student!"

Sōsan asked him: "What do you mean by studying Buddhism?" "Well," the old priest said, "the meaning cannot be explained in words." And he produced several Buddhist scriptures which he had never seen before and told him to read them carefully. What Sŏsan learned and practiced were the sayings and deeds of Confucius and Chu Hsi, and his supreme goal was to become a high-ranking government official complete with learning and virtue. However, Sungin's suggestive sayings and his cursory reading of Buddhist sutras opened a completely different world before him in which what mattered most was neither honor nor material gain but the eternal life in the world of Buddha. He at once recognized the uselessness of his Confucian studies. Reading the change in his mind, Sungin introduced Sŏsan to High Priest Yŏnggwan, a very famous Buddhist of the time.

Left alone behind his colleagues, Sŏsan became a novice under Priest Yŏnggwan, practicing Zen meditation and studying the deep meaning of various Buddhist sutras. After six years of apprenticeship under Yŏnggwan, he suddenly obtained "enlightenment" which was beyond verbal explanation. Exalted at his sudden awakening, he composed the following poem:

> "At the cooing of a cuckoo I looked out the window.
> Isn't it my native country, the spring hills that fill my eyes?"

The following day he composed another poem:

> "On my way home from the well with water, I turn my face.
> To see countless green mountains in the white clouds."

On the third day, he had his hair shaved off with a silver knife and took a vow of celibacy: "Even if I were to live my whole life as a stupid and illiterate person, I shall never become a Confucian teacher who lives by deciphering the meaning of characters."

With Sungin as his mentor and Puyong as his teacher of Buddhist Law, Sŏsan became a Buddhist priest. He was given the Buddhist name, Hyujŏng. Another of his pen names was Ch'ŏngho.

After the ceremony of ordination, he spent several years in the Tosol-san and Turyu-san Mountains, Samch'ŏl Cave and Taesŭng-am Hermitage, and then set out for a tour of scenic places. One day he was passing through a village called Yŏk-songch'on on his way to his friend's. Here he obtained great enlightenment at hearing the crowing of a cock at high noon. He picked up a fallen leaf and wrote the following poem:

> *"Even if my hair turns white,*
> *My mind stays young. The ancients have already said:*
> *Now hearing the crow of a cock,*
> *A man is able to finish a great work."*

Later this poem was called the "Ode of Obtaining Enlightenment."

Thereafter he spent half a year in the Odae-san Mountains, one year in the Diamond Mountains, and one summer at Mt. Hyangno-bong. Seven or eight years passed in his wandering like cloud and stork since he left Mt. Turyu-san.

During the times King Myŏngjong succeeded Chungjong and there were signs favorable for the revival of Buddhism. Queen Munjong, the regent for the young king, was a devout Buddhist. She reversed the anti-Buddhism policy of the previous reigns and helped re-establish the two Orders of Zen and Doctrinaire Buddhism and restored the state examination system for Buddhist clergy. Confucian scholars rose against the move, but Queen Munjong proclaimed the rehabilitation of Buddhism in 1550.

The first state examination for Buddhist clergy was held the following year, 1551, in which Sŏsan came out the first of the 406 successful applicants. Thus he was awarded the title of Taesŏn, the lowest grade in the hierarchy, and was promoted to Chŭngdŏk in 1553. He spent the summer of 1553 in Tondo-am Hermitage at Mt. Diamond, the hermitage located among soaring peaks of rock formations. From here he started for the Kwandong region. Passing through the famed Myŏngsasimni, or ten-*li* stretch of bright sand, he composed the following poem:

> *"The five-colored cloud over the Fairy Land*
> *Makes rain on the sobbing sand.*
> *The flowers of wild rose have all gone.*
> *We are three priests but there is only one ten-thousand-*
>   *house."*

Ten-thousand house refers to one of the three priests who happened to have the name, Chang Man-ho, meaning ten thousand houses.

The year when he turned 35 years of age, he returned to his native country after a long absence. Despite the long passage of time, his memories of miserable boyhood days were as fresh as ever. He was alone in his half-demolished house when a village girl passing by the house with her grandfather peeped through the broken window to find a strange man sitting there alone. The old man asked who he was, thinking it very strange to find a man in an abandoned house. It took some time before he could recognize the man was Yŏ-sin, the poor boy who had been orphaned some two and half decades ago. Despite the strong urging of the old man, Sōsan resolved to spend the evening in his old house, and before leaving the house he wrote a poem on the wall:

> *"Returning to my native village after 30 years.*
> *The villagers have gone, leaving the houses and the*
>   *village in ruin.*
> *The green mountain refuses to say any thing and the sun*
>   *sets over the spring sky.*
> *A cooing of cuckoo makes me sadder."*

In the following year when he was 36 years of age, he promoted to chief secretary of the Doctrinal Order and three months later he was appointed concurrently as the chief secretary of the Zen Order. In the spring of the same year he paid a visit to Pongŭn-sa Temple, which was then headed by Priest Pou and under the patronage of Queen Munjong. Later he became the chief of this temple, succeeding Pou. However, since he became the head priest of a temple and chief secretary of the two Orders of Buddhism, the knowledge dawned on him that the official duties imposed on him were not the concern of a priest who vowed to abandon worldly honor and wealth. Two years later, he resigned from his official duties on the pretext of eye disease and went back to Diamond Mountain.

The following poem entitled "Ode to Three Dreams," which he composed during his stay in the Diamond Mountain eloquently tells his spiritual attitude:

> *"The host tells his dream to the guest.*
> *The guest tells his own to the host.*
> *Now the two who are saying their dreams.*
> *Are they not also in a dream?"*

Leaving this poem behind him, he climbed Mt. Hyangno-bong which commanded a superb view below him, so grand and superb that he was ashamed of his life as the chief priest and the chief secretary of the Order. The following poem entitled "Hyangno-bong Poem" shows how he felt at the time on the top of the high mountain:

> *"The capital cities of the world are but an ant's nest,*
> *Heroes of the ancient times but mayflies.*
> *The moon shines through the window on my clean pillow,*
> *And the sound of ceaseless pine wind is ever more leisurely."*

He never thought this poem would implicate him in a conspiracy plot in later years.

He left Diamond Mountain and moved back to a hermitage on Mt. Turyu. When he was living there, a Confucian scholar in the neighborhood paid a visit to him at the hermitage. He said half-derisively: "You seem in needy circumstances compared to the pomp of your former years, and gloomier." "Well," Sŏsan said after a hearty laugh, "even before I became the chief secretary, I have slept on the pillow of Mt. Diamond with a single robe and a bowl. Now I have laid myself on the pillow of Mt. Turyu with a surplice and a begging bowl. Since I have lived my life in the mountains, not in the mundane world, worldly honor does not delight me nor the loss of it make me sad. These are things of the mundane world, not the world of mind."

In October 1589, an abortive revolt was staged by Chŏng Yŏ-lip from Chŏnju, which was soon pacified. But the rank and file Buddhist clergy were arrested in the wake of the revolt because many of them took part in the revolt. Many Buddhist temples scattered around Mt. Kyeryong and Kuwŏl in fact served as rebels' hide-outs, which put Buddhism in a very difficult position. As the event developed, many who had relations with Buddhism suffered directly or indirectly. The public security office arrested a priest by the name of Muŏp who during interrogation implicated Sŏsan in the incident by citing his "Hyangno-bong Poem" and also falsely accused Sŏsan's trusted disciple, Yujŏng (Samyŏngdang). Thus Sŏsan was arrested on Mt. Myohyang and Yujŏng in Kangnŭng.

Accused as he was of sedition, Sŏsan had no complaints and his answers to interrogation were clear, logical and perfectly calm. In no way did he look like a man who could plot sedition. King Sŏnjo sent for his book of poems for his personal examination, only to be struck with his outstanding talent in poetry and loyalty. The king had him acquitted and sent him a piece of bamboo painting in monochrome, asking him to compose a poem. Thus freed from custody, he composed the following couplet in his deep appreciation of the king's grace:

> "A bamboo branch from Hsieh-hsiang
> King's brush made its leaves grow.
> If I, a mountain priest, carry it with me
> Each of the leaves will bear the sound of autumn."

In answer to this poem, King Sŏnjo composed the following poem:

> "The leaves are given birth by the tip of my brush,
> The root did not come from the earth.
> Even the moon will not cast its shadow
> Nor the wind make any sound."

King Sŏnjo awarded him sumptuous gifts in recognition of the troubles and hardships he had undergone. Since then Hyujŏng's name became widely known.

Three years after the abortive revolt of Chŏng Yŏ-lip, the Japanese invaded Korea in 1592. Landing at Pusan on April 14, the Japanese army captured Pusan and Tongnae and moved up to Seoul. The king and his entourage fled as far north as the Amnok River. It was after the King's entourage reached Ŭiju that the king received news of the first victory, which however, was not won by the regular army but a militia unit led by Cho Hŏn. A detailed report said that Priest Kihodang played a significant role in the battle. This news reminded the king of Hyujŏng. He immediatly sent for him at Mt. Myohyang.

Hyujŏng was then an old man in his seventies. At the admonition of the king, he made a vow before him that he would mobilize all the priests and had those who could not fight pray for expulsion of the enemy and the able bodied priests fight the enemy with him. The king appointed him as the chief of the 16 Orders of Buddhism in eight provinces and ordered the creation of a priest militia unit under him. Thus appointed as the priest-general, Hyujŏng sent out appeals to his fellow priests to rise against the enemy to rescue the kingdom.

Thus aroused, Sōsan's disciple Samyŏngdang (Yujŏng) raised a priest militia unit in Kangwŏn Province and fought his way to P'yŏngyang; Priest Kihodang, who participated in the recapture of Ch'ŏngju under Cho Hŏn, fought the enemy in the Diamond Mountain; Priest Ch'oyong rose in the Honam area; and priest Haean in the Yŏngnam area. Later Samyŏngdang joined force with Sōsan and participated in the recapture of P'yŏngyang. Priest Kihodang was killed in the Kŭmsan Battle and Priest Ch'oyong participated in the battle at Haengju Fortress under General Kwŏn Yul.

Finally the Ming Chinese expeditionary forces helped the loyal troops and the militia units to drive out the enemy. The king returned to Seoul the following year. Confucian officials were jealous of Sōsan's frequent and easy access to the palace. Some complained that Sōsan had more frequent audience with the king than a minister. But his name was known even to the enemy camp and the Chinese expeditionary forces. The Chinese general wrote the following panegyric:

"You never cared for honor and profit.
But concentrated on the study of Buddhism.
But on hearing the urgency of the kingdom,
You came down from the mountain in a hurry."

Two years later, he resigned from the military services due to his old age and entrusted the duties to his disciples, Samyŏngdang and Ch'oyong, and returned once again to his hermitage in Mt. Myohyang. In recognition of his great services at the time of national crisis, the king bestowed on him the highest title of the Buddhist order, and had memorial shrines built for him. The first shrine thus erected was the P'yoch'ung-sa in Miryang, birthplace of Samyŏngdang in which the tablets of Sōsan, Samyŏngdang and Kihodang were enshrined. Another memorial shrine was built in Taehŭng-sa Temple where Sōsan's belongings were preserved. The third one was built in Mt. Myohyang where he lived the longest. His portraits and memorial stones were enshrined and erected in other major Buddhist temples of the country in later years.

After a short sojourn in Mt. Myohyang, he moved to Sŏg-wang-sa Temple and wrote *Unbong Sŏgwang-sa-gi*, the chronicle of Sŏgwang-sa Temple in Mt. Unbong, which described in detail the association between the founding king of the Yi dynasty and Priest Muhak and the history of the temple. At the time he wrote this chronicle, which was not included in his collected works, he was 79 years old. The book is a very important historical document and valued for his handwriting.

Time was running out for Sŏsan. It was on the morning of January 22, 1604. He called all the priests in the Wŏnjok-am Hermitage on Mt. Myohyang around him and gave them the last of his preaching. After the ceremony was over, he had his portrait brought before him and wrote the following on the back of the painting: "The portrait was I eighty years ago, and eighty years later I became the portrait." And then he composed another poem in praise of Buddha:

> *"Everything that calculates and schemes*
> *Is but a flake of snow that falls into a hot brazier.*
> *An ox fashioned with earth goes over the water.*
> *And then the earth and the heaven were broken in*
> *   pieces."*

Again he wrote two letters, one for his beloved disciple Samyŏngdang and the other for Ch'oyong who could not join him at his last moment, and then it is said that he passed away as he was seated.

Sŏsan's philosophy is best expressed in his *Sŏn-ga-gugam*, or The Paragon of a Zen Priest. It is an introduction to the Zen sect which was widely known in China and Japan. His motive and purpose in writing the book are well illustrated in the following quotations of his preface:

In ancient times, those who studied Buddhism did not

say what Buddha did not say, and did not do what Buddha did not do. Therefore what they cherished most was only the holy writings contained in sutras. However, what the students of Buddha recite nowadays are the writings the conventional scholars recite, and what they want to learn are the poems of scholar-officials. It is very sad to think that these are what the students of Buddha cherish the most. Although I myself am none too good a man, I have selected, in order to lessen the burden of my juniors with which they will plough the massive collection of Buddhist scriptures, about one hundred most essential sentences from the scriptures. Now that I have finished the selection, the sentences are very simple but replete with meaning. . . .

In the beginning of the book intended to establish a unified Order of Buddhism, he explained the general idea of Buddhism in the following words: "There is a thing which is by nature infinite, bright, supernatural, and ethereal, with no beginning and end, cannot be named or expressed in shape."

In *Sŏngyo-sŏk*, Explanation on Zen and Doctrinal Buddhism, which was written later than the above book, his views and thought came out clearer. In the book he comparatively analyzed Zen and Doctrinal Buddhism and pronounced that the Doctrinal sect is but a means to enter the Zen sect. He said Zen is the mind of Buddha and the Doctrinal is the word of Buddha. The word must go into the mind; thus one must go through the Doctrinal into the Zen. In this book he established his firm conviction on Buddhism and explained the fundamental tenet of unified Buddhism, which was then divided into the Doctrinal and the Zen sects, one blaming the other. His idea of going into Zen through the Doctrinal sect meant that Buddhism is one that cannot be divided into two. His idea was not a novel one but his strong advocacy of the unity of the two sects almost brought them into one, and many studied the Zen and the Doctrinal schools at the same time in order to achieve

Buddhahood.

Sōsan's idea of the unity of Zen and the Doctrinal school derived from Priest Pyŏksŏng who dwelt on Zen but did not abandon the Doctrinal, and Priest Puyong, his mentor, who, starting with the Doctrinal, later reached the conclusion that the essence of Buddhism lay outside the Doctrinal. His idea was not new, but it was he alone who could unify the two opposing sects of Buddhism which persisted since the previous dynasty. His position in the history of Korean Buddhism is eminent, and his presence marked a turning period in the Yi dynasty Buddhism.

His other books include *Sŏngyo-gyŏl* (the Secrets of the Zen and the Doctrinal schools), and *Samga-gugam* (Paragons of Confucianism, Buddhism and Taoism), *Ch'ŏnghodang-jip* (Collected Works of Ch'ŏnghodang), and others.

The Life and Thought of Sŏ Kyŏng-dŏk

CHŎNG CHONG-BOK

In Korea where the influence of Neo-Confucianism, which flourished in Sung China, was dominant, with dualism of the *li* (理; principle) and *chi* (氣; material force), advocated by Cheng Tzu and Chu Hsi, forming the mainstream. It was the vogue among Korean Confucianists to indulge in *li-chi* controversies once in their academic careers.

Contrary to the general trend of his times, Sŏ Kyŏng-dŏk (1489-1546, Pokchae by pen name but more familiarly known as Hwadam named after the place where he lived in what is now Kaesŏng) alone proposed *chi*-monism, thereby becoming Korea's first Confucian philosopher of originality.

There are, of course, criticisms that Hwadam was heavily influenced by Chang Heng-chu of China and his metaphysics was an imitation of the philosophy of Chao Kang-chieh of China. However, it should be made clear that Sŏ attained a stage neither Chang nor Chao arrived at. Hwadam became the founder of Korea's *chi*-monism. It should be added here that even if some of Sŏ's theories retain traces of partial influences from the phraseology or thought of Chang and Chao, the Korean philosopher made one step forward and created an entirely different world which the Chinese Confucians had never reached.

In a treatise, "*Wŏn-li-chi*" (Original Principle and Material Force), Sŏ discusses the Universe by dividing it into *Sŏnch'ŏn* (roughly comparable to Reality in the Western philosophy) and *Huch'ŏn* (World of Phenomena).

Sŏ explains *Sŏnch'ŏn* as *T'aehŏ* (Great Void), which is transparent and has no form, originally having no beginning and no ending, being infinite and omnipresent, filled only with *chi*. There is nothing which is larger than Great Void, which is preceded by nothing and whose origin defies human imagination. The *chi* which fills Great Void is so transparent and tranquil that it shows no form to grasp.

Great Void cannot be grasped as if it were Non-Being; yet it pervades the Universe without the slightest empty space. Therefore, it cannot be considered Non-Being. If one tries to seize it, one will find emptiness. As it is all pervading, Great Void cannot be called non-existent; as it is transparent, Great Void cannot be regarded as Being. It does not send forth a sound to be heard; nor does it emit an odor to be smelled. Therefore, Great Void is a void which is not void; such a void means *chi*.

Therefore, it would be a mistake to say that *chi* (material force) springs from the void, for if we say that *chi* is given birth to by the void, then it would mean that there was no *chi* before its birth. Any void without *chi* is a dead one; and such a void could not exist from the beginning. A dead void is incapable of giving birth to *chi*, and so such a void cannot be considered Great Void.

Hwadam's *chi* is a void that has no beginning, is transparent denying any effort to probe into its origin, but it is not really void, however.

This line of thought is basically different from the thought of Lao Tze when he said, "Being was given birth by Non-Being."

If we try to explain Hwadam's Great Void in the same way as we explain Lao Tze's thought on Being, our explanation would be that *chi* comes into being from the void, which certainly is far from what the former gave as an explanation of his Great Void, because he saw the void as *chi*.

What Hwadam meant by *chi* is the essence and substance of what is transparent and tranquil. Therefore, the essence and substance of Great Void are different names for *chi*, which he explained as "All that has no ultimate are manifestations of Great Ultimate." This is reminiscent of Chou Lien-chi's reference to the state which cannot be described with words.

In the beginning the Universe was filled with things which could not be perceived with their forms, colors, or voices; and so they were all called "void of the ultimate." However, there was an action in the midst of these things which could not be discerned by forms, colors, or voices, and the action came to be called. Great Ultimate.

Explaining *Huch'ŏn* (World of Phenomena), Hwadam said that movements arose in *Sŏnch'ŏn* where everything was transparent and tranquil, giving rise to a chain of creations. These movements, according to Sŏ, were not passive but inevitable; and this is called *li* (principle). This is also reminiscent of Chou Lien-ch'i saying that "*T'aegŭk* (Great Ultimate) moves and gives birth to *Yang* (the Positive)."

Sŏ already explained it as "One Material Force," which inevitably includes two, because the concept "one" presupposes the existence of the concept "two." One inevitably gives birth to two, which in turn gives birth to many others. That a chain of these movements occurred was due to the action of *chi*, which was the beginning of *Yang* (the Positive) and *Yin* (the Negative), as well as the essence of movement and immovability.

Divided, the "One Material Force" became *Yang* and *Yin*, *Yang* became Heaven after the end of all its movements and *Yin* became Earth after the end of its collections. The crystallization of *Yang* movements is the sun and that of *Yin* movements the moon. By-products of their movements were the stars, water, fire, etc., which Sŏ called *Huch'ŏn* (phenomena).

In a treatise, "Discourse on *Li* and *Chi*," Hwadam explained that *li* is one part of *chi* and cannot exist independent of *chi*. According to him, the essence of *chi* is oneness.

It is inevitable for one to give birth to two, thereby touching off one creation after another. What caused the series of creations through movement and quiescence was *T'aegŭk* (Great Ultimate) which is *li*.

Li cannot exist in separation from *chi*; nor can *li* be thought of without *chi*. It is said that *li* presides over *chi*; but *li* is not a presiding office who came from outside but is already in *chi* and hence on attribute of *chi*.

After a profound study on *chi*-monism, Sŏ finally realized the principle of indestructibility of matter. He said that birth and death are but gathering and dispersion of *chi*.

That *chi* remains the same without losing or gaining throughout its gathering and dispersion, Sŏ asserted, is due to its infinity and indestructibility. It is a mistake, he taught, to think that there is another world outside our universe. The material force, even that which resides in a tiny wild plant, never vanishes; all that pervades the universe is *chi* which has no beginning and no ending.

Even though things perish and disappear, the *chi* which existed in them never vanishes. The same can be said of humans. Even though men die and they can never be seen again, their souls never return to nil. *Chi* is eternally indestructible although there may be varying degrees in the scope and speed of gathering and dispersion.

"If one arrives at this stage after repeated studies, one will realize the subtlety of truth which sages of all ages may never have thought of."

Thus speaking, Hwadam was confident that he had realized it.

Sŏ Kyŏng-dŏk was by nature aloof and remote from officialdom. It seems that he was influenced decisively by a series of bloody purges of scholar.

Since the reign of King Sejo there had developed four factions among scholars and officials in and outside the government. One was a faction comprising ranking officials and government-patronized scholars who helped King Sejo usurp the throne. They included Chŏng In-ji, Ch'oe Hang, Yi Sŏk-hyŏng, Sin Suk-chu, Yang Sŏng-ji and Sŏ Kŏ-jŏng. Another was a group of scholars out of power who, indignant at the usurpation, decided to spend the rest of their lives in wandering. Most notable among them was Kim Si-sŭp.

The third faction consisted mainly of scholars in the Yŏngnam (presently Kyŏngsang Provinces) district, who, refusing to serve government posts, believed that they inherited the true tradition of scholars. They had included such notable as Kim Chong-jik, Kim Koeng-p'il, Chŏng Yŏ-ch'ang, Kim Il-son, and Yu Ho-in. The fourth group, also comprising scholars out of power, won a great acclaim from many scholars as they regarded authority and honor as something detestable and dirty, and decided to spend their time with scholarly talks and pursuit of literary refinement.

Factional feuding was ceaseless among the four groups, most fierce being the opposition between the scholars who had already established their positions firmly in the government and the Yŏngnam faction comprising scholars out of power. Their strife for power formed a remote cause of alienating scholars from officialdom and attracting them to life in the countryside, discussing philosophy with their disciples.

Their struggle finally entailed the scholar purges known as *Muo Sahwa* and *Kapcha Sahwa*. After the enthronement of King Chung-jong upon the ousting of King Yŏnsan, two more purges ensued, known as *Kimyo Sahwa* and *Ŭlsa Sahwa*, making scholars realize bitterly the futility of life in officialdom and inclined more and more to life buried in learning like the one Hwadam was leading. Especially the last two scholar purges had a decisive influence on the shaping of thought of Hwadam.

After the scholar purges, a number of Confucianists lost the desire to serve the government and returned to the mountains or their homes to spend the days not with political talks but with scholarly talks. Having realized the transitoriness of life

in the government earlier than anybody else, he firmly decided
to keep himself aloof from public life. Refusing repeated advice from his friends and the royal court to advance to officialdom, he returned to his home on Hwadam in Kaesŏng,
where he studied Neo-Confucianism with his disciples in
honorable poverty and uprightness. His devotion to learning
finally enabled him to establish such a creative theory as *chi*-
monism. Severing learning from politics, he dedicated himself
to learning throughout his life.

His seniors and illustrious scholars such as Cho Kwang-jo,
Kim Sik, Han Ch'ung, Kim Chŏng, Kim An-guk, and Kim
Chŏng-guk were sentenced to death in a scholar purge in the
14th year of King Chŏngjong's reign. This tragedy taught Sŏ
that while excellence in the learning of Confucianism served as
a tool for rising in officialdom, it could at the same time bring
about an appalling destruction.

Besides Sŏ Kyŏng-dŏk, there were many Confucian scholars
who preferred life in the countryside to life in officialdom. But
most of them were profoundly influenced by Sŏ, such as Yi
Ŏn-jŏk, Yi Hwang, Cho Sik, Kim In-hu, Ki Dae-sŭng, and Yi
I. Witnessing a series of bloody scholar purges, they severed
ties with officialdom and devoted themselves to philosophic
meditation and metaphysical inquiries.

To most Korean Confucianists, the basis was the learning of
Cheng Tzu and Chu Hsi of Sung China and they never
tolerated any slightest deviation from this line. Hwadam's attitude of learning and his practical life under these circumstances can be evaluated as perfect, showing a model for all
the emulate. Resolutely and courageously he replaced *li-chi*
monism, held in esteem as an unrefutable truth, with *chi*-
monism, a great achievement unprecedented in the history of
Korean philosophy. Before Sŏ Kyŏng-dŏk all Korean Confucianists believed that both *li* and *chi* are the central governing
forces of the universe, *li* more pivotal than *chi*. Sŏ maintained,
however, that *li* is part of *chi* and that as *chi* is Great Void,
li merely resides in *chi*.

Great Void, namely *chi*, has the capability to act and does not lose its justification, and its justified action is called *li* (principle). As *li* coexists with *chi*, *li* which has left *chi* cannot be thought of. Some say that *li* presides over *chi*, Sŏ maintained, but *li* is not anything which entered from outside but exists in *chi* which is ever moving; and this means that *li* did not exist before *chi*. This theory of Hwadam may have seemed to *li* advocates to be full of dilemmas. However, Hwadam's theory later stimulated the rise of a group of scholars known as the Kiho School, whose representatives were Ki Dae-sŭng and Yi I.

On the basis of his *chi*-monism, Sŏ Kyŏng-dŏk discovered the law of indestructibility of matter. Even though matter disappears, it means merely that *chi* changed from one position to another. Disappearance of forms does not mean any change or reduction in *chi* which is indestructible. Chemical changes in colors and forms or physical changes in nature do not bring about destruction to matter concerned. This thought is similar to the Buddhist theory of reincarnation.

The greatness of Hwadam can also be found in his life which was devoted to putting what he learned through reading and meditation into practice. Intelligent by birth, he did not aim at government service, and devoted his whole life to study. His lofty and upright character deserves everlasting admiration. As a philosopher he reached the stage where he could find truth by investigating things; and in such a stage he could not once be heard to grumble, never showing an attitude improper for a gentleman. It is more proper to say that Hwadam taught himself rather than to say that he learned under a tutor before he built up his scholarship to such an eminent height. Even though it cannot be denied that the Chinese classics served him as the basis for his learning, his attitude of study was quite different from ordinary scholars.

He was endowed with an exceptionally keen ability of observation. Even in childhood he never let himself overlook a strange thing without investigating its cause. When he had doubts, he pondered day after day until he found a satisfactory answer. Only after he understood the cause did he let himself move to another subject.

It is a well-known episode that he attentively observed the phenomenon of the earth's heat ascending in the morning and before dusk, and he devotedly probed into its cause. Another well-known episode is that at the young age of 18 he came across the passage "truth exists in investigation of things," while reading *the Great Learning* and realized its truth. In tears of overwhelming emotion, he stood up and wrote the character "things" on the wall, which became the theme of his meditation thereafter.

His learning was broad, encompassing not only metaphysics but astronomy, geography, medicine, pharmacology, divination, and astrology.

It is said that he was greatly delighted at seeing his disciples progress in learning. Though confined to the countryside, he deplored greatly when he was informed of a mistake in politics and of its evil effects. From this can we conclude that Sŏ's interest was not solely learning.

When his illness confined him to his bed and his last moments were approaching, one of his disciples asked him, "What is your thought today, sir?" Sŏ replied calmly, "I have already known the rule of life and death. My mind is at peace."

After his death in August 1546, he was buried on the hill at the rear of his home. The epitaph on his tombstone was simple: "The Grave of *Saengwŏn* Sŏ Kyŏng-dŏk." (*Saengwŏn* was a title accorded to those who passed the higher civil service examination in the administration department.) Twenty-eight years later the royal court accorded him the posthumous titles of Junior Deputy Prime Minister, Chief Royal Tutor, and Curator of the Ch'unch'ugwan Royal Archives.

Historical Review
of Korean Confucianism

PAK CHONG-HONG

Importation of Confucianism and
Its Development
until the 14th Century (An Outline)

According to a reliable book, *Samguk Sagi* (Chronicles of the Three Kingdoms), it was in 372 A.D., or during the second year of the reign of King Sosurim of Koguryŏ, that a national university dedicated to Confucian education was established in Korea. It is, therefore, safe to consider that the introduction of Confucianism to Korea took place long before that time—probably in the early days of the Koguryŏ dynasty when, according to historical records, the people of Koguryŏ had already learned (Chinese) characters and had put them to daily use. Wang Kyung of the Lolang district was invited to China in 69 A.D. by Emperor Ming-ti of Latter Han, where he distinguished himself by contributing to the improvement of irrigation methods in China and where he also devoted himself to the study of the Changes and became well versed in its teaching (Volume 82, Book of Latter Han). The kingdom of Koguryŏ, adjoining both the Chinese mainland and the Chinese colony of Lolang, must have benefited greatly from its favorable geographical position in establishing active cultural intercourse with China from early times. This made Koguryŏ the first kingdom in Korea to introduce

Confucianism. Besides the national university, in many parts of Koguryŏ there were private Confucian schools called *kyŏngdang*.

The Kingdom of Paekche established a doctorate system in the study of Confucian scriptures—testimony to the fact that there was a national university in the kingdom for the teaching of Confucianism. It was during the reign of King Kŭn-choko (371-374) that eminent Paekche scholars, such as Ajikki and Wang In, were dispatched to Japan to become teachers of Confucianism to Japanese princes and to the nobility. It is certain that Paekche established a national Confucian university almost at the same time as did Koguryŏ.

Silla, though a little behind Koguryŏ and Paekche in the early days of its history, also imported Confucianism from China. History reveals that in the year 648 Kim Ch'un-ch'u, a member of the royal family who later acceded to the throne to become King Muyŏl, went to T'ang China to inspect the Chinese national university. Remaining Silla inscriptions on gold plates or stone monuments tell how Silla youths made a pledge to devote themselves to the study of Confucian classics.

After Silla's unification of the Korean peninsula by destroying the kingdoms of Koguryŏ and Paekche in 669, a number of great Confucian scholars emerged, among them Kangsu and Sŏl Ch'ong. In order to make it easier for Koreans to read Confucian scriptures, Sŏl Ch'ong invented a new writing device by means of which the sounds of Silla words could be transcribed into Chinese characters. A large number of Korean students were sent to China for study, and those who gained a reputation in China for their scholarly achievements included Kim Un-kyŏng, Kim Ka-gi and Ch'oe Ch'i-wŏn. Especially the latter became the object of national admiration in China for his writing of a letter encouraging government forces setting out on a punitive expedition against insurgents led by Huang Chao.

During the Koryŏ era the government enforced the *Kwagŏ*

(Civil Service Examination System) and established the *Kukjagam* (a national university). Private Confucian schools began to be established by Confucian politicians during the reign of King Munjong (1047-1082) in order to expand the education of youth. There were 12 *kongdo* (student groups), such as the Munhŏn found by Ch'oe Ch'ung and the Hongmun by Chŏng Bae-kul. The former, the largest, consisted of nine schools. Ch'oe Ch'ung was familiarly called "Kung-tzu of the East" in praise of his great personality and his great influence. The private Confucian school system of Koryŏ can be regarded as an outgrowth of Koguryŏ's *kyŏngdang*. The foremost objective of these schools was to teach Confucian scriptures and history and to enhance morality.

Neo-Confucianism was first introduced to Korea from Yüan China during the reign of King Ch'ungnyŏl. Koryŏ scholar An Hyang visited Peking, the capital of Yüan, in 1290 (16th year of King Ch'ungnyŏl's reign) and returned home with a copy of a revised book by Chu Hsi and a copy of his portrait. At home An endeavored to restore Confucian learning from its temporary decadence caused by the prevalence of Buddhism and of shamanistic practices. With boundless veneration for Chu Hsi, he took as his pen name Hoehŏn which resembled Chu Hsi's pen name—Hoeam (Korean pronunciation). His disciple, Paek Yi-jŏng, remained in China for 10 years and, on his way home, brought with him books on Neo-Confucianism written by Cheng-tze and Chu Hsi. Kwŏn Bu studied Chu Hsi's *Ssu-shu Chi-chou* (Collected Annotations of the Four Books). U Tak is widely known as the first Korean who studied philosophy so deeply as to be able to comprehend Cheng Tze's *I-chuan* (Commentary on the Book of Changes). Yi Je-hyŏn accompanied King Ch'ungsŏn to China, where he maintained frequent contact with eminent Chinese scholars and gained a reputation for his profound knowledge of Confucian scriptures and Confucian literature. Yi Saek (whose pen name was Mogŭn), Chŏng Mong-ju (P'oŭn) and Kil Jae (Yaŭn) were also representative Confucian scholars of the period, being called

the *Sam Ŭn* (The Three Ŭns). Among them it was Chŏng
Mong-ju who introduced a new attitude toward the study of
philosophy. Not only is he highly admired because he suffered
martyrdom in order to defend his loyalty to Koryŏ at the time
of the dynasty's fall, but he resolved to comprehend the true
meaning of Confucian scriptures with his own meditation and
experience as a basis. As a result he won fame among scholars,
including Yi Saek who spared nothing in his praise of Chŏng
saying that not one of his theories contradicted truth.Chŏng's
interpretation, rich as it was in originality, made many
suspicious of its accuracy; but all were moved to admiration
once they found his theories in conformity with the expositions
conducted and published by Chinese authorities. Chŏng came
to be called the founder of Neo-Confucianism in Korea. Inheriting Chu Hsi's philosophy, he even tried to propagate *Chu
Hsi Chia-li* (Chu Hsi's Book on Family Rites). At any rate, he
was the first scholar to elevate Korean Confucianism to the
level of true philosophical meditation.

Confucianism, since its introduction, had been studied
from its literary aspects or as a means for politics or moral
cultivation. No scholar ever tried to study it with the depth
of philosophical meditation until Chŏng. Although the influence of Neo-Confucianism should not be overlooked, it is
true that Korean Confucianism, with the emergence of
Chŏng, started the process of deepening its inner, basic
attitude.

Laying the Foundation
for Yi Dynasty Confucianism
(From late 14th to early 16th centuries)

It was the Yi dynasty which designated Confucianism
Korea's state religion. In the early days of the dynasty Chŏng
Do-jŏn wrote an essay criticizing Buddhism and Taoism in
light of Confucianism. Kwŏn Kŭn fixed *kugyŏl*, a method of

reading Confucian scriptures by inserting Korean suffixes. A pioneer in the field of Neo-Confucianism, he also discussed the subjects of *hsin* (mind), *chi* (element or matter) and *li* (principle or reason). According to him, it is with *hsin* that Buddhism is mostly occupied in its desire to get rid man of earthly considerations but still interfering in everything, while Taoism, centering around *chi* and concentrating on preservation of life force, is apt to neglect the judgment of right and wrong thus abandoning everything and ending up by doing nothing. Therefore, he reasons, these two religions are inclined either to withering and self-annihilation or self-indulgence and extravagance, both harming to social morality. Confucianism, on the contrary, he says, is based on *li* and controls both *hsin* and *chi*, thus possessing every attribute of the highest good. It is the merit of Confucianism, he continues, that it teaches humble self-criticism with awe, thereby broadening what should be broadened and stopping what should be prevented. He explained the fundamental doctrine of Confucianism with a diagram, teaching that the Four Beginnings (sympathy, shame, concession and reason) originate from human nature which is the source of *li*, hence they are good and there is nothing intrinsically evil, and that the Seven Emotions (pleasure, anger, sadness, fear, love, hate, and desire) spring from *hsin* which is the source of *chi* and becomes either good or evil. With this theory he became a forerunner in the dispute on the Four Beginnings and the Seven Emotions which developed in the succeeding centuries. Chŏng Do-jŏn and Kwŏn Kŭn, so to speak, laid the basis for Yi dynasty Confucianism.

Toward the close of the 15th century a group of scholars emerged led by Kim Jong-jik and Kim Koeng-p'il who emphasized the practical aspects of Confucianism rather than concerning themselves with academic study. Thus they upheld and put into practice, as best as they could, sincerity and self-discipline. Inheriting their spirit, Cho Kwang-jo (Jungam, 1482-1519), a youthful and spirited scholar-politi-

cian, set in motion a resolute reform movement with a view
to establishing an ideal moral state. Rejecting such an academic
attitude as that of emphasizing poetry and letters, he took
the lead in practicing Confucian ideals and recommended the
appointment of qualified persons to government positions
from among young scholars in their thirties. In present-day
terminology, Cho advocated, so to speak, a shift of generations. He also gave himself to the task of distinguishing wise
men from the mean and of eradicating corruption and old
vices. The radical idealism of these young scholars, recognizing as it did no compromise, unfortunately aroused disgust
among the old conservative politicians. The dog-and-cat relations between the two groups resulted in the failure of Cho's
reform movement and he died tragically at the age of 38. A
scholastic purge accompanied almost every major shift in
political power throughout the Yi period and many able
scholars and politicians fell victims. One of its side effects
was party strife, which remained an incurable disease
throughout the five centuries of the Yi dynasty.

Yu Sung-jo (Chiniljae, 1452-1512), however, remained
eminent in the study of Neo-Confucianism. Devoting himself
especially to the study of the Changes, he theorized in his
Taehak Jam that when *li* moves, *chi* is inserted in it and that
when *chi* moves, *li* accompanies it. In *Sŏngni Yŏnwŏn Chŏlyo*
in which he first introduced the *li-chi* theories of preceding
Confucianists, he also said that *li*, once it starts its movement,
becomes the Four Beginnings and that *chi* moves to become
the Seven Emotions. The fact that he thus mentioned the *li-
chi* theory makes him another forerunner in the ensuing dispute concerning the Four Beginnings and the Seven Emotions which is the foremost characteristic of Korean Confucianism.

Philosophic Development of Korean
Confucianism and Its Influence (16th century)

The 16th century is the most glorious in the history of Korean Confucianism when this learning underwent the most profound and sincere philosophic meditation. It was also during that period that the most representative of Confucian scholars mushroomed in succession. That Confucianism had already been widely propagated as a state religion may have been one of the main causes for bringing about the golden age. However, this academic glory was chiefly the outcome, of a tendency prevalent among scholars at that time they would discard participation in government after seeing the tragedy of scholastic purges and devote themselves to learning in the solitude of the countryside. This tendency served as a foundation for the far-flung academic progress that followed.

Sŏ Kyŏng-dŏk (Hwadam, 1489-1546) maintained the monism of *chi* calling *chi T'aehŏ* or *T'aeil* (Great or Original Void or Great One). *Chi*, he theorized, divides itself into two to become *Yang* (the Positive) and *Yin* (the Negative); *Yang*, in turn, actively moves to turn into Heaven; and *Yin* condenses itself to become Earth. The difference between death and life or between human and demon is dependent upon the condensation or dispersion of *chi*. Therefore, the one *chi* is ever existent and has neither beginning nor end. Lao Tze told that entity springs from non-entity. This theory indicates Lao Tze's lack of understanding that the Void is nothing but *chi*. If we assume that the Void can give birth to *chi*, then we have to conclude that the Void before the birth of *chi* would be a dead thing. With this inference, Sŏ adamantly rejected the theory of Lao Tze and held fast to his theory although it was the monism of *chi*. He believed that the condensation or dispersion of *chi* is carried out under the power of its own force and is not influenced by outside elements. He was so confident about the soundness of his theory that he asserted that his was truth no sage had ever arrived at and left to posterity. Although he may have been influenced to a considerable degree by such Chinese scholars as Chao Kang-chieh and Chang Heng-chue, it is also true that his own meditation and experience played an important role in shaping his philosophy. Sŏ is widely known as one of the most original natural philosophers of Korea. His works are contained in *Ssu-k'u Ch'uan-shu* (Complete Writings in the Four Divisions) compiled in the days of the Ch'ing dynasty of China.

Yi Hwang (T'oegye 1501-1570) is the most representative Neo-Confucianist of Korea, a great philosopher who developed the most profound and precise thinking and whose influence was the most far-reaching of all Korean scholars. According to him, human nature consists of two aspects: one is the original, Heaven-bestowed nature which is pure good containing none of elements of evil; the other is a sensual nature originating in human passion which makes no distinction between good and evil. Likewise, he taught, the Four Beginnings are manifestations of *li* and therefore are pure good devoid of evil, while the Seven Emotions are manifestations of *chi* and therefore can become either good or evil. In short, he asserted that the Four Beginnings are revelations of *li* while the Seven Emotions are those of *chi*. Ki Dae-sŭng, one of Yi's ablest disciples, raised opposition to Yi's theory by terming it too dualistic. Ki maintained that since the Four Beginnings are also emotions, they do not reside outside the Seven Emotions and are manifestations of *chi* just as are the Seven Emotions, the difference being that the Four Beginnings are such that they are good ones among the revelations of *chi*. A dispute over this question between the two scholars continued for seven years while all scholars watched its outcome with keen attention. The discussion was carried out in the form of an exchange of dissertations containing the results of mutually sincere studies. Finally Yi came to soften his assertion by amending it so that the Four Beginnings are in manifestation of *li* followed by *chi* while the Seven Emotions the revelation of *chi* participated in by *li*. Ki, in the meantime, tended to approach Yi's amended theory, thus marking a temporary end on the dispute. The dispute on the Four Beginnings and the Seven Emotions, however, lingered on until the latter days of the Yi dynasty touching off heated disputes among scholars. No Confucian scholar after Yi did not express his own views on the dispute, and so the question underwent minute and elaborate analysis. The dispute in question involved philosophical inquiry into the moral values and psychological phenomena of man's emotions. It is one of the most characteristic aspects of Korean Confucianism that the same question aroused controversial disputes over hundreds of years.

Next we shall consider the conflicting views on epistemological problems between Yi and his disciples. For the recognition of the principle of things, Yi at first asserted that the human mind could arrive at the core of the principle and that *li* could be discovered only when the human mind was cleverly utilized. He maintained that since *li* of itself does not admit any emotion or scheming it does not emit itself by its own force. Stimulated by an opposing view raised by Ki and his disciples, Yi one month before his death became very much enlightened and admitted that since *li* was not a dead thing but something alive it was fully capable of emitting itself. It seems theoretically consistent for Yi, an advocate of the self-manifestation of *li* in the field of moral philosophy, to admit the positive operation of *li* in epistemology. His theory, so to speak, reminds us of European philosophy, such as that of Heidegger who believes that Being spontaneously manifests itself, or of Jaspers who says that Reason elucidates itself. That Yi was in no way hesitant about revising his theory is real evidence of the sincerity of his study and his scholarly honesty.

Yi, professing to follow the philosophy of Chu Hsi, compiled *Chu Hsi Sŏ Chŏlyo* (Essentials of Chu Hsi's Works) and defiantly rejected Sŏ Kyŏng-dŏk's monism of *chi*, Lo Cheng-an's theory of the union of *li* and *chi*, and Wang Yang-ming's theory cf the union of knowledge and conduct. As for the interrelation of knowledge and conduct Yi held that knowledge at times preceded conduct and at times conduct preceded knowledge as do the two legs in walking help each other in their mutual advance.

Yi's works were repeatedly reprinted in Japan from early times and exerted great influence on academic circles there. Ansai Yamazaki, a great Japanese scholar in Neo-Confucianism, praised Yi as the greatest Confucian in Korea. Gyokusui Muraji later compiled the 10-volume *T'oegye Shosho* (An Extract of T'oegye's Works). Toya Motoda, a lecturer to Emperor Meiji and the scholar who drafted the Imperial Rescript on Education, termed himself as an inheritor of Yi's philosophy.

Yi, late in life, compiled *Sŏnghak Sipto* (Ten Diagrams of Neo-Confucianism) and dedicated it to the king. An article printed in the Tong-A Ilbo newspaper on July 10, 1926, reported that Shangte Women's University in Peking had reprinted the Diagrams in 10 different minutely illustrated plates and was selling them to raise funds, believing that the Diagrams contained the gist of Confucian doctrine most perfectly. With this report it can be taken that Yi's philosophy has exerted far-reaching influence on China down to modern times.

A matchless pair of Confucianists in Korea were Yi Hwang and Yi I (Yulgok, 1536-1584). Yi I passed the Civil Service Examination at the age of 22 with a treatise entitled *Ch'ŏndoch'aek* (Treatise on the Way of Heaven), striking examiners with admiration due to his indisputable genius. His treatise soon found its way to China and, when Yi, in his declining years, received Chinese envoys visiting Korea, they mentioned this treatise and addressed Yi with the honorific title, "Teacher." Opposing Yi Hwang's dualistic theory that both *li* and *chi* manifest themselves, Yi I asserted that *chi* emanates of itself. The sympathy one would have on seeing a child drowning in a well, cited by Mencius as an example, is the

Beginning of Benevolence, in which case, Yi explained, such sympathy is a manifestation of *chi* as aroused by objects outside man. It would be absurd to infer that *li* manifests itself without being accompanied by the impression of *chi*, according to Yi I. Therefore, what reveals itself is *chi* which perceives outside objects while *li* merely participates in this revelation. It is against reason to assume that *li* manifests itself alone or that *li* manifests itself and *chi* accompanies it in its manifestation. The only thing that can manifest itself is *chi* and the reason for its manifestation is called *li*. This train of thought had already taken roots in him in his youth, which, after many years of repeated meditation, became a firm conviction, enabling him to express his self-confidence in this way, "Any eloquence, even though it is directed toward me by the thousand, will only eventually fail to make me abandon my view."

Li, essentially, has no form and is voiceless and odorless, Yi taught. It pervades the universe far and wide but can present its various phenomena only in accordance with the manifestations of *chi*. This resembles water conforming to the roundness or cubity of its container or the air yielding to the size of a bottle. While *li* is limitless, can penetrate everything and is free from every obstacle, *chi* possesses only onesidedness, such as being partial or fair, pure or turbid, docile or resistant. That pure and void *chi* remains undivided is due to the penetration of *li*, and that *li* can take on numberless varied forms is due to the limitations of *chi*. The expression, "*li* communicates while *chi* is limited," was coined by Yi.

Yi I's attitude of inquiry was not adherence to, or exposition of, the theories of foregoing scholars without due criticism but was a ceaseless search for truth from his own free standpoint. He even disputed Chu Hsi, despite the fact that he firmly believed in the latter, concerning the *li-chi* theory, pointing out that if it had truly been Chu Hsi's own view that both *li* and *chi* could manifest themselves, then he made a mistake that was unworthy of him. Furthermore, Yi said,

"My conviction cannot be subject to revision even though another sage emerges."

Not only as a philosopher but also as a politician, Yi was possessed of great aspirations and endowed with great statesmanship advocating reform and improvement in the government. Emphasizing the necessity of appointing public officials in accordance with ability, he called the government's attention, while serving as minister of finance and later as minister of war, to the eradication of unfair administration. He also asserted the strengthening of national defense by maintaining a 100,000-strong standing army, but people recognized his great foresight and came to admire him only after his death when the Japanese invaded Korea. In *Sŏnghak Jibyo* (Tenet of Confucianism), an elaborate work he dedicated to the king, he explained his concept of monarchism in a systematic manner, taking up such subjects as self-discipline, governing the family, politics and the genealogy of Confucian schools in that order. He also made a proposal for the development of education, specifying measures in detail in his *Hakkyo Mobŏm* (Manuals for Schools). He also laid stress on social education and put into effect his *Hyangyak* (Community Provisions). In Yi I, we can see the qualities of a truly awakened Confucianist and not those of a commonplace Confucianist.

Split of Schools and Party Strife

As Confucianism was the only learning with which the government's Civil Service Examinations dealt, differences in academic tradition and theory arising from the wide dissemination of the learning not only in the capital but also in the provinces eventually resulted in the establishment of schools. As Yi Hwang lived in Yŏngnam (Kyŏngsang Province), the group of scholars inheriting his teaching came to be known as the Yŏngnam School. Meanwhile, Yi I was a native of Kyŏnggi Province and, as scholars succeeding to his teaching mainly came from Kyŏnggi and Hosŏ (Ch'ung-ch'ŏng Provinces), they became known as the Kiho School. Such a rift in the schools, however, was hardly thought of during the life of Yi Hwang and of Yi I. At first, however, in the field of politics, two political parties—the *Tongin* (East Men) and the *Sŏin* (West Men)—emerged, a division mainly resulting from collisions due to differences in lineage and age or disparity between progressives and conservatives. Generally speaking, the mainstream of the East Men consisted of scholars belonging to the Yŏngnam School while almost all of the West Men were politicians affiliated with the Kiho School. As the years passed, the East Men split into the *Namin* (South Men) and the *Pugin* (North Men) while the West Men divided into the *Noron* (Old School) and the *Soron* (Young School), their antagonism and friction becoming ever intensive. Although the period did not lack persons of exceptional ability the rift between the schools and party strife made it impossible for them to unite so as to be able to display their ability and, making matters worse, the nation was subjected to two invasions, i.e., the Japanese encroachment of 1592 and the Manchurian invasion of 1636. The land was in utter crisis, and Confucianism was unable to make the progress it had in the foregoing period.

With the death of King Hyojong in 1659, politicians split into two rival groups due to a dispute on how long the late king's stepmother should remain in mourning. The West Men asserted that the queen dowager should mourn for one year while the South Men, a ramification of the East Men, maintained that the period of her mourning should be extended to three years. The disparity in ceremonials developed into full-scale partisan wrangling. As political changes recurred, the party in power utilized the ceremonials as a means of inflicting deadly blows on its rival. The result was excessive concern about ceremonials, the study of trivial and minute formalities-works on the subject being fabulous—thereby giving rise to the evil and also obstinate custom of attaching importance to the merely formal.

Nevertheless, Song Si-yŏl (Uam, 1607-1689), one of the West Men, embarked on the writing of a voluminous book. *Chu Hsi Ullon Dongiko* (A Comparative Study on the Sayings of Chu Hsi), as the first step toward a thorough study of the great thinker's philosophy. The work was completed in 1741 by Han Un-jin, a scholar belonging to the same clique, a professional achievement requiring half a century. Yun Hyu, an East Man, who held a position opposed to that of Song in connection with theories concerning ceremonials, attempted a new exposition of the classics by means of an original and unique analysis and inquiry without sticking to the phraseology of foregoing Confucianists, especially that of Chu Hsi. Certainly he stood out all alone in the history of Korean Confucianism which attached the highest importance to unconditional obedience to Chu Hsi's doctrine.

New schools came into being during the first half of the 18th century as a product in the process of further disruption of schools. The birth of new schools took place in a dispute in which the main problem in question was whether the nature of man and that of things was different or the same. Yi Kan, a disciple of Kwŏn Sang-ha, who in turn was Song's disciple, asserted that the two were the same while Han Un-jin, although he studied with Yi under Kwŏn, expressed the contrary view. The dispute lingered on for seven years from 1709 to 1715, their arguments being so voluminous that the dispute became second only to the dispute over the Four Beginnings and the Seven Emotions. Han and scholars supporting his view being natives of Ch'ungch'ŏng Province were called Horon (Lake—Ch'ungch'ŏng—School), while the other group, despite the fact that Yi himself came from Ch'ungch'ŏng Province, consisted of natives of Kyŏnggi Province and thus became known as the Nangnon (Kyŏnggi School).

According to Horon, nature means sensuality or, in other words, *li* as it permeates *chi*, and, because man and things are governed by different types of *chi*, the nature of man and that of things cannot be the same. Nangnon, on the contrary, claimed that both man and things are endowed with the same nature, oriented by Providence, and that what is different between them is in the aspect of sensation and not of original nature. In other words, Horon understood nature as something sensual on the basis of the opinion that nature is *chi* and held the view that the nature of man and that of things is not the same. Nangnon, regarding nature as innate and God-given on the basis of the opinion that nature is *li*, considered the nature of man and of things the same. These different views of nature sprang from the choice of *chi* or *li* as the universal substance.

The Rise of Silhak Philosophy
Dedicated to Popular Welfare
and Acceptance of Modern Science

The poor living conditions of the people, already aggravated by foreign invasions, were becoming worse as politicians busied themselves with party strife. Scholars, who indulged in nothing but partisan wrangling or academic dispute, were incapable of contributing to the settlement of current problems. Long recognizing this drawback, a group of Confucianists set a campaign in motion emphasizing the necessity of *Silhak* (Real Learning) by means of discarding abstract and empty argument so as to give a new aspect to public welfare. During the first half of the 17th century such scholars as Yi Su-gwang and Kim Yuk led the new movement. Succeeding to their spirit, Yu Hyŏng-wŏn (Pan'gye, 1622-1673) proposed concrete measures by which he attempted to create new systems and improve public welfare. Yi Ik (Sŏngho, 1681-1763) inherited Yu's spirit and methods and brought Real Learning to full bloom. An Jŏng-bok, Yi's disciple, conducted an overall study even on Korean history. These Real Learning scholars, although well versed in Neo-Confucianism, devoted themselves mainly to the discovery of measures by which to solve current problems impeding the improvement of popular living conditions.

Toward the close of the 18th century a group of progressive and spirited scholars, Hong Dae-yong, Pak Chi-wŏn, Yi Dŏk-mu and Pak Che-ga to name a few, emerged. Stimulated by the new civilization of Ch'ing China, they stressed institutional improvement and better living methods. Hong endeavored to introduce and absorb modern West European science, including mathematics and astronomy. Making instruments for celestial observation himself, he introduced the rotation theory after intensive research. For this he was greatly admired by Chinese scholars. Pak Chi-wŏn, in his *Yŏlha Ilgi* (Cheho Diary), an account of his trip to Peking, satirically described and ridiculed the tyranny and false prestige of the *Yangban* (ruling class) and severely criticized Korea's institutional shortcomings. In the journal he also stressed the promotion of public welfare and the exaltation of national self-consciousness. Pak Che-ga wrote *Pukhak-ŭi* (Discourse on Northern Learning), in which he emphasized, citing examples, the necessity of learning new institutional methods from Ch'ing China.

The philosophy of the Real Learning School found its consummation in Chŏng Yak-yong (Tasan, 1762-1836). His broad learning encompassed not only Confucian scriptures and history but also administration and social welfare. He left behind many writings on the results of his research while at the same time doing his utmost to understand modern science. He not only participated in the construction of a sampan bridge but also proposed the use of pulleys in the construction of a castle wall and even conducted research into smallpox vaccination.

The Real Learning School, the gist of whose philosophy is illustrated above, vehemently rejected the study of false and frivolous poetry or literature and learning merely for the sake of passing the Civil Service Examinations. It would be far better for the improvement of the welfare of the common people to engage in the production of vegetables and fruit than to waste paper and ink on meaningless arguments. However, the School by no means neglected the practice of Confucian morality. They emphasized, among all else, a sincere and pious attitude of mind. In other words, the School took up the problem of public welfare as a means of preserving the dignity of man rather than of pursuing utilitarian goals considering them alone to be the ultimate goal.

This attitude is best illustrated by Yi Wŏn-gu, a Confucian of the early 19th century, when he said that morality and industry are as closely related as husband and wife and that to honor morality alone and ignore industry is equal to being a widower and to stress industry and neglect morality is like being a widow. He saw the two united so closely that they are inseparable.

The introduction and dissemination of modern scientific techniques inevitably brought about contact with Catholicism, a religion strange to the Korean people. Many young scholars thirsty for the most modern in respect to knowledge competed with each other to obtain and devour Catholic publications. Even the students of *Kyŏnghagwŏn*, the Confucian institute of highest learning, read Catholic scriptures in secret.

However, the closed-door policy enforced by the government during the last days of the Yi dynasty for fear of any intercourse with European countries entailed the strict prohibition of Catholicism along with cruel persecution. This ended a movement aimed at the absorption of modern science. Deprived of the opportunity to participate in world developments, Korean Confucianism could not escape falling behind the advancement of the times. Korean Confucianism, since it had not experienced confrontation with new Western thought in the true sense, was not in a position to overcome its own weakness—the self-righteousness of the frog in the well.

Even the philosophies of China's Wang Yang-ming and Lu Hsiang-san were labeled heretical and strictly prohibited in Korea soon after their introduction. Deploring the partiality and prejudice of Korean scholars Chang Yu (Kyegok, 1647-1698) studied the philosophy of Wang Yang-ming with his friend Ch'oe Myŏng-gil and became well versed in it. But what he left are mere fragmentary jottings and he can hardly be considered to have accomplished anything scholastically profound. Following him, Chŏng Je-du was fascinated by Wang's philosophy, gave up the Civil Service Examinations and was contented with a simple and earnest life in retirement in his native village. Later accepting advice from his seniors and friends, he changed to Neo-Confucianism—hardly a student of Wang in the strict sense. The study of Wang's philosophy in Korea was at such a low ebb and so no scholars left to posterity any results of study worth mentioning. This is another aspect of Korean Confucianism, i.e., its domination by Chu Hsi's philosophy.

Neo-Confucianism during the Last Days of the Yi Dynasty

With the suppression of Catholicism and the decline of the Real Learning, Neo-Confucianism again emerged to the forefront, with discussions on *li* and *chi* becoming active.

Early in the 18th century Im Sŏng-ju (Nokmun, 1711-88) asserted the absolute monism of *chi*, by expounding that *T'aegŭk* (First Cause) was the original *chi*, and that human nature also is *chi*. He maintained that there is no human nature except the sensual nature and that the reason why human nature is good is that sensual nature is good. Rejecting the widely accepted view that *li* can express itself in various ways, Im explained that we cannot grasp *li* without considering *chi* and, therefore, that which specifies itself in various forms is *chi*.

In the 19th century Ki Jŏng-jin (Nosa, 1798-1879) asserted the absolute monism of *li*, quite antagonistic to Im's theory, after his own unique meditation. *Li* is the most respectful and absolute and what we call *chi* is that which abides in *li*. The monist of *li* claims that when *chi* acts it does so by its own force and not under the influence of others. Opposing this view, Ki maintained that *li*, itself heaven's decree, set *chi* in motion and that, therefore, man and things share the same nature, or *li*. Furthermore, he bitterly rejected Catholicism by recognizing it as a body of doctrine supporting the monism of *chi*. It was, however, his mistake to confuse Catholicism with a scientific attitude due to his lack of understanding of European philosophy.

Another *li* monist was Kwak Jong-sŏk (Myŏnu, 1846-1919). According to him, *chi* is merely material of the mind and what governs its activity is *li*. When *li* governs, the human mind can restore its originality. This he regarded as the Confucian creed. He further maintained that *li* is mind—the extreme of the monism of *li*.

Kwak once mentioned ancient Greek philosophy and criticized European philosophy as being entrapped in the transformation of *chi* and contented with leading up to wondrous effects in science, not advancing beyond the utilitarian ego and unable to fathom the way of the sages. Although he deserves some praise for his interest in a strange alien thought, it cannot be denied that his criticism of European philosophy was biased because it was based on scanty and partial knowledge introduced by way of China.

Another inheritor of Yi I's tradition in the last days of the Yi dynasty was Chŏn U (Kanjae, 1841-1922) who asserted that the mind is *chi* and human nature is *li*. According to him, if the mind were *li* it would be incapable of thinking and perceiving, for *li* itself does not act. Therefore, he reasoned, the mind is *chi*. The mind, because it is *chi*, can act and is based on human nature. He was so confident concerning his theory that he said he would not revise it even though a sage emerged to refute it. He continued to say that human nature can be compared to a teacher, while the mind is his disciple. This he called his own invention. Concerning the probable question of how *li* which is devoid of activity can function as a teacher, Chŏn clarified that a sage, although uttering no word, can leave everlasting influence on posterity and that, likewise, human nature can manifest itself to be discovered in daily life as the highest good. The mind, the disciple, should listen to the voice of human nature most humbly, and then virtue will fill the universe and abide in it eternally. What he called human nature, or *li*, might be compared to Aristotle's concept of God which, remaining motionless, can orient everything toward itself.

Chŏn continued to say that *li*, devoid of activity, resides above the mind and functions as its original sources. He saw it the duty of Confucianists to set human nature in the highest place and allow the mind to obey its directions and glorify it. He termed it heretical to prevent the mind from glorifying human nature and instead glorifying itself. He denounced emphasis of *chi* as the main cause of demoralizing the world and destroying the country, terming it the enemy of all creatures. Although he defended Yi I's theory, he should not be regarded as a mere monist of *chi*.

To summarize, the foregoing illustrates how Korean Confucianism achieved its development, to the very last, centering around the theory of *li* and *chi* under the influence of Yi Hwang and Yi I.

Confucianism's Bequest to the Mental Life of the Modern Korean

Politics throughout the Yi dynasty era was completely dominated by Confucian thought as applied by Confucianists. And it is hardly conceivable that the concern of present-day Confucianists for politics has totally disappeared in spite of the complete difference in the situation. Most so-called "patriotic old men" are those who have soaked in Confucian culture. Confucianists such as Yi Hang-no and Ch'oe Ik-hyŏn, seeing Korea placed under Japanese control, did not yield to Japanese oppression and to the last were loyal to their country, thereby providing'immense moral support to the people. Confucianism, although it sticks to obstinate formalities on the one hand, it undoubtedly remains on the other the last fortress of national morality. Usually a Korean, unless he belongs to some specific religion, associates ethics or morality with that of Confucianism and attempts to find the criterion of moral·value in Confucian virtues. Confucianism has taken deep roots in the living mode of the masses as is found in their observance of the three-year mourning or in their reverence for the aged, to say nothing of the minute details governing their family system. In the provinces virtually every community has a *hyanggyo* (Confucian shrine); and on the campus of Sŏnggyun'gwan University in Seoul—the successor to the national Confucian university of the Yi dynasty—still stands the stately shrine known as the Taesŏng-jŏn where, strictly in accordance with procedures observed during Yi dynasty days, Confucianists conduct solemn rituals on Confucius' birthday every year with the education minister usually attending, thereby making the occasion an important one.

Besides, in places related to past eminent Confucian scholars there still remain the *Sŏwŏn* (Confucian school) in which are enshrined their memorial tablets to the memory of their greatness as a virtuous scholars. The *Sŏwŏn*, in olden times, fulfilled, along with *hyanggyo*, the functions of an institute dedicated to the training of Confucian scholars, as well as to studies of Confucianism. Also engaged in the publication of Confucian classics and of the writings of distinguished scholars, these institutes served as centers of local enlightenment. Most of these *Sŏwŏns* were either destroyed by the authorities or lie in ruins, but they have not yet completely vanished from the memory of the local people. Some places still retain the latent influence of a Confucian group uniting itself with their *Sŏwŏn* as a rallying point.

This is no place to discuss the merits and demerits of Korean Confucianism in connection with its influence on the mental life of the Korean people. Although it sometimes showed its conservative facet, seeming to go against the tide of the times, as long as phenomena are concerned, Korean Confucianism is considered to contain in its fundamental spirit something which should be restored to life. Anyhow, Confucianism still continues to exert a die-hard influence and it is concluded that without sufficient knowledge of Korean Confucianism it is difficult to predict what the future of Korean thought might be.

T'oegye and His Thought

PAK CHONG-HONG

Yi Hwang (T'oegye by pen name) was born in On'gye-ri, Yean-hyŏn (now Togye-dong, Tosanmyŏn, Andong-gun) North Kyŏngsang Province, on November 25, 1501, in the seventh year of the reign of King Yŏnsan of the Yi dynasty. He was the youngest son of Yi Sik, a *chinsa*, a title conferred on a scholar who passed the civil service examination in the literary department.

Only seven months after his birth, his father died, leaving behind seven sons and one daughter. These children, only the eldest having been married, found it difficult to make a living. Their mother, who was widowed at the age of 32, was, however, determined to maintain the lineage, and devoted herself ever more diligently to farming and silkworm raising at a time when severe taxation drove many families to impoverishment and bankruptcy.

As her children grew up, she managed to eke out educational expenses from the destitute circumstances, and enabled them to get an education. She always admonished her children that it was more important to cultivate the virtue of discretion rather than to devote themselves to literary arts. She also encouraged them, "As people are apt to criticize the children of a widow as being devoid of education, you must exert yourselves far more diligently than others, or you will be unable to avoid such a criticism."

Under their mother's influence they studied with diligence, and as a result, all of them, except two who died early, made a success in learning and brought honor to their family. Especially the youngest one, T'oegye, grew up into a sage, whom we admire as our greatest Confucianist, and from whom we draw an eternal source of national morality.

At the age of six, Yi Hwang started to learn the Book of One Thousand letters from an old gentleman in the neighborhood. Dressing himself spotlessly clean, the little child used to visit his teacher early in the morning, presenting himself only after he had succeeded in committing to memory what he had been assigned on the previous day. His manner was so solemn that he impressed all who saw him.

At the age of 12, he learned the Analects from his uncle, Yi U (Songjae by pen name) who had held the posts of Andong magistrate and Kangwŏn governor. When a welcoming reception was held downstream of the On'gye in honor of the visiting governor one year before, T'oegye had had the honor of taking part in the party. As a teacher, however, his uncle was relentlessly stern. A man of simplicity and severity, his uncle had T'oegye learn by rote the Annotations to the Analects from the first to the last chapter without missing a single letter.

Impressed deeply by the passage of the Analects describing the disciples of Confucius as men who were devoted to filial piety at home and to reverence in dealing with others, T'oegye gave himself the caution: "A son should observe this principle rightly." One day while reading the Annotations, he was attracted by the meaning of the character *li*. After deep thinking, he asked his uncle, "Does the rightness of a thing constitute its meaning?" His uncle was greatly pleased and praised his nephew, "You have already grasped the meaning of letters."

T'oegye's father, as was expected, had a large collection of books. After his father-in-law died, his mother-in-law, pleased at his fondness for learning, gave all of her deceased husband's books to him, saying, "Books must be public properties and should be returned to a scholar's house." T'oegye's father, together with his younger brother, could read extensively all the works of great thinkers. Once he admonished his children, "I read books even at meals, I see them in dreams, I am with them when I sit or when I walk, I never left them. You should do as I did. If you while away time without reading them, when can you attain your aspiration?" Since boyhood, T'oegye was surrounded with a scholarly atmosphere, though born to a family not well-off.

At the age of 19, T'oegye obtained the two-volume *Sŏngni Taejŏn*, which he finished, to find himself in a process of great awakening. Having read through the Book of Changes at the age of 20, he almost forgot his meals and sleep in order to inquire into its true meaning. His excessive devotion to study at that time impaired his health badly, causing him indigestion throughout his life.

He came up to Seoul when he was 23 years old and resumed his study at the National Academy. As a byproduct of the purge of scholars four years before, he found Confucian students depressed in morale. Rather than devoting themselves to study, they were generally stained with a frivolous current, so much so that they even jeered at T'oegye's moderate words and deeds. Greatly disappointed at their decadence, T'oegye refrained from making friends with them, except Kim Ha-sŏ, a Neo-Confucianist noble in purpose, who became T'oegye's lifelong friend, both exerting themselves to criticize heresies and protect Confucianism.

While studying in Seoul, Yi Hwang obtained *Simgyŏng Puju*, whose annotations, being a collection of sayings of Cheng-tzu and Chu-tzu, were very difficult, even denying correct reading, not to speak of understanding. Confining himself to his study for several months and after repeated reading and referring to other materials, T'oegye finally penetrated into their meaning. Later he confided, "Having read the book, I realized for the first time how deep the science of mind is, and how minute the law of mind is. For all my life I trust this book as if it were God, and I revere it as if it were my rigorous father." In his late years, T'oegye often suffered much from an eye disease, and it is presumed that it was caused by his excessive reading.

Yi Hwang passed the higher civil service examination in March in the year when he turned 34 years in age, making the first step into officialdom. However, his poem one year before can perhaps reveal his true mind.

> *Alas, people in the secular world,*
> *Do not cherish high office.*

One evening while he was on night duty at the Royal Archives in the year when he turned 42 years of age, he versified the following poem, revealing his yearning for a return to home away from the disorderly turn of events.

> *All the branches of that plum tree in the garden are*
>   *buried in snow,*
> *How disorderly this world is, as it is hit by storms.*
> *I sat here at my office facing the spring moon,*
> *The wild geese crying to stir my mind.*

In October the following year, T'oegye returned home on the pretext of visiting the graves of his ancestors, making a firm determination to quit the government. T'oegye by nature was disgusted at earning his livelihood by obtaining a government position through the civil service examination. This disposition was well attested when, at the age of 28, he underwent a government examination, but set out on his journey back home without seeing its result. When he was about to reach a ferry on the Han River, he received the news that he was successful in the examination but, without showing any sign of happiness, he continued the journey. He was only forced to undergo the government examination and obtain a government position by the destitution of his family, by the old age of his mother, and by exhortation of his friends. Later he himself regretted it, attributing it to his superficial ideas, in youth. Although he was summoned by the king to serve in the government and accepted many illustrious positions, it was evidently not his lifelong aspiration.

In a poem written when he turned 56 years of age, he likened wealth and fame to drifting smoke and honors to a fly in the air. He taught how pleasant it was to devote oneself to one's profession, confining oneself to one's home, and warned against the danger that might accrue from frequent association with nobility. These examples may make one think that T'oegye was a passive hermit lacking positive character. Nevertheless, he was filled with firm conviction springing from his vitality, deriving its source from his minute and meditation and profound experience in life.

With a relentless attitude he took part in purges of corrupt government officials. In a report to the monarch after an inspection tour of Ch'ungch'ŏng Province as a royal secret inspector at the age of 42, he ruthlessly attacked a provincial official who, neglecting an order from an honest magistrate, busied himself in amassing an illicit fortune by taking possession of government articles. He gave the advice to the king that only after punishing corrupt government officials would it be possible to save the people from destitution.

In a lecture to the king when he was 68 years old, T'oegye resolutely defended the scholarship and personality of Cho Kwang-jo, the scholar-politician who was purged in the scholars' persecution, and clarified that the incident was an outcome of an intrigue by Nam Kon and Sim Chong. The king finally deprived Nam Kon of his office and rank.

During forty years of public life, he served four kings (Chungjong, Injong, Myŏngjong, and Sŏnjo). He followed only the dictates of righteousness. By birth, T'oegye was endowed with the ability to follow the Way. He was warm in heart, clear, sincere, and pure. All of his deeds originated from the Way, and not from momentary outbursts.

A multitude of students knocked at his door for teaching. He treated them as his friends, and spoke to none in terms accorded generally to one's juniors, however young they might be. With a modest attitude, he received and sent off his guests. His first greeting whenever he received a guest always concerned the health of his parents. Whenever his disciple asked a question, however shallow it might be, he paused a little before answering, and never gave an answer in an instant without thinking it over. Even when a person engaged in debate expressed a view contrary to his, T'oegye never refuted it as wrong at once, but showed him reasons why he himself reached other conclusions, while upholding a definite answer.

He was earnest in loving his disciples. He even foresaw in a dream a misfortune that would befall one of his disciples and wrote a letter to him to give him a warning. Though not well-off himself, T'oegye once sent rice to one of his disciples who was troubled with destitution. Even when he was ill, he never suspended lecturing. One month before his death, he gave lectures as usual, and his disciples never got an inkling of his critical condition.

Scholarly Attitude and Achievements

T'oegye's scholarship, viewed from the angle of philosophical methodology, surprises all on account of its minuteness and profundity. He expressed even a single phrase only after deep meditation with prudence, far from an attitude of a genius who is in the habit of asserting his view in the way it comes to his mind. No doubt T'oegye is the philosopher who conducted the most sincere philosophical meditation among Korean Confucianists. Although it is true that Chu-tzu's philosophy constituted the main body of T'oegye's scholarship, he was not like would-be Confucianists who were satisfied with interpretation of unessential phrases and words, or with committing them to memory. He had not a bit of interest in passing the civil service examination by manipulating prose and verse.

According to T'oegye, philosophical meditation has many methods, and no one should be confined to one method. Among the four methods mentioned in *the Book of the Mean*, that is, erudition, inquiry, prudent thinking, and clear vindication, T'oegye considered prudent thinking most indispensable, saying that one achieves if one thinks prudently and one fails to achieve without prudent thinking. What is thinking? According to him, it is that which leads one to acquisition of a solution to a question. It concerns not an interpretation of words, but meditation and experience. Those who have great doubt will reach great realization. Those who do not think and act cannot have doubts, and therefore they cannot experience realization. What is necessary is not recitation but self-experience of the Heavenly Way by thinking over what one learned from books at night when one's mind recovers serenity. As taught in Zen Buddhism, truth cannot be comprehended all of a sudden, but only after devotion to learning for a long period of time.

T'oegye was disgusted with the attitude of asserting one's opinion without examining details. He realized that there is a difference between two which are the same, and that there is sameness between two which are different. Even when a thing is divided into two, their inseparability should not be impaired, and when the two are united into one, there should not remain the ugliness of mixture.

As modest as he really was, T'oegye did not hesitate in revising his theory once he discovered its shortcoming, even when he was 70 years of age, an old master whose scholarship and virtue all the people admired.

All of T'oegye's writings have philosophic depth. Even a simple poem is filled with profound truth. His letters addressed to his disciples often attain the height of excellent philosophical theses. A good example is his correspondence with Ki Kobong. Japanese Confucianists cherished *Chasŏngnok*, a collection of T'oegye's letters, drawing from it permanent influence.

T'oegye resided near the West Gate whenever he came up to

Seoul, and his residence in Seoul amounted to a total of twenty years. But he had no contact with his neighbors. One day in October of the year when he was 53 years of age, he happened to know *Chonmyŏng Tosol*, authored by Chŏng Chu-man, his next-door neighbor. The two soon became friends. T'oegye revised one passage of the original text, "The four beginnings spring from *li*, while the seven emotions spring from *chi*." into "The four beginnings are a product of *li*, while the seven emotions are a product of *chi*." Ki Ko-bong later wrote to T'oegye expressing his view that his theory was too much dualistic. The famous debate between the two about the Four Beginnings and the Seven Emotions started.

Li can be considered Reason in present-day philosophical terminology, while *chi* represents Sensation. The Four Beginnings, or buds of human nature, expounded first by Mencius, are Compassion, Declination, and Discrimination between Right and Wrong. The Seven Emotions, pointed out in the Book of Rites, are joy, anger, sorrow, fear, love, hatred, and desire. Concerning the relations between the two, Ki Ko-bong stated that the Four Beginnings cannot reside outside the Seven Emotions and that *li*, likewise, cannot exist away from *chi*. To him T'oegye explained that as there is in human nature an intrinsic nature which is pure-good and an emotional nature which cannot be considered either good or bad, it is proper rather to distinguish emotions which are more closely connected with *li* from those which are related more closely to *chi*.

The debate, which started in the year T'oegye was 60 years old took seven years until it reached a conclusion. As correspondence between the two grew in volume, T'oegye softened his dualistic view a little: Although the Four Beginnings are not different from the Seven Emotions in that they, too, are stimulated to function by Matter, as are the Seven Emotions, the former are manifestations of *li*, with *chi* exerting a lesser influence while the latter are the manifestations of *chi*, with *li* exerting a lesser influence. Ki Ko-bong finally confessed his shortcoming and expressed his general support of T'oegye's theory.

T'oegye's theory on the Four Beginnings and the Seven Emotions won great admiration from Japanese Confucianists, who praised it as a clarification of what his predecessors had not attempted. The debate on the Four Beginnings and the Seven Emotions attracted attention of all Korean Confucianists, becoming the central theme of philosophical meditation. Their views differed according to which school they supported and the debate came to be viewed in connection with partisan strife. The most salient characteristics of Korean Confucianism can be found in the theory concerning the Four Beginnings and the Seven Emotions. What was wrong is that the theory was utilized for partisan feuding and, from a scholarly view, the theory should be regarded as a task for modern philosophers to further develop in the light of modern philosophy.

Li is generally considered reasonableness, and therefore it may sound strange to say that *li* acts upon something, and the general tendency may be that Yi Yulgok's monistic theory is superior in stating that *chi* alone operates. However, *li* is limited to reasonableness and, as Western philosophy regards Reason and Understanding as things that are positive and Sensation as something that, being passive, operates only when stimulated by outside caused, *li* is something positive that can operate by itself. As knowledge is possible when Understanding and Sensation and combined into one, not only *li* operates but *chi* rides on it. In this manner T'oegye viewed the world as a whole.

It is generally thought that T'oegye blindly followed Chutzu's philosophy, and therefore his theory lacks originality. However, the fact remains that T'oegye explored his theory of the Four Beginnings and the Seven Emotions through his own meditation, and only later found a similar expression in Chutzu's work, thereby confirming his conviction further.

The true greatness of T'oegye does not lie in his theoretical depth. The fundamental task T'oegye assigned to himself was to find out reasonableness in theories. It was his unshakable conviction that reasonableness exists in our daily life. *Tahsueh* and *Mencius* teach that knowledge should precede conduct, while *the Book of the Mean* says that knowledge can be acquired after conduct. According to T'oegye, neither is true. He asserts that knowledge and conduct should assist each other, as the right and left legs do in walking. He sees that sincerity is the fundamental force enabling knowledge and conduct to cooperate with each other. Sincerity is the way of heaven, and man's effort to become sincere is his duty.

The ultimate aim of T'oegye's scholarship and view of life can be found in his devotion to reverence. It was T'oegye who practiced reverence throughout his life. It is for this reason that we respect T'oegye not only as a scholar devoted to the search for truth, but as our true teacher.

T'oegye's Influence in Japan

As is well known, it was during the Tokugawa Shogunate period that Confucianism was established in Japan. In the year before the Hideyoshi invasion, Kim Hak-pong went to Japan as a Korean envoy and met with Seiko Fujiwara, a great Japanese Confucianist. It cannot be denied that many works of Korean scholars which were taken to Japan during the war made a great contribution to studies of Japanese Confucianists. During the reign of King Injo, Im Tong visited Japan as a Korean envoy and met with Rasan Hayashi, a disciple of Seiko Fujiwara, and the two engaged in a discussion of the theory of the Four Beginnings and the Seven Emotions. Confessing that his knowledge was too shallow to meddle in the debate to any appreciable depth, Hayashi sided with T'oegye rather than with Ki Ko-bong, and expressed his hope to learn more of Kobong's theory. As his teacher had already supported T'oegye's theory, it became an established truth in Japan as far as the theory of the Four Beginnings and the Seven Emotions was concerned.

T'oegye's *Essentials of Chu-tzu's Works* was introduced to Japan and exerted great influence on Japanese scholars, including Ansai Yamazaki, who held the author in high esteem and lectured on his scholarship. Naogata Sato, who inherited Yamazaki's learning, paid tribute to T'oegye, regarding his scholarship as so deep as to defy comparison with that of the Chinese Confucianists of the Yüan and Ming dynasties. T'oegye's *A Collection of My Self-Reflections* and *Essentials of Chu-tzu's Works* were published in Japanese editions. In a preface to the latter publication, Jian Kuroiwa, a disciple of Yamazaki, stated that T'oegye was very diligent in intellectual pursuits, and made a significant contribution to encouraging his junior scholars.

Moreover, Gyokusui Murashi, who belonged to Sato's school, authored a 10-volume *Excerpts from T'oegye's Works.* Seriri Koga, a Professor of Shoheiko, the highest academy of the Tokugawa Shogunate, wrote a preface to the *Excerpts*, in which he stated that the more one reads his works the greater one's admiration becomes in acknowledgment of the purity of his scholarship, that he is truly a great teacher, and that his works are filled with his modest, clear and sincere spirit. The Japanese published the *Excerpts* with a view to promoting local Confucianism by introducing T'oegye's philosophy, as T'oegye authored *Essentials of Chu-tzu's Works* for a similar purpose.

Taino Ozuka, another great Japanese Confucianist, believed in Wang Yang-ming's philosophy in youth but, after reading T'oegye's *A Collection of My Self-Reflections*, was initiated into the true meaning of Chu-tzu's philosophy. He cherished T'oegye's *Essentials of Chu-tzu's Works* so much that he copied all of its 20 volumes. He confided: "When I was young, I read the *Essentials of Chu-tzu's Works* carefully, and could understand what his philosophy was. Lest I should forget it, I keep the book carefully, and for the past forty years I have placed my unswerving faith in it and served it."

Tono Motoda, a lecturer for Emperor Meiji, won fame as the author of the Imperial Edict on Education, which elucidated Japan's educational aims. Belonging to the school of Ozuka, Motoda took pride in the fact that he gave Emperor Meiji lectures on T'oegye's scholarship. It may not be too much to say that T'oegye's basic spirit as manifest in his "Ten Diagrams for the True Learning" was adopted as the core of his lectures to the emperor, and constituted the gist of the imperial edict.

Kisui Tokutomi, father of the great Japanese historian Soho Tokutomi, recorded T'oegye's sayings in his diary a few days before his death.

Shikita Koyanagi, a Japanese scholar, explained in the Japanese Encyclopaedia that "Yi Hwang is a scholar who penetrated into the true essence of the learning of Cheng-tzu and Chu-tzu. He did not follow their theory blindly. In discussing the relations between *li* and *chi*, Yi Hwang did not interpret them from a dualistic viewpoint, but grasped them as two ingredients of a whole. All happenings in the universe show that *li* and *chi* help each other; *li* cannot exist without *chi*, nor *chi* without *li*. However, *li* and *chi* are two things and not one. It is Mind that combines the two."

Yi I (Yulgok) and His Thought

AN PYŎNG-JU

His Life

A baby was born in Pukp'yŏng Village, Kangnŭng, Kang-wŏn Province, on December 26, 1536 (31st year of the reign of King Chungjong of the Yi dynasty). Named Yi I, Yulgok became his pen name when he grew into a great Confucian scholar revered as the "Greatest Teacher in the East," the East indicating Korea, as it was situated east of China.

Serious disruption arising from partisan feuding began to plague Yi dynasty in the latter half of the 16th century, exposing many political dilemmas. It was a period which witnessed a gradual economic bankruptcy on account of disorder in land ownership and the government's excessive exploitation.

In addition to instability in domestic affairs, the Japanese in the south and barbarians in the north threatened Korea's security. A storm, it was felt, would befall the Koreans at any moment. Korea's political leaders were not sagacious enough to accept Yulgok's far-sighted view concerning national defense, and the people soon had to undergo the bitter experience of invasions by the Japanese and then by the Manchurians. Such disorder and instability, and the lack of effective defense measures and armament, characterized the period in which Yi I grew up.

Yulgok was of distinguished family—his father, Yi Wŏn-su, had served as an inspector at the Office of Government

Supervision, and later had been conferred the title of Senior Assistant to the Prime Minister; and his mother, Madame Sin Saimdang, won great admiration not only from her contemporaries but from posterity as a woman who was well versed in Chinese classics, prose and poetry, calligraphy, and painting. His great endowment, lofty personality, grand aspiration, and far-reaching vision enabled Yulgok to excel others in endeavors to transform the corrupt Yi society into a Confucian utopia.

The primary duty of a Confucian is moral self-cultivation and aspiration for right government. Yulgok was truly Confucian in nature, displaying to the fullest extent combined ability in learning and politics. He was the greatest philosopher, scholar, statesman, man of letters, and educator Korea produced at that time.

Social confusion is apt to generate the tendency among scholars to confine themselves to the ivory tower, where they are able to search for truth in seclusion. Yulgok warned against such a disparity between learning and politics. He formulated social reform measures, while engrossed in theoretical inquiry. He was a great thinker who possessed both learning and statesmanship, and who exerted earnest effort to save the nation from corruption and the danger of collapse.

That Yulgok was born of a mother as eminent as Madame Sin Saimdang was a piece of luck denied to ordinary persons. Besides, a mysterious story is told of his birth. One day Madame Sin had a dream, in which a fairy from the East Sea, carrying a boy baby, placed it on her breast and disappeared. Soon she became pregnant. Before childbirth, she dreamed another dream, in which the Black Dragon flew into her bedroom from the ocean. Soon Yulgok was born.

By the age of seven, Yulgok had finished his lessons in the Four Books and the Three Classics. There lived in his neighborhood a man named Chin Pok-ch'ang. Having seen through this man's small mindedness, Yulgok wrote his biography, warning that such a man as Chin would cause misfortune if he gained high position. True to the forecast, Chin later masterminded a persecution of scholars. Yi's foresight was so accurate since his childhood.

He became a *chinsa* (a title conferred on scholars who passed the civil service examination in the literary department) at the age of 13. Nevertheless, he showed no sign of self-conceit and exerted himself more diligently in study, winning praise from all who knew him that he would become a great man. In the meantime, Yulgok indulged in reading the Taoist classics and Buddhist scriptures. It seems that by that time he had already read extensively most books on Taoist philosophy and Buddhism.

His mother's death when he was 36 years old brought him deep sorrow. That he could no longer see his mother made him feel bitterly the transience of life. In March of the year he finished the three years' mourning in memory of his beloved mother, he left his home for the Diamond Mountains. Many arguments may arise on the question of Yulgok's temporary renunciation of the world by secluding himself on the Diamond Mountains. However, his decision is understandable if we consider his feelings. First, he may have thought after three years of lamentation that the Buddhist phrase, transience of life, would erase his sorrow. Second, he may have understood that the Confucian teaching, "Preserve your mind and nurture your nature," was synonymous with the Buddhist teaching, "Open your mind and see your nature." Third, he may have regarded it as a pleasure to rest in the countryside, as it is said that a gentleman and a good governor are fond of enjoying mountains and rivers.

Thinking along this line, Yulgok may have reached the decision to enter the priesthood. His decision is fully understandable, and, moreover, it can be said that his renunciation of the world, giving himself an opportunity to reexamine the truth contained in the Buddhist scriptures, together with his Zen Buddhist practice, proved a great help to achieving a mature philosophy in later days.

Yulgok's philosophy shows great influence from Taoism, especially the thought of Chuang-tzu. Even if the Taoist influence is denied, it is evident that Yulgok's writing contains many phrases unique to Chuang-tzu. It is interesting to compare this fact with the apparent Zen Buddhist influence on the philosophy of Chuang-tzu.

The philosophy of Chu Hsi, or Metaphysical Confucianism, which is called Neo-Confucianism in order to distinguish it from Primitive Confucianism, exerted a predominant influence on the Yi kingdom, and it was Metaphysical Confucianism that was adopted as the object of their academic inquiry by such eminent scholars as Yi I and Yi Hwang (T'oegye). It is pointed out by many scholars that Metaphysical Confucianism is a system of thought influenced greatly by the thought of Lao-tzu and Chuang-tzu, and by Buddhism. It is not valid, however, to say that Neo-Confucianism is something like Taoism or Buddhism because of its being influenced by the latter. It is as invalid as to say that a lion which ate too many rabbits resembles a rabbit when dissected.

The same can be said of Yi I. His renunciation by no means changed his Confucianism into Taoism or Buddhism. The experience rather helped him deepen his theory of philosophy.

Yulgok, who was well grounded in Metaphysical Confucianism, rather won admiration from Buddhist priests in the Diamond Mountains; they were, in fact, so struck with admiration that they called Yulgok a reincarnation of the Buddha. After a year-long stay on the mountain, he converted again to Confucianism and returned back to the secular world, believing that the Buddhist cultivation of mind by severing all ties with worldly affairs was less valuable than the Confucian principle of moral training, home management, wise government, and pacification of the whole world.

When he turned 23 years of age, he called on Yi Hwang at his home in Yean, North Kyŏngsang Province, and his encounter with the great aged Confucian infused in his mind many inspirations. Fully recognizing Yulgok's talent as a scholar, T'oegye wrote in a letter to his disciple Cho Mok. "After meeting Yulgok, I realized for the first time the truth of Confucius' saying that 'fearful is criticism by posterity.' "

In winter of the year he visited with T'oegye, Yulgok passed another civil service examination called *Pyŏlsi* with the highest marks. His excellent thesis on the subject of *Ch'ŏn-doch'aek* struck all the examiners with great admiration. They praised Yulgok as a true genius who could produce such a wonderful thesis in so short a time, its subject being so difficult that they themselves spent several days for meditation before reaching an agreement on its adoption for the examination.

The thesis written by a 23-year-old man was a literary masterpiece interwoven with erudite knowledge of history and Confucian philosophy of politics, also reflecting his profound knowledge of Taoism, especially the philosophy of Chuang-tzu. The thesis won a high reputation not only at home, but the masterpiece was introduced to Ming China and read widely there.

It was when he turned 29 years of age that Yulgok passed the higher civil service examination, and his government service started that year. He was promoted to a higher position nearly every year until he could join the elite class, a group of ranking government officials who, forming the nucleus of politics, were entitled to express their opinions concerning measures to establish an ideal Confucian society.

The provincial positions Yulgok held included magistrate of Ch'ŏngju and governor of Hwanghae Province. The central government posts he held included the royal secretary, deputy president of the National Academy, chief remonstrator, and chief government supervisor. Besides holding these important positions in the fields of education and government supervision, Yulgok also served as minister of finance, national defense, and home affairs. He also gained experience as a diplomat when he went to the capital of Ming China as a member of a Korean mission to the Chinese court. His life was truly a serious and busy one, in which learning and politics were never separated from each other. On some occasions he submitted a petition to the monarch beseeching royal permission for retirement from government service, in order to enrich his learning and search for truth. Nevertheless, he was a great man who made many achievements in government during his short life before his death at the age of 49.

When he was granted a vacation for study by the king at the age of 34, he submitted to the monarch *Tongho Mundap*, an 11-article treatise devoted to clarifying his conviction that righteous government could be realized even in his days, showing measures to achieve it and his aspirations for it.

Now Yulgok reached the age of 37, and exchanged letters with Song U-gye discussing the human mind, the essence of truth, and *Sadan Ch'iljŏng* (the Four Beginnings and the Seven Emotions). Numbering in the scores, their letters constitute the most detailed, logical, and systematic exposition of Yulgok's philosophy of *li* (principle) and *chi* (element).

In September of the year he turned 40 years of age, he authored *Sohak Chibyo* (The Essentials of Confucianism), which can be rated as a most valuable book showing examples for life. Based on the teachings of the Confucian classics and patterned after the style of the Sung dynasty Chen Hsi-shan's *Ta-hsueh-yen-i*, the book clarified the close relation between learning and statecraft by making references to theories of deceased Confucian scholars and historical facts.

His far-sighted vision was revealed on such occasions as his proposal for the establishment of an Office of Economy, made when he was 46, while he was the minister of finance, and his assertion of the need for training 100,000 soldiers, which he advanced at a lecture to the monarch when he was 48 years old and serving as the minister of national defense. His advocacy of strengthened national defense capability met frustration as it was opposed by Yu Sŏng-yong, who held the view that to train soldiers for no particular reason would rather entail a disaster. When the Japanese invaded Korea soon afterwards, Yu sighed his admiration of Yulgok at the royal court, praising him as a true sage.

Yulgok suddenly became ill, and his health was quickly deteriorating. On January 14, 1584 (17th year of the reign of King Sŏnjo, when he turned 49 years of age), Sŏ Ik, who was appointed an inspector of the northeastern provinces of Korea, called on him before his departure for consultations. Rejecting his sons' advice not to meet him for fear that their father's ailment would grow worse, Yulgok called the visitor in, and, with the help of his sons, he aroused himself on his bed to discuss grave matters of national security, and made his younger brother write down what he said. The dictation, his last writing, was a six-article strategy.

He took a sudden turn for the worse after the meeting. Two days later he woke up early in the morning, had his bed changed, put on a new hat and attire, and quietly breathed his last breath.

Yulgok, who lived but a short life of 49 years, was extraordinary in realization and excelled all others in wisdom. He was a man who needed no teachers, but could all of a sudden arrive at the core of truth himself, without going through developmental stages. In the field of learning whose aim was moral self-cultivation, Yulgok aspired to become a sage, an ideal human figure envisaged in Confucianism. In the field of politics, he strove to realize righteous government, inheriting the tradition of Mencius, who rejected the rule of might and utilitarianism.

He possessed a clear view of history which made him advocate expedient means in reforming maladministration by revising even rules handed down from the ancient times if they were not appropriate. His vision being clear and far-reaching, Yulgok advocated appointment of illegitimate sons to government positions and liberation of talented slaves, both public and private, while doing his utmost to reconcile the East and West factions.

An In-sik concluded his "Life and Achievements of Yi Yulgok" by saying, "Heaven was stingy in granting life to Yulgok, and that was related to the national destiny. The early death of Sung's Cheng Ming-tao was mourned as a misfortune of the entire world. Yulgok's unhappiness can be called an unhappiness of the Yi kingdom."

His Writing

Yulgok Chŏnjip (The Complete Works of Yulgok) was compiled after his death on the basis of the writings he bequeathed. Soon after his death, his disciples started arrangement and editing of his writings. Under the guidance of Sŏng U-gye, his disciple Pak Yŏ-ryong compiled Yulgok's prose, while Pak Chihwa edited his verse. These manuscripts were printed with wood blocks in 1611 (the third year of King Kwanghae's reign) in Haeju, as the first collection of Yulgok's works. Afterwards Pak Se-ch'ae added 10 volumes to the collection with a view to supplementing what was lacking in it. The additional volumes were published in 1682 (the eighth year of King Sukjong's reign).

The necessity of publishing his complete works was felt keenly, and in 1744 (the 20th year of King Yŏngjo's reign) Yi Chae compiled a 38-volume collection, adding *Sŏnghak Chibyo* (The Essentials of Confucianism) and *Kyŏkmong Yogyŏl* (The Cardinal Principles for Inculcating into Youth). Six years later, it was published. Later, six more volumes were added to it.

As years passed, the need of a reprint was felt, and in 1814 (the 14th year of King Sunjo's reign), all of these works were printed again with wood blocks. This is the edition still extant. The East Asian Cultural Research Institute of Sŏnggyun'gwan University published this edition in one volume through phototype process in 1958.

Introduced below are the contents of Yulgok's Complete Works.

Vols. 1 and 2—Prose and poetry.

Vols. 3 to 7—Memorials submitted to the throne.

Vol. 8—Recommendations.

Vols. 9 to 12—Letters (including those exchanged with Pak Hwa-suk and Sŏng U-gye which contain the gist of Yulgok's metaphysical Confucianism, and other letters which show his views on politics, morals, economy, and philosophy).

Vol. 13—Essays written by royal order, prefaces, notes, and epilogues.

Vol. 14—Expositions, eulogies, epitaphs, memorial addresses, and miscellaneous writings No. 1 (including such great theses as *Yŏksuch'aek* and *Ch'ŏndoch'aek*).

Vols. 15 and 16—Miscellaneous Writings No. 2 (including *Tongho Mundap* and *Hakkyo Mobŏm*).

Miscellaneous Writings No. 3 (including *Sŏwŏn Hyangyak* and *Sŏkdam Hyangyak*).

Vols. 17 and 18—Writings for inscription on monuments biographies.

Vols. 19 to 26—*Sŏnghak Chibyo* (A treatise Yulgok dedicated to King Sŏnjo while he was the deputy president of *Hongmun'gwan*. A collection of the essentials of Neo-Confucianism, it discusses the essence of righteous government. Dealing with methods of study, it is a valuable manual for all, regardless of their position, and especially for younger scholars. As Yulgok stated in the preface, it is a result of his indefatigable and earnest labor.)

Vol. 27—*Kyŏkmong Yogyŏl* and *Cheuich'o* (A book Yulgok wrote when he resided at his native town. Sŏkdam near Haeju, *Kyŏkmong Yogyŏl* is designed to provide guidance for young students, and is a fine introduction to

Neo-Confucianism. A great manual the like of which can never be found since Chu Hsi's *Hsiao-Hsueh*.)

Vols. 28 to 30—*Kyŏngyŏn Ilgi* (A Diary of Lectures Before the Throne) Covering the 17-year period from 1565 (the 20th year of King Myŏngjong's reign) to 1581 (the 14th year of King Sŏnjo's reign), the diary contains events that took place at the royal court, records debates that were exchanged between courtiers, and states his sharp criticism without reservation.

Vol. 31—A Collection of Yulgok's Sayings, No. 1.

Vol. 32—A Collection of Yulgok's Sayings, No. 2. (These collections contain Yulgok's philosophy of *li* and *chi*, especially his theory on *chi*, in the style of question and answer.)

Vols. 33 to 38—Supplements (These volumes describe Yulgok's life in chronological order.)

Addenda (six volumes).

His Thought

In spite of Chuang-tzu's influence (or frequent references to his phrases) and the influence of Avatamska Buddhism, as is evident in his letters discussing the philosophy of *li* and *chi*, in his treatises like *Ch'ondoch'aek*, and in *Li-il-bun-su-bu*, it cannot be denied that Yulgok's basic thought has its roots in the Neo-Confucianism of the Sung dynasty. It is also undeniable that Yulgok could not free himself from the category of the Confucianism of Confucius and Mencius, in view of his scholarly attitude, his philosophy of moral training and conduct of life, and his philosophy of politics.

The philosophy of *li* and *chi*, which roughly corresponds to the ontology section of Sung's Neo-Confucianism, attained much development in the Yi dynasty through considerable argument between Yi T'oegye and Yi Yulgok. As pointed out by Sŏng Nak-hun in his "History of Korean Confucian

Thought," however, the argument merely exposed the self-contradiction of the Sung dynasty's philosophy of *li* and *chi*, and was but a theoretical dispute, having no influence on actual politics and moral training of Korean scholars. As pointed out again by Sŏng Nak-hun, an interesting aspect of the philosophy of *li* and *chi* of T'oegye and Yulgok is that it exposed the dilemma of Sung's Neo-Confucianism. That T'oegye's theory won support from the Southern Faction and Yulgok's from the Western Faction had nothing to do with the theory itself.

As the Neo-Confucianism of the Sung dynasty, from which Yulgok drew the origin for his philosophy of *li* and *chi*, was formed under influence from Taoism and Buddhism, a similar influence on Yulgok's theory cannot be excluded. However, it can be said that as in the case of Sung's Neo-Confucianism, Yulgok's philosophy of *li* and *chi* cannot be regarded as something similar to Taoism or Buddhism due to their direct influence. Yulgok's philosophy cannot be called by a name other than Confucianism.

In fact, the ultimate aim of Yulgok's learning, as is evident in his own warning against disparity between learning and politics, was to realize once again the government of the ancient Chinese kings Yao and Shun, whom Confucianism regarded ideal monarchs.

Yulgok's political philosophy looked to a wise king who had completed his self-cultivation for the realization of moral government. In other words, Yulgok aimed at righteous government or politics by a philosopher. In this regard, he can be compared to Cho Chŏng-am, a great statesman during the reign of King Chungjong in the middle part of the Yi dynasty period. In fact, Yulgok admired Cho. However, this had no connection with his philosophy of *li* and *chi*.

As a politician, Yulgok admired Cho, and as a scholar, Yi T'oegye. He stated in *Kyŏngyŏn Ilgi*, "Although T'oegye cannot match Chŏng-am in terms of talent and capacity, Chŏng-am cannot be considered an equal of T'oegye in minuteness of learning." He again said, "Chŏng-am upheld learning, while

T'oegye was deeply immersed in righteousness."

However, Yulgok did not revere Cho Chŏng-am uncondi-tionally as a politician. He was sceptical of Cho's radicalism, and, instead, advocated gradual reform.

Yulgok also did not revere Yi T'oegye unconditionally as a scholar. In the philosophy of *li* and *chi*, he rather showed a greater interest in Lo Cheng-an of Ming and Sŏ Hwadam of Korea. He was generous in praising them, saying that their theory of inseparability between *li* and *chi* was full of originality. While paying deep respect to T'oegye for the pro-fundity of his learning, Yulgok criticized his theory as being devoid of originality, and voiced dissatisfaction at his follow-ing Chu Hsi's theory.

Sŏ Hwadam's philosophy also failed to win Yulgok's full support. However, we can notice that Hwadam's theory had greater influence on Yulgok than T'oegye's. If Hwadam's theory can be considered as being heavily *chi*-centered, in that it shows a materialistic tendency, T'oegye's theory is *li*-centered, or thoroughly speculative. Yulgok, who also could not liberate himself completely from the restrictions of Chu Hsi's theory, assumed a speculative position centering around *li*, and, in this respect, he is similar to T'oegye. However, in his logical development of *chi*, he shows a considerable similarity to So Hwadam's theory.

Particulars concerning Yulgok's philosophy of *li* and *chi* can be found in his correspondence with Sŏng U-gye contained in Vols. 9 and 10 of his complete works. The letters exchanged between him and Pak Hwa-suk are also important.

As is shown in his correspondence with Pak Hwa-suk, Yulgok opposed Sŏ Hwadam's theory of *chi*-monism, theory of the Void, and theory or regarding Yin (the Negative) as the ori-ginal source, while supporting his and Lo Cheng-an's theory of inseparability of *li* and *chi*. On the other hand, Yulgok's cor-respondence with Sŏng U-gye reveals his refutation of T'oegye's theory of simultaneous emanation of *li* and *chi*, while coming one step closer to the thought of Lo Cheng-an and Sŏ Hwadam, which centered around *chi*.

In a letter addressed to Sŏng U-gye, Yul-gok expounded his famous theory: *Chi* emanates and *li* rides on; or *li* pervades and *chi* accommodates it as a vessel.

While holding the view that *li* and *chi* cannot be separated from each other, Yulgok could not free himself from the influence of the dualism of the Sung philosophers Cheng I-chuan and Chu Hsi, who strictly discriminated between *li* and *chi*. He states:

> As *li* and *chi* are inseparable from each other, they seem one and the same. But they have differences: *Li* does not act, while *chi* acts. It is *li* that, being formless and unable to act, can become master of *chi*, which has form and is able to act. It is *chi* that, having form and being able to act, can become a vessel for *li*, which is formless and unable to act. As *li* has no form and *chi* has form, the former can pervade and the latter contain. As *li* is unable to act and *chi* is able to act, the latter emanates and the former rides on it.

According to Yulgok, *li* by nature has neither beginning nor end, neither front nor back. Therefore, *li* rides on *chi* and goes aboard it. Even when it is not uniform, *li* never loses its original nature of being mysterious. When *chi* is partial, *li* also becomes partial, but it is not *li* but *chi* that is partial. When *chi* is impartial, *li* also becomes impartial, but it is not *li* but *chi* that is impartial. *Li* is present everywhere—in clearness, turbidity, purity, motleyness, dregs, ashes, manure, and filth—but it retains its mysteriousness. Therefore it is said that *li* pervades.

According to Yulgok, *chi*, as it has already taken form, has both beginning and end, front and back. It is not impartial and generates thousands of changes. *Chi* is quite unlike *li* which retains its mysteriousness in all things. This is why *chi* is called a vessel.

By way of explaining his theory that *chi* emanates and *li* rides on it, Yulgok said that Yin (the Negative) is static while Yang (the Positive) is dynamic; and that when Yang moves, *li* rides on its movement and *li* does not move by itself; and when Yin remains static, *li* rides on its being static and *li* is incapable of remaining static by itself. In order to clarify causality between *li* and *chi*, Yulgok explained; "What emanates is *chi* and what makes *chi* emanate is *li*. Without *chi*, there is no capacity of emanating, without *li*, there is no emanation."

Based on the view that *li* can become the cause of *chi*'s emanation, but cannot emanate by itself, Yulgok refuted T'oegye's theory that both *li* and *chi* can emanate. If T'oegye's theory of simultaneous emanation of *li* and *chi* had its origin in Chu Hsi, Yulgok went on, Chu Hsi himself made a mistake. Through his theory of *chi*'s emanation and *li*'s riding on it, Yulgok took a step closer to Lo Cheng-an's and Sŏ Hwadam's theory of the inseparability of *li* and *chi*.

Clinging to the *li-chi* dualism of Cheng I-Chuan and Chu Hsi, Yulgok could not develop his theory into a thorough *chi*-monism upholding that *li* is nothing but *chi*, but he took an eclectic position by advocating the theory that *li* and *chi* do not mix themselves together. Warning against an attempt to bring Sŏ Hwadam's *chi*-monistic tendency to the extreme, Yulgok advised in a letter to Sŏng U-gye that one should rather follow T'oegye's adherence to Chu Hsi than to follow Sŏ's originality.

Yulgok explained that without *li*, *chi* has no ground to stand on, and, without *chi*, *li* has no basis to rely on, and that *li* and *chi*, therefore, are inseparable as they are not two different things. In another passage, however, he explained that although *li* and *chi* are inseparable, *li* remains *li* and *chi* remains *chi* even when they are combined, and that, therefore, they cannot be mixed together. On the basis of this theory of incapability of mixing *li* and *chi*, he asserted that *li* and *chi* are not one and the same. The relation between the two, Yulgok explained as being one and two, and two and one. Their causality to him was immanent causality.

In "An Essay on Yulgok," Yi Pyŏng-do points out that Yulgok's *li* and *chi* are comparable to Spinoza's God and various
phenomena, respectively. He also points out that Yulgok's
theory of *li* pervading and *chi* accommodating reminds one of
Avatamska Buddhism.

This writer wants to add one thing in this connection.
Yulgok's philosophy of *li* and *chi* retains an influence it received from the philosophy of Chuang-tzu. There may be
some who deny the influence, but they nevertheless cannot
deny the fact that Yulgok's writings are interspersed with
phrases smacking much of Chuang-tzu's philosophy.

His essay, entitled "*Li-il-bun-su-bu*," reveals that his thought
contains a considerable number of elements originating in
Chuang-tzu. His famous thesis, "*Ch'ŏndoch'aek*," which he
wrote at the age of 23, also shows much influence from
Chuang-tzu. Among Chuang-tzu's phrases, those contained in
the chapters of *Soyoyup'yŏn* and *Chemullon* were referred to
by Yulgok most frequently. These clearly testify that Yulgok
read Chuang-tzu's works carefully, especially the two chapters
mentioned above.

Especially the thought, which Chuang-tzu introduced in
Chemullon, that all things in the universe, when viewed from
the standpoint of Tao (the Way) or from the standpoint of Absolute Knowledge transcending relative knowledge, are one
and the same in spite of their multifarious phenomena, exerted
profound influence on Sung dynasty Cheng Ming-tao's
"benevolence as oneness of all things in the universe." The *chi*-
monism of Chang Heng-chu, a Sung philosopher, had its
origin in influence from Chuang-tzu's philosophy, as pointed
out by some scholars. Cheng Ming-tao's *chi*-monistic tendency
and Chang Heng-chu's *chi*-monism present an attitude different from that of the *li-chi* dualism of Cheng I-chuan and
Chu Hsi, who strictly distinguished the two, although they
were all rated as most representative Neo-Confucianists who
revered the teachings of Confucius and Mencius.

The thought of Lo Cheng-an of the Ming dynasty, whom

Yulgok rated as superior to Yi T'oegye or Sŏ Hwadam, and from whom he received much influence, that all things in the universe are one and the same in spite of their multifarious phenomena, and that *li* and *chi* cannot be separated, can be regarded as belonging to the same school as Cheng Ming-tao and Chang Heng-chu. In view of this genealogy of philosophical development, it is apparent that Yulgok's philosophy, his conception of *li* and *chi*, which has no special connection with his political philosophy and his moral philosophy, received profound influence from Chuang-tzu.

In fact, Cheng I-chuan and Chu Hsi, whose dualism restricted Yulgok, forcing him to adopt the eclectic theory of impossibility of admixing *li* and *chi*, kept Cheng Ming-tao at a distance and guarded themselves against him.

In a chapter of *Chibukyŏp'yŏn*, Chuang-tzu said in question and answer with Tonggwakcha that Tao can be found in an insect, in barnyard grass, in a roof-tile, even in urine and dung, thus advocating the omnipresence of Tao. In a letter to Sŏng U-gye in which he asserted the theory of *li* pervading and *chi* accommodating, Yulgok maintained the omnipresence of *li*, showing striking similarity to Chuang-tzu's theory of the omnipresence of Tao. As already referred to, Yulgok in another passage said, "*Li* is present everywhere—in clearness, turbidity, purity, motleyness, dregs, ashes, manure, and filth."

Although there may have existed minor differences among their theories concerning details, it should not be overlooked that a pantheistic idea gave birth to Chuang-tzu's theory of the omnipresence of Tao, Spinoza's theory that God is nature, and Yulgok's theory of the omnipresence of *li*.

In spite of restrictions from Chu Hsi's dualism, Yulgok, in his theory of *chi* emanating and *li* riding on it, observed that Yin is static and Yang is dynamic, and that their being static or dynamic is so of their own accord; nothing forces them to be so. In *Ch'ŏndoch'aek*, he said, "what makes Yang quick and Yin slow is *chi*, and the reason why the former is quick and the latter is slow is *li*. I do not know what makes them so. I merely say that they are so of their own accord." The phrase, "of their own accord," is a proof that Yulgok's theory was formulated under the influence of Chuang-tzu.

As has been pointed out already, his basic thought, in spite of elements originating in Chuang-tzu, had deep roots in the philosophy of Confucius and Mencius, who revered Kings Yao and Shun as ideal monarchs.

It seems that Yulgok's philosophy of *li* and *chi* had no close relation to his moral philosophy, political philosophy, or his actual conduct in life. It is also interesting to note that the important contents of the philosophy of *li* and *chi*, in the case of both Yi T'oegye and Yi Yulgok, were published not in the form of theses with express titles, but through correspondence with contemporary scholars—with Ki Ko-bong in the case of T'oegye, and with Sŏng U-gye and Pak Hwa-suk in the case of Yulgok.

In short, there existed so close logical connection between Yulgok's philosophy of *li* and *chi* and his moral philosophy or political philosophy.

In *"Ch'ŏndoch'aek*," as has been referred to, Yulgok said that "what makes Yang quick and Yin slow is *chi*. . . . I do not know what makes them so. . . . I merely say that they are so of their own accord." On the other hand, however, he said, "Human mind is Heaven's mind," asserting that both harmonious movement of celestial bodies and occurrence of any degeneration in it are result of good or bad government of the ruler. Saying that *"chi* is responsible for making the celestial movement take such a turn, and this also depends upon human affairs," Yulgok made an assertion contradictory to his previous statement that ". . .they are so of their own accord."

It is again evident that his philosophy of *li* and *chi* had almost no relation to his political philosophy. In fact, his primary concern was not the philosophy of *li* and *chi*, but the realization of ideal moral government based on Confucianism.

Yulgok applied his theory of *li* and *chi* to his explanation of

Mencius' teaching that compassion is the beginning of Benevolence, a feeling of shame is the beginning of Righteousness, modesty is the beginning of Civility, and discrimination of right and wrong is the beginning of Wisdom; and of the teaching of *li-chi* about the seven emotions—pleasure, anger, sadness, fear, love, hate, and desire. His theory of *li* and *chi* also had a relation to his explanation of the Mind of Tao and Human Mind, as mentioned in the Scripture of Documents. It is convincing to say that his explanation of the Four Beginnings, Seven Emotions, and the like was made not as a result of his inquiry into *li* and *chi*, but for the motive of providing philosophical depth for his Confucianism.

REFERENCES

1. An In-sik: "The Life and Achievements of Yi Yulgok"
2. Yi Pyŏng-do: "An Essay of Yulgok"
3. Sŏng Nak-hun: "The History of Korean Confucian Thought"

On the Criticism of Confucianism in Korea

YI SANG-ŬN

The more the problems of modernization are discussed, the more important becomes the question of the relation between tradition and modernization. Hence, a re-examination and new understanding of traditional culture is of great academic importance. Considering the tremendous influence exerted by Confucianism on the various facets of Korean history, culture and social life in general becomes an even more important one. This paper will attempt to probe this problem.

Evaluation requires standards. An evaluation that is not based on certain set standards is mere personal opinion, the more so when a judgment concerns a great historic philosophy or religion. If a philosophy or religion has exerted a profound and wide influence on mankind while maintaining its own life, that philosophy or religion must contain elements of eternal truth, for without such elements it could never have survived. At the same time, since a philosophy or religion is a product of a certain era, it takes on different forms in the course of its development in order to adapt itself to society in a certain age. These adopted forms are not the essentials but rather the means of its adaptation to the surrounding circumstances. Such means can take on different forms and are subject to change according to the creative ideas of the adaptor and to the situation in a given society and at a given time. Unless we draw a distinct line between the essence and the adopted form of a philosophy, we are most likely to mistake the one for the other or confuse the nature of both, thus losing the chance of gaining correct understanding. In our discussions concerning the merits and demerits of Korean Confucianism, our judgment will surely be prejudiced unless we have the necessary standards for our judgment.

There has been much criticism of Confucianism in Korea, and so it is necessary to re-examine and gain new understanding of traditional values from the historical as well as ideological viewpoint. However, critics in the past did not base their criticism on sound standards of judgment; and most of them have been prone to point out only the defects in Confucianism. The first work which deals with both the merits and demerits of Korean Confucianism and its influence on Korean Society is Dr. Hyŏn Sang-yun's[1] celebrated work *Chosŏn Yuhak-sa* (The History of Korean Confucianism). In the introduction to his book, Dr. Hyŏn has a separate chapter titled "The Merits and Demerits of Korean Confucianism" which devotes itself to a criticism of Confucianism in Korea. His criticism may be said to have embodied the opinions of all critics ever to have appeared in Korea. This paper, therefore, will attempt to re-examine the merits and demerits of Confucianism on the basis of Dr. Hyŏn's book.

Dr. Hyŏn comments on the influence of Korean Confucianism on the history of Korean thought as follows:

> In spite of the fact that Confucianism is, comparatively speaking, an intellectual, aristocratic and academic ideology, its influence on the life and thought of Korean society has, indeed, been profound. It gave direction to Korean philosophy and character to the nation and it wrought important national changes, politically, culturally, and economically. Some of this influence can be considered as both a service and a disservice to Korea.

As merits Dr. Hyŏn enumerates:

1) Encouragement of the "Learning of the Superior Man" (君子學);
2) Respect for ethics and morality;
3) Respect for "probity, loyalty and righteousness" (清廉節義).

As demerits, he lists:

1) Respect for China (慕華);
2) Factionalism;
3) "Family-ism" (家族主義);
4) Class-ideas;
5) Effeminacy (文弱);
6) Deterioration of industrial capacity;
7) Respect for personal honor (尚名主義);
8) Trend to retroactivity (復古思想).

We shall now consider to what extent the evaluation of merits and demerits by Dr. Hyŏn corresponds to the recognized standards of judgment which draws a line between the essence of Confucianism and the adaptations it has made.

On the whole, the merits and demerits Dr. Hyŏn points out are in accordance with those of past and present critics although it is doubtful whether they correspond to the aforesaid standards of judgment and whether Dr. Hyŏn's explanation of merits and demerits is adequate. We shall examine these point by point.

New Understanding of the Meritorious Service of Confucianism

1. *Encouragement of the "Learning of Superior Man"*[2]

Dr. Hyŏn enumerates the contents of the "Learning of Superior Man" as "learning for one's perfection" (爲己之學), "sincerity in solitude" (慎獨), "self-reflection" (反求諸己), "to subdue one's self and return to propriety" (克己復禮), and "do not deceive oneself." He further explains that what matters first in Confucianism is "to cultivate one's person, to rectify one's mind, and to make one's intentions sincere." Thanks to Confucian learning, he said, many sages and Superior Men appeared during the 500 years of the Yi dynasty (1392-1910), some at the court and others throughout the country, to ennoble mores and to foster filial love and respects for elders. Thus foreigners came to call Korea "the most courteous country in the East." Dr. Hyŏn says that "Make oneself a Superior Man instead of an inferior man" exerted a greater reformative influence than did punitive justice. He says it was possible for the Yi dynasty politics to "govern not by law" and to "purify not by punishment" solely due to the fact that the people strove to attain the "learning of Superior Man."

Dr. Hyŏn's commentary points out quite correctly the merits of Confucian influence on Korean culture, even though it contained certain exaggerations and ameliorations when viewed in the light of the political reality of the latter period of the Yi dynasty.

Will such a form of education be necessary in the future? Those who lament the present educational reality, the lack of moral instruction and the degeneration of popular morality and who desire to rectify the situation will draw the conclusion that it is necessary to resuscitate such traditions that were once inherent to the Korean mentality. The question here is the correct understanding of the spirit of the "learning of Superior Man" and how to realize it in modern Korean education.

2. *Respect for Ethics and Morality*

"Be filial to parents, serve the king loyally, be prudent in associations with the opposite sex, respect elders, keep faith and preserve justice among friends." On the basis of this principal thought, Confucianism contributed much to the Korean state and society; i.e., harmony reigned in families, subjects were loyal, sons filial, wives chaste, social order was preserved and decency between men and women fostered, states Dr.

Hyŏn.

These are the Five Moral Stipulations (五倫) in human relations rooted deep in Korean thought. Even when the legal system was incomplete and when the administration fell prey to chaos, at least the semblance of social order and justice was maintained due to the fact that the five moral stipulations were observed in all walks of life. Indeed, the philosophy underlying the five principles contributed greatly to the enhancement of popular morality in old Korea.

Certain questions arise, however. Is it still necessary to uphold such principles under the present liberal democratic political system? Many have already voiced their opposition and, in China, this issue gave rise to heated controversy in the earlier days of the New Cultural Movement. Few in Korea advocate that these five principles be strictly followed; those who do are traditional Confucianists. Some modification seems necessary. To what extent, then, can these principles be modified? Or are they to be completely ignored? Their total neglect, even in a democratic society, seems impossible because, as long as we maintain our present mode of family life, such human relations as those between father and son and brother and sister are inevitable. Unless we are to leap overnight into the world of a Platonic society of communal wife, relations between husband and wife will continue to have their meaning. Faith among friends becomes even more necessary in today's open democratic society. From such points of view the five moral stipulations certainly cannot be ignored even today, although the form of their application should be modified. The only point here is loyalty to the king as the king is no longer required but the concept of the king has been changed to that of the state or government while loyalty to the king has been replaced with loyalty to laws which the people's representative body formulates with the people's consent and with loyalty to the public position which individual officials occupy. What matters here is a correct modern interpretation of the ancient yet equally valid concept.

Some hold these five moral stipulations as a mere feudal morality constituting moral coercion imposed from above. However, such is not in the true spirit of Confucianism. Confucianism rather takes the attitude that morality constitutes basically reciprocal obligations imposed on all parts concerned and that therefore one-sided obligations can never become morality. Thus the original meaning of the five moral principles—father-love, son-filiality; elder brother-brotherly love, younger brother-reverence; king-justice, subject-loyalty; husband-initiative, wife-obedience; and friends-faith—stipulated mutual obligations which both sides must fulfill. Therefore, when one side demands that the other fulfill its obligations without first fulfilling its own, the five moral principles are negated.

The only apparent exception is the rule that "men and women shall not share the same seat after they have reached the age of seven." This cannot be strictly adhered to, since free association between male and female has become an inevitable social phenomenon in the modern world. Another phrase, "the activities of the master lie outside the house and that of the mistress inside the house," cannot become absolute for it naturally changes according to the social condition of the times. The present vogue for what might be called "open sex" comes from the West with its different cultural traditions and it not only runs counter to Korean tradition but it is also feared that it will result in lowered social discipline and a degeneration of man's spirit.

3. *Respect for Probity, Loyalty and Righteousness*

Dr. Hyŏn states:

As seen from such Confucian catch-phrases as 'the superior man is in search of the right way, not of food,' or 'the superior man contents himself in poverty but delights in the right way,' or 'to die of starvation is rather trivial while to betray one's loyalty is really grave,' or 'the commander of forces many be carried off, but the will of even a common man cannot be taken from him,' Korean Confucianists esteemed probity, loyalty and righteousness as they did their own lives because they considered that these had important connections with Confucian morality. Thus, the politicians of old Korea esteemed honesty and honorable poverty as much as they despised injustice, wealth and nobility. Therefore, corrupt government officials and national traitors appeared only in the latter days of the Yi dynasty when Confucianism began to loose its hold over Korea.

It is a fact, gleaned from ancient literature and from the collections of writers, that the Yi dynasty Confucianists, whether they were government officials or ordinary citizens, strove to uphold probity, loyalty and righteousness as "literati" (士). This can be interpreted to mean that the Korean people, on the basis of their inherent purity of character, furthered ethical and moral values by their veneration of Confucianism. The Three Scholars (三學士)[3] and the Six Martyrs (死六臣)[4] proved this conviction by their martyrdom.

Re-examination of the Demerits of Confucianism

1. *Respect for China*

We cannot deny Dr. Hyŏn's allegation that the respect of Korean Confucian scholars for China thwarted the development of an independent spirit and of a national self-consciousness in Korea. However, this was not due to any defect in Confucianism itself for Confucianism embodies only the concept of the Universe (Tien-hsia) and not that of the nation-state, just as Christianity calls for world brotherhood and an end to discrimination among nations. Nevertheless, Great Britain, France and Germany embraced Christianity and then went on to form nation-states respectively. Japan, which imported Confucianism from China as did Korea, nevertheless asserted her independence from China. If Korean politicians had adopted an independent foreign policy, their nation certainly would not have had to pay tribute to China for so long (of course, we cannot ignore the fact that Japan's geographical situation in relation to China is different from that of Korea). We must say that this particular defect can be attributed more to Korean politicians than to Confucianism itself.

On the other hand, I would like to probe into the reasons for Korea's respect for China from another angle. It may be assumed that the Korean people are, by nature, inclined to love culture and spiritual values. In ancient times, China was the only country bordering Korea that had a higher civilization than Korea. In this connection it was quite natural that the Korean people, who love culture, looked upon China as a highly-civilized state and consequently came to love and respect that country for what it represented. We now think of America and England in more intimate terms, than we do of other countries, because in our estimation, the thought of liberal democracy is more closely related to them. Furthermore, the concept of nationalism is a modern import from the West while, in the Orient, there was only Universalism (Tien-hsia) manifested in the expression, "There are not two suns in the sky nor are there two kings above the people." Under the feudal system it was the rule that feudal lords received their titles from the king in the place where tribute was paid to the king. Under such circumstances, the Korean people easily accepted the thought of Great Unity (大統一) in "the Spring and Autumn Annals" (春秋) and the historic record that Kija (箕子) came to Korea from China because the ancient Korean people probably thought that, since Kija was a man of high virtue, if they installed him in the position of founding king of their country their cultural position would be so elevated as to make it equal to that of the Chinese people.

In brief, I am of the opinion that if we consider the admiration of things Chinese in the light of nationalism, it is certainly undesirable, but if we take it as meaning a love of cultural values, it testifies to the fact that the Koreans are a culture-loving people. The fact that Korea introduced Buddhism during the Silla dynasty, and Christianity and liberal democracy during this century must be considered to mean the same thing as love of Chinese culture.

I must add one thing here. Dr. Hyŏn uses *Mohwa* (慕華 : respect for China or admire for Chinese or admire for Chinese Culture) instead of the more-commonly used term *Sadae* (事大 : to serve a large country) in his book, but from the context he seems to have confused the two terms. We must distinguish the one from the other. The latter is concerned with political affairs while the former is concerned with culture. The size of a country does not matter when we evaluate its culture. The West still longs for Greek culture and the Greek spirit not because Greece was a large country but rather because Greek culture typifies what is beautiful and her spirit what is lofty. However, in the case of China many are apt to confuse the cultural "admiration of China" and the political and diplomatic "respect for China" due to the fact that China happens to have developed a high form of civilization and to be a large country at the same time. That "the Korean people called China 'Big Brother' while calling themselves the 'Eastern Barbarians'," or that "they used the era name of Ming China" was due to Yi dynasty's submissive foreign policy toward China. Korea never voluntarily adopted flunkeyism which has nothing to do at all with cultural love of China.

One more point I would like to make clear here is the fact that although the term "*Sadae*" was written in historical records and diplomatic documents, Korea never used the term '*Sadae Juŭi*' (事大主義) or '*Sadae Sasang*' (事大思想) before the Japanese annexation of Korea. This means they never considered *Sadae* as an 'ism' or thought. Official Japanese scholars first used the term with a view to showing that the Korean people were inveterate sycophants. We must not fail to detect the political scheme the Japanese advanced when they did so. Because many independence fighters during early Japanese colonial days were Confucianists, because Confucian scholars resisted Japanese rule long after Japan's annexation of Korea, and since the Japanese considered the Korean people's disdain for the Japanese to be the result of their love for Chinese culture, the Japanese tried to separate Korea from China spiritually as well as emotionally and to plant the seeds of hatred and contempt for the Chinese in the hearts of the Korean people. This hidden political scheme resulted in official Japanese scholars forging the term "flunkeyism" with a view to provoking the national sentiment of the Korean people to China-hating. The Japanese thus purposefully encouraged confusion of the two terms. Did the Japanese themselves not once love things Chinese? Some ignorant Korean scholars use the two terms indiscriminately as if to acknowledge that the Korean people are sycophants and they hold Confucianism responsible for this.[5] To repeat, Korea as a nation paying tribute to China was in effect forced to adopt a foreign policy submissive to China. Moreover, under the feudal system the concept of paying tribute was nominal and allowed total autonomy in domestic affairs. We know of many historical occasions in which Korean kingdoms did not hesitate to send expeditionary forces to the north to counter Chinese attempts to interfere in their affairs.[6] In short, the Korean people were forced to adopt *Sadae* (serve a large country) policy, and voluntarily love Chinese culture. This is the true historical meaning of *Mohwa* (慕華) in the Korean term. If we confuse *Mohwa* with *Sadae* we commit the fault of distorting Korean intellectual history.[7]

2. *Factionalism*

Factionalism refers to struggles among political forces and not to competition among academicians. However, since in Korea Confucian scholars often took charge of state affairs, as was the case in China also, factionalism was considered to have inseparable ties with Confucianism. Dr. Hyŏn alleges that factionalism appeared in Korea because Confucianism drew a distinct line between the superior and the inferior man. But it is a contradiction that Dr. Hyŏn, who considers the "learning of the Superior Man" as a merit of Confucianism, condemns at the same time the distinction between the superior man and the inferior man, which is an essential of "the learning of the Superior Man," as a demerit of Confucianism. What is worthy of blame here is not Confucianism, which laid stress on the moral distinction between superior and inferior groups, but rather the people who abused one another by alleging "I am a superior man and you are an inferior man," or "we are the party of superior men and you are the party of inferior men."

I view the long history of Korean factionalism and the subsequent massacres of the literati in this way. The prime cause of factionalism lies either in the fact that our politicians failed to grasp and translate the essence of Confucianism into their political life or in the fact that the political and social situation of the time made factionalism inevitable.[8] Confucianism itself cannot be held responsible for the rise of factionalism. This also holds true in the case of China. Confucianism is already a phenomenon of the past as far as Korea is concerned but factionalism still lives on. Does Korea's current factionalism have anything to do with Confucianism? Rather, if the "learning of superior men" had been correctly put into practice, factionalism would not have become so severe as it now is.

3. Defects of "Family-ism"

Dr. Hyŏn points out that "Confucianism laid too much stress on filial duties, to the extent of slighting the state and society." It is true that Confucianism held filial piety in higher esteem and that in a Confucian state the concept of "home" and "family" was stronger than that of "state" and "society."

Today's world, which is swayed by surging waves of nationalism and in which the nation-state proceeds to form an international society, reveals the weakness of this "family-ism." This is one of the key issues concerning the essentials of Confucianism. Gone are the days when "nine generations lived in the same house." Such large families are impossible to find in these days when more people find it more convenient to break up families and live in separate homes.

Since this family-ism was the product of an agricultural society, the contents of filial piety have inevitably become simpler today when it is no longer possible for the majority of the people to observe elaborate rituals and practise cumbersome manners as in olden times.

Then, in what way can filial duty, which constitutes a key element in Confucianism, be adapted to modern social life? This is one area in which Confucianism must modernize. First it is necessary to re-examine the concept of filial piety. If we strip away the ritual associated with filial piety we find that filial piety is derived from the concept that holds family succession and multiplication in high esteem as can be gathered from the sayings of the sages: "The beginning of filial piety is not to impair the body, even one hair or one piece of skin, which is given by parents," or "There are three things which are unfilial; to have no posterity is the greatest of them."

If mere succession of family life and multiplication are meant, there is no difference between men and animals. Men, however, have respect for life and they desire to sublimate life. He who is conscious of the precious gift of life is entitled to be called a man. It is natural, too, to have affection for one's life and to be grateful to the parents who gave that precious life. Thus filial piety comes from a feeling of affection for and gratitude to one's parents and, if one really has such a feeling, he naturally needs to express it. Filial piety is the embodiment of the expression of such a feeling.

The feeling of filial piety can be expressed in many diverse ways such as parties to celebrate parental birthdays, taking good care of parents during their old age and, after their death, burying them with appropriate ritual and observing memorial rites to them, etc.

Seen in this way, filial piety is a natural and spontaneous revelation of human nature that will continue as long as the family system lasts whether in an agricultural society or in an industrial society. There is no reason to hold that Confucianism laid too much stress on the family, due to the stringent dictates of filial piety at the expense of society and the state. Dr. Hyŏn, indeed, points out, "Toward the end of the Yi dynasty corrupt government officials did not work as true government officials for the good of the state, because they placed their personal interests before those of the state and their homes above the state."

However great the importance Confucianism placed on the family, there is no call for linking Confucianism to corrupt officials pursuing their personal gains, because Confucianism strictly distinguishes public from private matters and righteousness from selfish gains, so much so that when a son who fulfills his filial duties is selected to fill a government post, he is strictly enjoined to observe the distinction between public and private affairs. This is one of the characteristic features of the code of conduct for government officials in a Confucian state. Thus, such phrases as "To kill selfishness and serve the public" (滅私奉公) or "even a parent is to be sacrificed for the purpose of greater righteousness" (大義滅親) are concrete expressions of the importance of Confucian "public matters" and "righteousness." Even if corrupt government officials in Korea's past placed personal interests above those of the state, it cannot be said outright that this was due to Confucian influence. If such government officials had grasped the true Confucian spirit they would have learned the distinction between private and public matters, between righteousness and personal gain.

In brief, we still live in a world which, in its stage of evolution from nation-states to a universal state, stresses nationalism so much as to make the defects in family-ism more pronounced and in which the concept of the home and the family loses ground while that of social organization gains momentum. However, if the world evolves into "Great Unity" (Universal State) from its present state, then nationalism will no longer be necessary and life in the small unit of an autonomous community, like Lao tzu's ideal society, will become the ideal of politics. In this sense, the family has an eternal meaning. Indeed, the political ideals of Confucianism point toward the ultimate realization of such a universal world. Confucianism held the home in greater esteem as the basic unit of a viable community in a world of the future which transcends boundaries and distinctions of mere nations and states. Therefore, it seems that the Confucian family system is not merely a remnant of agricultural society because it also has an inherent value that must be further explored as an ideal form of life in future society.

4. *Class Idea*

"Of Confucianism, which regards the observance of order and moral obligation (名分) according to the basic moral hierarchy of the Three Fundamental Principles (三綱) and the Five Moral Rules (五倫), class idea is an inevitable attribute," Dr. Hyŏn says. Quoting Confucius, "The people may be made to follow a path of action, but they may not be made to understand it" (T'ai-po, ba. 3. Analects), and Mencius, "If there were not men of a superior grade, there would be none to rule the countrymen. If there were not countrymen, there would be none to support the men of superior grade" (Teng-Won-Kung. Part II, Work of Mencius), Dr. Hyŏn reaches the conclusion, "From this originated the custom of putting the government over the people and the distinction between aristocrat and commoner. The distinction between first wife and mistress was derived from the prohibition of intermarriage between the offspring of the first wife and mistress. Thus all class ideas in Korea originates in Confucianism." Dr.

Hyŏn's commentary concerning this issue is a most authentic representation of the general opinion of the anti-Confucianists of the past. We must re-examine his commentary in order to formulate the new social ethics.

As a conclusion to this part of our discussion I would like to point out that Dr. Hyŏn seems to confuse the true nature and application of Confucianism on the one hand while, on the other, his understanding of the true nature of Confucianism is incomplete. First, it is not clear what he means by the term 'class.' I gather that Dr. Hyŏn does not use the term in its usual Western social and economic sense, for example, as in "middle class," "capitalist class" and "working class." When he refers to "The Three Fundamental Principles and the Five Moral Rules," "Order and Moral Obligations," and "The Custom of Placing the Government above the People," he seems to refer to hierarchy in the government system. When he says, "Confucianism has a strong class consciousness," he misunderstands the term if he uses it as a socio-economic concept because such classes did not develop in the Orient, especially in a Confucian society governed by the literati.

However, if he means hierarchy in the government system he is close to the mark. This hierarchical system, originating in the feudalism of Chou (周), developed in the Ch'in and Han periods, when a centralized system of government was established to replace the feudal system, and reached fruition in the T'ang period. Thus emerged the five divisions in social position, namely, Kung (公) first-class official, Ch'ing (卿) second-class official, Tai-fu (大夫) third-class official, the literati (士) fourth-class official, and commoners (庶人). The development of this hierarchy in the central government was completed during the Yi dynasty period in Korea. It has been said that European nations used this form of hierarchical bureaucracy as a model when they established centralized modern states to replace their aristocratic feudalism. If this is true, the hierarchical bureaucratic system of a Confucian government must be considered one of its meritorious aspects since it helps maintain order and security in a state. Is the bureaucracy of modern states also not organized on the basis of the Confucian hierarchical system, only under different names?

By the class philosophy of Confucianism, Dr. Hyŏn seems to imply what he calls the thought of "putting the government above the people," quoting the following sayings of Confucius and Mencius as evidence of the connection of this thought with Confucianism:

"The people may be made to follow the path of action, but they may not be made to understand" (Confucius), and

"If there were not men of superior grade, there would be none to rule the countrymen. If there were not countrymen, there would be none to support the men of superior grade" (Mencius).

But we must understand that these sayings do not imply the thought of "putting the government above the people (官尊民卑)."

The above saying of Confucius, of course, does not mean a policy of mass illiteracy (愚民政策). The Confucian educational ideal that "every town and village has its school" cannot be considered to advocate a policy of mass illiteracy. Does the *Great Learning* not expostulate in its first chapter the "illustration of illustrous virtues and the renovation of the people (新民, 明明德)?"

Mencius' saying, also, does not imply, as critics allege, the protection of the superior man's class, the ruling class, and the exploitation of the countrymen, the ruled. This is evidenced in his debate with the Hus-hsing school which advocated the "joint tilling of the land by the superior men and the countrymen." The gist of Mencius' saying is summed up: "The politicians (superior men) are so engrossed in politics that they cannot find time to farm and the countrymen (the commoners) are so preoccupied with their farm work that they cannot find time to engage in politics. So let the superior men and the countrymen do their respective work: the countrymen work hard and pay taxes so that the superior men may rule the country on a government salary." Mencius countered the Hsu-hsing school's theory of "joint tilling by the superior men and countrymen," by saying that cooperation among traders as traders, artisans as artisans, farmers as farmers alone will make social life smooth. If one man tries to meet every and all of his necessities, he will find it an impossible task.

Thus it is wrong to try to interpret the above two sayings to mean "putting the government above the people."

The idea of putting the government above the people is derived from the teachings of Legalist Han Fei. The system of absolute monarchy originated from Shin Huang T'i of Ch'in China, based upon the philosophical foundations laid by Han Fei whose monarchism influenced the Chinese political system in such a way as to ultimately give rise to the concept of placing the government above the people. Following the Han dynasty period, the civil service examination system was adopted to pave the way for Confucian scholars to take charge of the affairs of state. However, the Confucian scholars felt the need to check the arbitrary rule of the monarchy and so they established the office of prime minister and a system whereby ministers were appointed and made responsible for various fields in the government. The ministers formed a consultative council to advise the king. Thus, Confucian politics was primarily concerned with the protection of the commoners' rights and interests by holding the arbitrariness and despotism of the monarchy in check. Therefore, it is wrong to equate despotism and the idea of placing the government above the people with Confucianism. The reason all evils are attributed to Confucianism is that Confucian scholars held government power for too long. It is not necessary to enumerate those evils of Confucianism because the history of the later days of the Yi dynasty are only too well known. When we had no place to appeal our national grievances we attributed every evil to Confucianism, and this, I consider, is the main reason we have condemned Confucianism. However, considering the fact that

Confucian Japan prospered while Confucian Korea did not, we should blame not Confucianism but those who misapplied its principles and the disadvantageous socio-economic situations which resulted from successive Japanese and Chinese invasions.

5. *Effeminacy*

Dr. Hyŏn describes the defect of Confucian effeminacy by saying: "Confucianism admired letters at the expense of military affairs. While Confucianists repeated that, 'when there is a matter of civility, there must be a backing of military preparedness,' they not only actually neglected but also slighted things military. As a consequence, the sons of the literati easily evaded military duty and despised arms and those who bore them. During the period when society despised its military the Korean people fell victims to effeminacy. This nation displayed military heroism during the Three Kingdoms and Koryŏ dynasty periods alone."

The above comment seems to distinguish the nature of Confucianism from its application. "To despise things military and admire letters" is the ideal of Confucian politics because Confucianism stresses pacifism and the politics of benevolence and righteousness or righteous government, while holding military government or government by might in contempt. As a political ideal it cannot be questioned. The ultimate hope of mankind has always been and still is peace, not war; the political ideal today is also "to limit things military and cultivate letters" i.e., to limit armament as much as possible while promoting peaceful construction and not waging wars but establishing military rule. The minimum in armament is needed when a state could not defend itself armed with letters alone. "When there is a matter of civility, there must be a backing of military preparedness" is a phrase that was not only spoken but also put into practice by Confucius.[9] The blame must go to those Korean and Chinese Confucian politicians who took charge of state affairs in Yi dynasty and latter-day China.

However, even in Korea those who comprehended the true spirit of Confucianism did not neglect military affairs even in times of peace. Yi I (李珥), one of the leading Confucianists at the time of King Sŏnjo (宣祖), advocated "the training of 100,000 soldiers" in the period of peace before the Japanese invasion of Korea in the 16th century but his reasoned advocacy was drowned in the flattery and cajolery of those Confucian scholars and officials who competed for the attention of the king. The humiliation Korea suffered at the hands of the Japanese in the 16th century was not due to Confucian effeminacy but to the fact that the Yi dynasty politicians failed to translate the real meaning of Confucianism and put it into practice.

Another of Dr. Hyŏn's tenets, that the ancient Korean people "displayed military heroism. . ." must be re-examined from another angle. Maintaining a triangular position on the not-yet unified Korean peninsula, the Three Kingdoms fought with one another to gain hegemony throughout the peninsula just as the warring states did during the "age of the contending states" in China. The climate of the period was such that a state's policy naturally oriented toward faith in militarism and everybody respected military heroism. However, on a closer examination of the tales of military heroism of that time such Confucian sayings as "Do not retreat from the battlefield" or "Serve the king with loyalty and the state with patriotism" constituted the basis of such tales rather than did Buddhist or Taoist elements. The *Hwarangdo*, sometimes translated as the Flower Boys, were protagonists of such heroic tales and they were Confucian in their spirit rather than any combination of Buddhism and Taoism.

However, the situation reversed itself in Yi society. Domestically, the Yi dynasty enjoyed peace on its unified peninsula under a centralized system of government with no need for rivalry as in the case of the Three Kingdoms; externally, the Yi dynasty was not, as were preceding kingdoms, compelled to make military preparations against a northern enemy because Ming China was content with maintaining Korea as a tributary in light of past futile attempts to conquer Korea militarily, attempts made by the Sui through the T'ang to the Yuan dynasties of China. This is the background of the age in which Yi Confucian officials tried to carry out the Confucian ideal of "suppressing the military and cultivating letters" which consequently led to national development of a high culture around the period of King Sŏnjo. Had there been no Japanese invasion of Korea in 1592 and Manchurian invasion in 1637, the Confucian ideal of "suppressing the military and cultivating letters" might have helped the Yi dynasty develop a more brilliant culture.

Lastly, Dr. Hyŏn's statement that "sons of the literati easily evaded military duty and honest civil officials despised arms and those who bore them" does not express a special feature of the time. It is common among intellectuals in any country in any age and so can hardly be considered a feature exclusive to a Confucian country.

6. *Deterioration of Industrial Capacity*

Dr. Hyŏn, advancing reasons why Confucianism inhibited industrial capacity, says, "Confucianism despised the commercial and artisan classes. This comes from the sayings of the sages that Confucian scholars devote themselves to attaining purity of conscience and sincerity while traders and artisans give themselves only to personal gain and deception; the literati ($\pm$) classes, known as the *yangban*, had the notion that 'superior men govern the commoners who feed the *yangban*' and did not engage directly in industry; and the spirit of dependence arising from the notion of a large family caused the nation to eat the bread of idleness. Thus Korea's industrial capacity and will to work gradually deteriorated to the ruin of industry and a rise in poverty." Dr. Hyŏn states, in essence, that

1) contempt for the commercial and artisan classes reigned, 2) the *yangban* class did not engage directly in industrial endeavors, and 3) the large family gave rise to a spirit of dependence and an idle life.

Of the three, the third has nothing at all to do with the nature of Confucianism for the size of families can vary according to changes in time and circumstances. However, it is true that the large family hindered the growth of the people's spirit of economic independence.

The first two items concern Confucianists, 'the scholars,' their way of thinking and living, but it is doubtful that those who belonged to the '*yangban*' class were really Confucian scholars.

The term *yangban* refers to two classes—the civil and military services of the government which recruited their personnel through the civil service examination. The term distinguishes such officials from the commoners who held no official positions. Thus, the term at first vaguely referred to those who held official positions, regardless of their hierarchical level, but later it came to mean the privileged hereditary classes, the sons of the *yangban*.

Thus, *yangban* cannot always be taken to mean the Confucianists. What makes a scholar is not a man's official position but rather his learning, behavior and virtue. According to this standard, only one out of every ten thousand *yangban* in the past would qualify as a true scholar while the rest would be pretenders or self-styled literati who dared to commit every kind of evil only to disgrace Confucianism. They were the cause of all the ills and the eventual downfall of the state. So, if industrial capacity deteriorated it is rather they who must be held responsible and not Confucianism itself.

If we attribute the deficiency of despising the commercial and artisan classes to Confucianism, then it is to be blamed accordingly.

Confucianism did look down on such classes and this contempt so influenced the national psychology that agriculture, the financial base of the scholar-literati, became a major vocation and commerce and industry on occupation for the lowly. Naturally few wanted to engage in commerce and industry and so technical know-how for development could not be accumulated resulting in the gradual deterioration of industry. (Here the word "deterioration" is used in a relative sense in comparison with foreign countries because, even though they were despised by the scholar-literati, as the landless population increased, more people engaged in the trades to accumulate experience and slowly better their techniques. But in foreign countries knowledge and techniques grow very quickly due to the participation of specialists from the intellectual class.) Why then did Confucianism despise traders and manual workers? This is the crucial point.

It is true that Confucianism contains such unjust elements but they are actually concerned with personal morality and, not with government policy. Even Confucianists, as politicians, could not despise all traders and manual workers who were subjects in the same royal domain because of their ideas regarding personal morality. We must realize that the way of living and the way of thinking concerning politics and economics, derived from the Confucian idea of righteousness and benefit, provided the basis for class discrimination.

Concerning the notion of benefit and righteousness, Confucius said: 1) The superior man concerns himself with righteousness, while the inferior man thinks only of benefit; 2) If one pursues benefit alone he will begrudge good to others; 3) To become rich and noble by unjust means is for me (Confucius) like a cloud floating in the sky; and 4) I cannot discourse with those scholars who intend to achieve the Way and who are ashamed of their crude clothing and food. Mencius said that those who rise at the first crow of the cock to do good are the people of Shun (舜) and those who rise at the first crow of the cock to seek benefit are the people of Chih (跖)[10]. Tung Chung-shu (董仲舒) said that the right attitude in life is "to conform to the virtue of righteousness and not to take into consideration the question of profit; to make clear the Way and not to think of reward." This is why Confucianists hold the distinction between righteousness and benefit (profit) in such high esteem. Here "benefit" means private gain and "righteousness" means public good. Traders and industrialists were considered to be those who pursue only private gain and hence the distinction between the superior man and the inferior man.

It is written in the section entitled "The Government of a State" in The Great Learning, "By gaining the people through the Way the kingdom is gained, and by losing the people the kingdom is lost. On this account, the ruler will first take pains to ensure his own virtue. [11] Possessing virtue will give him the people. Possessing the people will give him territory. Possessing territory will give him wealth. Possessing wealth, he will have the resources for the expenditure. Virtue is the root; wealth is the result. If he makes the root his secondary object and the result his primary, he will only wrangle with people and teach them rapaciousness. There is a great course also for the production of wealth. Let the producers be many and consumers few. Let there be activity in production, and economy in expenditure. Then the wealth will always be sufficient. . . . Rather than to have a minister who collects wealth, it would be better to have a robber-minister. This is in accordance with the saying that in a state pecuniary gain is not to be considered prosperity; its prosperity will be found in righteousness."

According to this, virtue comes first and wealth last in the government of a state and, if the government does not try to achieve virtue and collects wealth, fighting will ensue among the people for wealth and profit.

In brief, the political aim of the Confucian economic policy does not lie in the increment of national wealth by positively developing industry but rather in maintaining the people "in their given vocation with ease."

The saying that a state should not have a wealth-collecting

minister means that if government policy is oriented toward the increment of wealth the people will also vie with one another for wealth and profit. Everybody craves profit and so when people start to fight over profit competition among them will last forever since man's craving for profit is endless. Social injustice and distinctions between rich and poor and victor and vanquished will result. Thus, Confucian politicians could not adopt policies that would promote commercial and industrial development. In conclusion, if Confucianism really aided the deterioration of industrial capacity, it is rather because of the nature of Oriental civilization, in contrast to that of the modern Western world. The East is oriented more toward stability and peace than competition; toward moral cultivation rather than the pursuit of wealth and power.

7. *Respect for Names* (*Honor*)

"The Confucian idea that the ultimate of filial piety lies in making one's parent prominent by means of establishing himself and making his name known to the world gave rise to the custom of honoring false names as in borrowing and buying other's official titles, maintaining an official title after death, erecting innumerable statues, and creating many important executive positions in companies and banks. People sold and bought official titles during the last days of the Yi dynasty, not with a view to carrying on their political ideals but to procure an official title to be used until their death. For these evils Confucianism must be held responsible," says Dr. Hyŏn.

Thus, according to Dr. Hyŏn, respect for names seems to have come from Confucian filial piety. It is true that the Korean people had and still have this defect. But it is necessary to examine why this defect is related to Confucian teachings on piety. Respect for names originally resulted from man's desire to be honored which, along with the desire for power and wealth, is common to all people in any society and time. It does not seem reasonable to attribute this defect to the Korean people and to Confucian filial piety alone.

The desire for honor itself cannot be called an evil or a defect unless it turns out to be admiration for false names. Everybody has a sense of the dishonorable. It is man's immanent good nature that makes him displeased when abused and delighted when praised. If man has no sense of honor and no sense of shame then he will commit any crime unashamedly thus rendering the social system of reward and punishment null and void. Therefore, man's sense of honor is relative to his sense of shame and in the moral sense of respect for human nature it promotes the spiritual values of human civilization.

Does Dr. Hyŏn then consider that the phrase "to establish oneself and to make oneself known to the world to make one's parent prominent" promotes the worship of false names? From this commentary he seems to believe so. His quotation from *The Book of Filial Piety* is precisely: "To establish oneself and practise the Way, and to place one's name in posterity to make one's parent prominent, these are the ultimate achievement of filial piety." Latter-day scholars deleted the five characters that translate "to practise the Way" and "in posterity." *The Book of Rites* classified filial piety into three different stages, "The great filial piety is to revere parents, the second is not to make them ashamed and the third is to be able to feed them." To reverse the order of the above, the first stage in filial piety is to care for one's parents, then not to commit sins and crimes that will shame one's parents, and finally to revere one's parents to make them prominent. Deletion of the five characters is crucial because it makes a vast difference in the true meaning.

If "establishing oneself" means the cultivation of one's character, it is only a step toward the realization of the second stage of filial piety—"not to shame one's parents"—and a move to the stage: "practising the Way will not only end in the cultivation of individual character but will be the last step toward man's ultimate achievement of filial piety. After accumulating knowledge and virtue man goes out into the world to serve his fellow men, his nation and his state and then mankind as a whole i.e., he translates the Way, lofty ideals, into actuality through his accomplishments. His contempories, or even the next generation, may not recognize him but someday he will be recognized and hence he will "pass his name to posterity."

Interpreted in this way, the phrases "to establish oneself" and "to pass one's name to posterity" contain nothing to induce man to seek "false names" and pursue vanities. Such filial piety means the actualization of the pure moral ego with no hint of such extraneous properties as honor and material gain. The parent is honored not because the son had any prior motive to do so but as a natural result of the son's actualization of his moral ego. If the son does whatever is possible merely to make his parents honored it is an indication of a selfish motive and egoism and certainly not moral practice. Not only that, as Confucius said, the superior man feels ashamed when his popularity runs higher than his status actually requires. It is a basic spirit of Confucianism that if the name of a man does not fit his reality he has cause to be ashamed.

However, during the last days of the Yi dynasty very few among the pseudo-aristocratic scholar-literati who sought official titles and empty names through the civil service examination were imbued with even a modicum of the true Confucian spirit. They were not ashamed to sell, buy or borrow someone else's official title. They had no sense of honor or shame and no capacity to discourse on moral practice. Such persons are more ubiquitous than ever before in today's underdeveloped countries and utilitarian society, in the political, business, religious and academic fields and so we can hardly attribute the ill to Confucianism. Rather, we must say that such ills became more inveterate due to the lack of the true Confucian spirit. It seems that the present age demands a return to Confucian morality more than any previous age ever did.

8. *Retroactivism*

Dr. Hyŏn says, "The habit of referring to the ancient world is a natural result of Confucianism. Confucianism, which praises the golden age of the Three Eras (三代) and which habitually quotes Yao and Shun, sowed the spirit of retroactivism among the Korean people as a logical consequence. Thus, the Korean people habitually quoted and referred to Yao, Shun and Chou Kung and refused to wear what was not traditional and obey what was not commanded by their ancestral kings. Tradition became the standard of their behavior and thought. Scholars and statesmen always admired and modelled themselves after the ancient sages, condemning as an illusion attempts to seek the standard of happiness and prosperity in the future and in a new world. On this basis Catholicism was persecuted, Taewŏn-gun (大院君) adopted a closed-door policy, the Kaehwa-dang ("Enlightenment Party") was suppressed, new education was opposed and the people resisted a decree that men's hair be cut short and that no longer wear a top-knot."

Critics of Confucian retroactivism, including Dr. Hyŏn, tend to imply two things by the word, namely, a return to the old (復古) and conservatism (保守). In Dr. Hyŏn's above comment, Taewŏn-gun's closed-door policy, resistance to the short-hair decree and suppression of the new education refer to conservatism and not a return to the past. Conservatism is a way of thinking and manner of living derived from man's force of habit, insecurity in the face of renewal and progress, complacency with the present, the pursuit of peace and indolence, and the maintenance of the status quo, while "return to the old" is a way of thinking derived from man's impulse to modify and revolutionalize present absurdities by having recourse to the past. Conservatism lacks the spirit of reform and renovation and the ideal code of conduct with which to distinguish right from wrong and the good from the bad in order to translate what is good and right into everyday life. However, the cult of the return to the past due to discontent with the present has a strong idealistic element to reform. One characteristic of the followers of this cult is that they always model themselves after the sayings and deeds of former kings and of the sages and wise men of the past. Thus the two terms must be carefully distinguished one from the other and never confused.

We cannot say Confucianism is conservative simply because at the time of Confucius and Mencius its teachings were spread in order to change (易) the unreasonable (無道) world into a reasonable (有道) one. But Confucianism has been called retroactive since Confucius and Mencius referred to Yao and Shun in expostulating their own revolutionary ideas. This did not, however, mean a simple return to the past as some later commentators have held. Confucius' attitude toward learning is well illustrated in that the master himself "loves the old and inquires swiftly" and "cherishes old knowledge and is continually acquiring new knowledge." According to a commentary of the Kung Yang School on the Spring and Autumn Annals, Confucius had implicitly entertained a three-stage-progress (三世進化) view of history—pacification of the war-like, the promotion of peace, and the great peace (T'ai p'ing)—by having recourse to Kings Won and Wu (文王, 武王), Yao and Shun. Thus, a clear distinction should be made between "recourse to" (託) and a "return to" (復) the old.

The term "revolution" also derived from the "Commentary on Ko Kua" (革卦象傳) of the Book of Changes (易經) in which it is written, "Heaven and earth revolve to give four seasons; the revolution of T'ang (湯) and Wu (武) is in accordance with the call of heaven, and thus is in response to the call of the people. The meaning of time in the revolution is great indeed." If the "Ten Commentaries" (十翼) can be attributed to Confucius we cannot call such teachings "retroactive." Mencius, too, employed the land distribution system, Ching T'ien (井田), that originated with the Chou dynasty. He modified the system for the benefit of the people and not for that of the feudal lords. He also endorsed the T'ang and Wu revolution while praising the peaceful transfer of government power from Yao to Shun.

Such government conduct cannot be said to have existed in the past and so it must be considered an ideal for the future. However, the old-scripture commentators (古文經學家) alleged that the two sages advocated that it existed in the past while the new-scripture commentators (今文經學家) countered that the two sages expostulated their future political ideals in recourse to Yao and Shun. Thus the Great Unity (大同) in the Liyun (禮運) of the Book of Rites must be seen as a description of a utopia. Of course, we cannot say that the interpretation of one school is entirely right while that of the other is completely wrong since both allegations are not entirely without foundation. But from their sayings and deeds we cannot consider that the two sages were retroactive in their thinking. It is closer to the philosophy of the two sages to hold that Confucianism purported to reform reality by "recourse to the past" (託古).

On the other hand, Confucianism gradually became official after the Ch'in and Han dynasties established a unified and centralized imperial state in China and adopted a conservative attitude in order to maintain the existence of the regime it served. Thus Confucianism came to take on conservative and exclusive colors as a state cult and, therefore, the conservative nature of Confucianism is by no means an essential feature but a product of the conservative habits of Confucian officials. Those Confucianists who stood aloof from politics so often criticized their colleagues in power that they were even more bitterly criticized in return for "deviating from the Way." In the case of Korea we see such an ex-

ample in Cho Kwang-jo (1482-1519) who was poisoned at
the instigation of the conservatives when his movement to
reform the government ended in failure. He, too, tried to reform the reality of his time by recourse to past knowledge.
The publication of Pak Chi-wŏn's *Yangban-jŏn*, ("Tales of the
Yangban")[12] attests to the fact that Korea's Confucianism even
had its reformist, progressive, forward-looking aspects and
that it did not indulge exclusively in "conservatism" and "a
return to the past." Thus if retroactivism is an attribute of
Confucianism, we must not forget that the revolutionary idea
of negating political reality in order to realize its reform is
equally an attribute of Confucianism. The reason I stress this
point is that all critics of Confucianism have laid and are laying two much stress on one defect, that of retroactivism and
conservatism, while ignoring its revolutionary spirit and
achievements.

To sum up, eight demerits of Confucianism Dr. Hyŏn enumerates in his *History of Korean Confucianism* are not the
outcome, as he claims, of the true nature of Confucianism but
rather appearances in the course of applying of Confucianism
to Korea's political life. Some these defects were inevitable
results of the socio-political and economic conditions of the
time while others resulted from spiritual indolence and the
lack of self-reflection on the part of Confucian officials. The
former may be attributed to national fate but for the latter
neither Confucianism nor national fate but only man, can be
held responsible. If the spirit of Confucianism had been correctly understood and practised Korea could have avoided
more than half of the ills she suffered. The worst of these ills
was factionalism.

From the viewpoint of modernization, only the sixth item,
economic deterioration, can be validly said to have been due
to Confucianism. This defect became all the more pronounced

as Korean Confucian scholars identified themselves with Sung and Ming Confucianism. Confucianism in Sung and Ming China and the Shing Li School of Yi dynasty overemphasized the Confucian notion of "righteousness before profit" and "inwardness before outwardness" at the expense of "utilization" and "welfare." As a result the so-called "Real Learning School" rose in revolt. The ancient Confucianists laid equal stress on "the rectification of virtue" (正德), "utilization" (利用) and "welfare" (厚生) but later Confucianism came to give more stress to the rectification of virtue rather than to utilization and welfare under the influence of Lao Tzu, Chung Tzu and Buddhism. The Yi dynasty was so wrapped up in the Shing Li School of Sung Confucianism that she lost the strength to counter her enemies to the south as well as to the north. The Real Learning School appeared under these circumstances.

Some say that Japan prospered because she imported the Wang Yang-ming School of Confucianism while Korea did not do so because she imported the Cheng Chu School of Confucianism. Korea was fortunate, however, to have imported the Cheng Chu School instead of the Wang Yang-ming School because the latter stressed the Confucian notion of "righteousness over profit" and "inwardness over outwardness" far more than the Cheng Chu School. Chu Hsi's interpretation of "ko-wu chih chin" ("investigate things and increase knowledge") left room for development into the utilitarian-realist school of "Real Learning." Wang Yang-ming's interpretation of the phrase, however, only opened the way for Zen Buddhism.

The reason why I demanded, at the outset of this article, that a distinction be made between the true nature and application of Confucianism is that all historical philosophies and religions must be comparatively evaluated without prejudice or preoccupation. But my complaint is that the critics of Confucianism, branding Confucianism as the cause of the ruin of the state, took a biased attitude with no intention to comparatively evaluate Confucianism along with other religions, philosophies and academic schools. A comparative evaluation of Confucianism with other schools will reveal that its defects are not its own exclusively but common properties of any religion. Then, and only then, can we measure the advantages and disadvantages of Confucianism in comparison with other religions.

As in the case of China, with the growth and prevalence of the *Silhak* School, criticism against *Sŏngnihak* (性理學) became intensified in Korea. Their charge was, after all, that Neo-Confucianism only indulges in academic controversies rather than setting itself to solve practical problems for the welfare of the people through state planning. This sort of criticism was a natural consequence in the past when learning was not specialized. However, today learning is highly specialized, and this criticism is not necessarily valid, for the so-called learning for the welfare of the people through state planning advocated by *Silhak* scholars has been specialized today into politics, economics, law and sociology, and the Neo-Confucianism which they claimed was indulging only in empty theorization has been specialized today into philosophy, religion and ethics. Thus, from the contemporary viewpoint, *Silhak* belongs to social sciences and Neo-Confucianism is within the realm of philosophy, both having their own status and significance. The fact that the *Silhak* School criticized Neo-Confucianism might lead one to the mistaken conclusion that *Silhak* is not Confucianism. But they are merely two different types of Confucianism that came into being in its developmental process. The features of the two schools are that Neo-Confucianism emphasizes the "inner world" while *Silhak* stresses the "outer world." If human life comprises inner life and external life, then Neo-Confucianism and *Silhak* are both indispensable factors of Confucianism. Viewed from the standpoint of modernization, the spirit of *Silhak* is closer to the present needs of modernization than that of *Sŏngnihak*. The cry of modernization in Korea today can be safely said to be the continuation and revival of the cry which was shouted by the *Silhak* School in the later period of the Yi dynasty. At the same time, recent public opinion that moral subjectivity should be emphasized in order to prevent several defects attendent upon the process of modernization reflects the succession of the spirit of *Sŏngnihak* or the "learning of superior man."

NOTES

1. Dr. Hyŏn Sang-yun, 74, was one of the nationalist leaders who directed the famous "March 1st Independence Movement" against Japanese rule. After the Liberation in 1945 he became the president of Korea University, Seoul (1946-1950), from which he received in March 1953 the degree of Doctor of Literature for his work on the history of Confucianism in Korea. He was kidnapped by Communist agents and taken to North Korea in the early days of the Korean War, July 1950.
2. In Confucianism, what is called 君子 "the Superior Man" and 小人 "the Inferior Man" may, in some cases, mean relative rank, high or low, of social status or position, but it must be noted that in most cases it points to the relative grade, high or low, of personality, virtue and dignity.
3. This signifies the three men—Yun Jip (尹集), O Tal-je (吳達濟) and Hong Ik-han (洪翼漢)—who were detained by Ch'ing soldiers during the Manchurian invasion of 1636 on the ground that they objected to the amicable settlement asked by the Manchurians. They were sent to Shenyang (瀋陽) and met a tragic death in prison there.
4. This signifies the six men—Sŏng Sam-mun (成三問), Yi Kae (李塏), Yu Ŭng-bu (兪應孚), Yu Sŏng-wŏn (柳誠源), Pak P'aeng-nyŏn (朴彭年) and Ha Wi-ji (河緯地)—who objected to the usurpation of power by the seventh Yi dynasty monarch, King Sejo, and because of this were arrested and sentenced to death by King Sejo.
5. Among Korean historians, the scholar who used the term "*Sadae Sasang*" (the idea of serving a large country) for the first time was Sin Ch'ae-ho (申采浩). However, the underlying motivation in which he used the term was to enhance the thought of national independence by attacking the view of history which Kim Pu-sik entertained. He by

no means used the term in the sense that the Korean people themselves are a nation harboring *Sadae Sasang*. However, when government-patronized Japanese scholars used this term, they recognized it not as meaning an 'ism' or thought of any particular person but as a condition inherent to the Korean people.

6. The outstanding examples are those of King U (禑王) at the end of the Koryō dynasty who resolutely dispatched expeditionary forces to Liao-tung (遼東) on the problem of Chul-Ryong-Ui (a Chinese outpost located inside the northern territory of Korea), and that of Yi dynasty King Hyojong who contemplated a northward expedition.

7. That *Mohwa* (respect for China) and *Sadae* (to serve a large country) is mutually distinguishable, can be testified by the attitudes of the Korean people toward the different dynasties of China. Although, from the time of Han China, Korea had been placed by name in a subordinate position to the dynasties of T'ang, Sung, Yüan, Ming and Ch'ing, the attitude and sentiment of Korean intellectuals toward the T'ang, Sung and Ming dynasties differed from their attitude toward Yüan and Ch'ing. Toward the former they assumed an attitude of respect and toward the latter one of contempt. This can only be rightly explained in terms of Korean affection for cultural values.

8. The reason why factional strife became fiercer from the middle to the end of the Yi dynasty must be explained in terms of political and economic causes. After the Japanese and Chinese invasion of Korea in the 16th century, the state's economy and finance were bankrupt and the prolonged effect dealt a hard blow to the everyday life of the people. Accordingly, the people made it their prime goal of living to advance into the bureaucracy in the belief that it was the only way of solving the problem of their livelihood. On the other hand, those who already occupied government posts did everything to maintain themselves. Many wanted to grab the few government posts and the bankrupt government was no longer capable of feeding them all. Under such circumstances, the people fought for official posts in those days as now. Therefore, it is superficial to explain away the causes of factional strife in terms of alteration between the self-assumed Superior Man and the Inferior Man. Rather the causes must be found by digging into the history of factional strife.

9. See the part regarding the Chiaku Meeting (夾谷之會) in the biography of Confucius as contained in Shih-chi (史記).

10. The name of a great robber recorded in Chinese history as a subject of Emperor Huang (黃帝), usually known as 'Taochih' (盜跖) meaning

"Robber Chih."

11. Virtue here means the consciousness of public good or righteousness which Confucianists regard as one of the four cardinal virtues rooted in human nature.

12. This is a literary work in the style of a biography which satirized the *Yangban* class. Pak Chi-wŏn (1737-1805) was one of the leading figures of the *Silhak* School during the reign of Chŏngjo (正祖).

Confucian Politics in Chosŏn Period and the Existence of Sallim

YI U-SŏNG

There ·is an old saying that goes: "One queen was un-rivalled by ten prime ministers, but one *sallim* (山林) outdid ten queens." This saying subtly illustrates how much the ruling class of the late Yi dynasty needed *sallim* in order to maintain its power.

That one queen was unrivalled by ten prime ministers alludes to the fact that the ruling class was dominated by relatives of a queen in the late Yi dynasty. Members of the ruling class related to the queen exercised political influence to the extent that they could dismiss a prime minister from office and exile him at will when they were so inclined. This means that the power of a prime minister was virtually nothing as compared to that of a queen.

The saying emphasizes that a *sallim* is even more impor-tant than ten queens. This is certainly an exaggeration, but we cannot ignore the pointed meaning contained in this phrase. In fact, the role of a *sallim* was so important for some time during the late Yi dynasty. *Sallim* were actually able to settle various issues which a queen was incapable of dealing with. They were competent in solving controversial government issues with their scholarly dignity and judge-ment. Their judgements were closely associated with Con-fucian teachings, and their role had a vital political meaning especially in settling cases involving the succession to the

147

throne.

It is strange that such an important role of *sallim* in the development of the Yi dynasty has seldom been dealt with by Korean historians at large. This is probably due to the general tendency of historians to view the history of the Yi dynasty within the framework of the history of party strife. Of course, we cannot discuss the existence of *sallim* independent of party strife. Nevertheless, there is room for us to consider *sallim* beyond the realm of party strife and to attempt a new analysis of *sallim* from the angle of political history. By so doing we can understand the politico-social structure of the Yi dynasty in general, and the realistic situation of the late Yi dynasty in particular.

Unfortunately, however, their paper is incapable of fully dealing with the subject in question. It remains to be an attempt to consider the importance of *sallim* and how it was associated with the political history of the late Yi dynasty which was dominated by Confucianism as a political instrument.

The Meaning of Sallim

Sallim, literally meaning the mountain and forest, is the antithesis of *chosi* (朝市), which means the court and city. Unlike the officials serving at the court and city offices, *sallim* may be defined as *ch'ŏsa* (處士), or hermits, who lived an upright life studying in the countryside without seeking the official status coveted by commonplace scholars. The officialdom was often vulgarized. But *sallim ch'ŏsa* remained noble and upright in contrast to officials in *chosi*.

Confucian ideals were aimed at achieving integrity, moral discipline and home management and ultimately peaceful government administration. *Sadaebu*, or the class of scholar-officials, were those devoted to study and government service.[1] They were meant to serve in the government in accord with Confucian teachings. But the ideals of the *sallim ch'ŏsa* were not derived from Confucian learning.

Sadaebu of the Yi dynasty were called *yangban*, or men of the noble class or the learned class. *Yangban* meant those taking part in civil or military service. When did people begin to respect the hermits called *sallim* who remained in the countryside in spite of their remarkable scholarly caliber? This tendency can be partly traced to the general disappointment of people over heated partisan dissension. But more importantly, it was derived from the corruption of the *kwagŏ* (higher government service examinations) system. All government servants of higher posts had to pass the examinations. Entering the later Yi dynasty, however, the *kwagŏ* system became extremely corrupt and became the target of public criticism. Speaking of the *kwagŏ* system, Tasan (Chŏng Yak-yong, 1762-1836) wrote:

> Today, *sŏnbi* (honest scholars) are ashamed of what is called *kwagŏ*. In the early Yi dynasty, upright scholars applied for the examinations. Cho Chŏng-am and Yi T'oegye were among such upright scholars. From the time of the reign of King Injo onward, however, no man of self-respect dared to take the examinations.[2]

Maech'ŏn (Hwang Hyŏn, 1855-1910) made a similar remark as well:

> Entering the late part of the Yi dynasty, government practices became disorderly to the extent that the *kwagŏ* examination hall was as boisterous as a marketplace. Many people derided the situation. This is why men of pride refused to apply for the examinations.[3]

An increasing number of proud *sŏnbi* came to denounce the *kwagŏ* system as corrupt. This brought about an abnormal element in the management of the political system of the period. In this connection, Tasan pointed out: "As a result, those who remained in the spirit of *sallim* circles alone were revered as men of learning and virtue, but those career officials who passed the *kwagŏ* examinations could no longer take pride in their status as Confucian scholars."[4] This social trend was certainly unprecedented in Yi society. The term "Confucianist" equipped with the Confucian learning and virtue was applied to the *sallim* scholars who had nothing to do with *kwagŏ*. The *sallim* scholars were more respected than those officials who won *kwagŏ* degrees.

We must bear in mind, however, that the *sallim* did not necessarily denounce politics though they did denounce *kwagŏ*. If they had remained hermits throughout their lives without having participated in politics, their role could have been of little historical importance. They could not belittle politics for two reasons. In the first place, it was natural for a Confucian state to try to use Confucianists. The government had to treat them well in whatever form. Secondly, even though they were in a mountain retreat, they had the Confucian moral obligation not to betray their country. They could not totally sever themselves from the fate of their nation.

Thus the *sallim* participated in politics, but they never abandoned the status of *sallim*. They had to be in *sallim* physically. They were faithful to "the spirit of *sallim*" even if they had to leave the countryside to serve the government or to take part in political affairs, for they would lose the qualification as Confucianists as they left the *sallim* and became a career official.

At first, those Confucianists who cultivated themselves in the countryside aloof from the secular city life were generally called *sallim hakcha* (scholars in hermitage) or *sallim yang-dŏkchisa* (gentlemen accumulating virtues in the mountain and forest). The title was shorted to *sallim*. But later those who received various special privileges as they responded to the call of the government were called *sallim*. Then the term *sallim* was not applied to ordinary scholars in the countryside. Therefore *sadaebu* Confucian scholars who became career officials could not become Confucianists in its intrinsic sense because they entered officialdom through the *kwagŏ* system. And those ordinary country scholars could not become *sallim* because they had not been called upon by the government. This is very paradoxical.

Political Importance of Sallim

From when did *sallim* take part in politics? Maech'ŏn traces the beginning in Chŏng In-hong (1535-1623):

> When Yi I-ch'ŏm came to power during the reign of King Kwanghae, he made Chŏng In-hong a prime minister and used him fully as a political instrument for the abuse of his own power on the pretext that Chŏng In-hong was a Confucian sage. Following his suit, subsequent strongmen chose a scholar in hermitage and made him a puppet leader. Every man in power invariably used a *sallim* to exploit his own fortune.[5]

After the reign of King Kwanghae, however, with the downfall of the *Pukin* group Chŏng In-hong was dismissed from office and was exiled. This brought disgrace on him and he was never able to restore the honorable status of *sallim*. The *sallim* rose to power after the reform in 1623. Yŏngjae (Yi Kŏn-ch'ang, 1852-1898) explained the new situation:

> After the so-called Injo Reform, the reformists who attempted to dethrone an incompetent king pledged to keep their relations with the court by marriage and to put *sallim* into important government positions.[6]

That is, the main elements of the reform were the vassals of the *Sŏin* group who maintained close relations with the queen and *sallim* for political purposes. By maintaining kinship with the king through royal marriage, they could enjoy power with the support of the queen. At the same time, they needed political stability. Yŏngjae further said: "When Song Si-yŏl rose to fame as a virtuous Confucian scholar, such vassals as Kim Cha-jŏm, Wŏn Du-p'yo and Yi Hu-wŏn tried in competition to use him as their political tool by recommending him to the king to the position of their party leader. The leader was sometimes called *kamju*. Ch'oe Myŏng-gil (1586-1647) explained the role of *kamju* in his memorial addressed to the king:

> After the development of partisan strife, the government structure was based on *chŏnjo* (the office of personnel administration) and three offices dealing with political affairs—Hongmun-gwan, Sahŏn-bu and Saganwŏn. The functions of these offices were indispensable. The *kamju* was selected from among competent officials of these government branches. He alone dealt with grave political and personnel affairs of the government.[7]

The three vassals attempted alike to entrust such an important position to Song Si-yŏl since he was a reputed Confucian scholar of the *sallim* school. This illustrates well what the political weight of the *sallim* was like during the late Yi dynasty.

Rise of the Sallim and the New Government Systems

The government institutionalized new systems in order to provide *sallim* Confucian scholars with a privileged official treatment.

The first to be installed was the system of *saŏp*. *Munhŏn Bigo* (Records on Official Systems) states:

> Such scholars as Kim Chang-saeng, Chang Hyŏn-gwang

and Pak Chi-gye were given privileged official treatment during the first year under the reign of King Injo. They were given important positions, such as *saŏp* at Sŏnggyun-gwan, Sahŏn-bu, and a teaching post responsible for the education of crown prince. Kim Chip, Song Si-yŏl and Song Chun-gil were recommended to such posts.[8]

A chapter in *Injo Sillok* (The History of the Reign of King Injo) dealing with editorship of historical books states: "After the reform, the official post of *saŏp* was installed in Sŏnggyun-gwan. Kim Chang-saeng was appointed *saŏp* and made responsible for training Confucian students."[9]

At the suggestion of Kim Sang-hŏn, a junior prime minister, new official posts were added to the system of *Seja Sigang-wŏn* (the institute for the education of the crown prince), namely, *ch'ansŏn, chinsŏn*, and *chaŭi*. The new posts were installed during the 24th year under the reign of King Injo, and the *sallim* scholars were assigned to such posts:[10]

> Kim Chip was appointed *ch'ansŏn*, Song Si-yŏl, *chinsŏn*, and Kwŏn Si, *chaŭi*. Song Si-yŏl and Kwŏn Si were especially reputed as Confucian scholars, though they held to official positions. Government post horses were made available to them. This was an exceptional treatment given to *sallim* scholars because there were few post horses after Manchurian invasion in 1636.[11]

Im Tam was once appointed a cabinet minister, but under pressure he had to concede the office to Kim Chip. The advent of *sallim* became active as Kim Chip took over the post held by Im Tam. *Sallim* scholars were given high government posts one by one. They included Song Chun-gil, Song Si-yŏl, Yun Sŏn-gŏ, and Yi Yu-t'ae among the *Sŏin* group, and Kwŏn Si, Hŏ Mok, and Yun Hyu among the *Namin* group.[12]

The rise of *sallim* scholars invited the resentment of career officials, such as Sin Myŏn and his group. Sin Myŏn was of a reputed scholarly clan and Song Si-yŏl had informed him of his desire to serve in the government. Sin Myŏn wondered what *sanin* (mountain people) would do for the government. Song Si-yŏl's side declared: "We pledge to revenge ourselves on Ch'ing for our disgrace at Namhan Sansŏng and to compensate for the death of Kang Pin (the wife of crown prince Sohyŏn)." In response, Sin Myŏn's side wrote:

> You are like phoenix. You are welcome to make a flight in the secular world occasionally. But you would be derided if you make a noise like domestic fowls.[13]

This remark angered the Confucian school of *sallim*.

Thus the *sallim* group itself came to be regarded as a political faction. It was labelled as the *san-dang* (mountain party) or *han-dang* (han party). Yŏngjae wrote of this:

> *San-dang* was headed by Kim Chip. Song Si-yŏl and Song Chun-gil supported him. These people were all from the mountainous region of Yŏnsan and Hoedŏk. Meanwhile, *han-dang* was a group of Seoul people led by Kim Yuk and Sin Myŏn.[14]

Sin Myŏn and his friends were aristocratic bureaucrats residing in Seoul, hence the name *han-dang*. And Song Si-yŏl and his group came from the countryside of Hoedŏk and Yŏnsan, hence the name *san-dang*.

San-dang and *han-dang* were antagonistic toward each other for some time. For instance, there was some talk that Sin Myŏn was accused of having collaborated with Ch'ing. And he was flogged to death as a result of the animosity held against him by the *san-dang* faction.[15] But both factions belonged to the *Sŏin* group and they allied with each other when threatened by the *Namin* group. In the long run, they had to compromise with the powerful *sallim* group, and the names of the *san-dang* and *han-dang* began to disappear. From this time onward the *sallim* group steadily rose to power.

New official posts were necessitated with the promotion of *sallim*'s political status. The official post of *chwaeju* (祭主), was established in Sŏnggyun-gwan during the ninth year of the reign of King Hyojong. *Saŏp* which had been established in *Sŏnggyun-gwan* held the seventh official grade, while the newly-installed *chwaeju* held the higher rank of fifth official grade. *Chwaeju* was the highest post given to the *sallim* group and was used as a synonym for *sallim*. The head of Sŏnggyun-gwan was *taesasŏng* with the same rank as *chwaeju*. But *chwaeju* exercised a stronger political and social influence than *taesasŏng*. The honorable post of *ch'ansŏn* at *Sigang-wŏn* also held the fifth official grade, but *chwaeju* was considered by the public as the more honorable government position to offer to a *sallim* scholar. The position was held first by Song Chun-gil and next by Song Si-yŏl. *Chwaeju* was an exceptionally privileged post. Even the prime minister was able to serve concurrently as *chwaeju*. During the year in which Hyŏnjong was enthroned, there was a debate as to whether Song Si-yŏl should be honored as *chwaeju* as well. But he was able to held the concurrent post of *chwaeju*.

Chwaeju, literally meaning ritual wine or officiant of wine, was pronounced not as *cheju* but as *chwaeju* in order to give a special privileged meaning to it.

Chwaeju was indeed a specific official term and was like an epithet of the powerful *sallim* school. Its gravity increased as ages went by. A man who had once served as *chwaeju* was honorably called *chwaeju* even when he left the position.

Changes in the Character of Sallim

The prestige of *sallim* was at its height during 1650-1720 in which Hyojong, Hyŏnjong and Sukchong reigned. At the same time, this period witnessed the most serious factional strife. During the second year of the reign of King Sukchong, Yŏngp'yŏng-jŏng, a relative of the king, read a memorial before the king in tears: "The factional dissension was derived from Song Chun-gil and Song Si-yŏl and later from Hŏ Mok and Yun Hyu. This has come to threaten the fate of the nation."[16]

The four persons were alike of the *sallim* group. But Song Chun-gil and Song Si-yŏl were political *Sŏin*, while Hŏ Mok and Yun Hyu were *Namin*. They were all leaders of their political factions. On the surface, their antagonism was a kind of dissension among the *sallim* group. But their strife was rooted in political antagonism. The most controversial issue concerned the official costume of the queen mother of a deceased king. It concerned ceremonial affairs, but it was derived from the power struggle between the two groups. The understanding of the dissension requires a complex explanation.

At any rate, the *Namin* group led by Hŏ Mok and Yun Hyu, temperarily succeeded in holding the reigning power but could not overcome the persistent counterattack of the *Sŏin* group. As we have already seen, the *Sŏin* group maintained kinship with the king and solidified its traditional power with the support from the queen. They occasionally retreated from the forefront, but they could easily restore their power. But the *Namin* group collapsed at the time of the so-called *Kapsul Kyŏnghwa* of 1694. From this time onward, the *sallim* group was dominated by those of the *Sŏin* party.

During the reigns of Hyojong, Hyŏnjong and Sukchong the principal figure in the *sallim* group was no doubt Song Si-yŏl. He was revered widely as *taero* (the great authority). He became a victim of factional strife when he was 80, but many of his disciples dominated both political and academic circles and his fame grew even greater after his death.

Having risen to power, the *Sŏin* faction was divided into the *Noron* and *Soron* groups. The *Noron* was the mainstream of the *Sŏin* group that had high regards for Song Si-yŏl. The *sallim* group was naturally dominated by the followers of Song Si-yŏl.

The followers of Song Si-yŏl, however, did not take part in politics. And with the rise of *Noron*, changes occurred in the role of *sallim*. Times changed. The following record explains the new situation:

> The king offered *Uŭijŏng* (a minister of the right) to Kwŏn San-ha (1641-1721) because Kwŏn was respected as the most distinguished disciple of Song Si-yŏl. On each occasion Kwŏn did not accept a high office offered to him. The king was more impressed and offered him the office of the prime minister. But Kwŏn never accepted the post. Thereafter, the *sallim* scholars did not enter the government even when they were offered high posts.[17]

The *sallim* scholars did not lose their social prestige though they did not become high officials at the call of the throne. In 1728, the fourth year of the reign of King Yŏngjo, Yi Se-jin, a censor, proposed to King Yŏngjo that two high officials of the *sallim* group, Pak P'il-chu who held the office of *chipŭi* and Yang Tŭk-chung who was *changnyŏng*, be relieved of their offices because they did not intend to appear at a ceremony of a national mourning. Thereupon, the king reprimanded Yi Se-jin for having belittled respectable Confucian scholars. The king emphasized: "To treat *sallim* scholars with respect has been our royal tradition. Our national fate depends on the development of Confucian learning."[18]

Yŏngjo's remark draws our attention. Yŏngjo's real intention was not to expect policy planning from the *sallim* scholars, but he had to treat the *sallim* scholars with respect as symbolical existences in the Confucian country. In fact, he treated them with full courtesy.

Chŏngjo, the succeeding king, was a distinguished ruler like Yŏngjo. The two kings were remarkable administrators and the factional strife became gradually declined during their reigns. The *sallim*'s prestige in this period was not as great as it had been in the period of Song Si-yŏl. Nevertheless, they enjoyed high respect from the king.

As the king's relatives of the distaff side became powerful after the reign of Sunjo, the status of *sallim* scholars was on the wane. No longer were they accorded respectable treatments. Tasan explained the tendency of this period:

> A superior man could have been selected from among *sallim* Confucianists and have been given a post as a prime minister or a minister. But only several selected *sallim* scholars were treated as a *pinsa* (honorable master) and were assigned to a post responsible for Confucial worship. They appeared like sinners and barely survived as *pinsa*. They were unable to restore their traditional honor; they were even ridiculed.[19]

Discussing *Sŏngnihak* (性理學) in his *Ohak-non* (The Theory of Five Sciences), Tasan wrote of *sallim*:

> In ancient times, a man devoted to learning and self-cultivation was defined as "*sa* (士)". *Sa*, by implication, was "serving." Today, who study *Sŏngnihak* consider themselves *ŭn* (隱), a term that can be interpreted as hermits. They did not serve in the government. Even those who had been reared in Seoul were called *sallim* if they studied *Sŏngnihak*. They were made to lecture on the Confucian classics or to take part in the education of the crown prince. When the government tried to assign them to the posts dealing with finance, defense, law or diplomatic posts, many people objected to the idea insisting that such treatment could hardly be adequate to "respectable Confucian scholars". Then where could the king use them? They used to say, "I follow the teachings of Chu Hsi." Does the teaching of Chu Hsi really agree with him?[20]

Tasan criticized the inflexible government policy that led to the ridicule of *sallim* scholars and criticized the *sallim* scholars as well for their unrealistic attitude towards the nation and society.

As Tasan said, a few Confucian scholars were selected from among *sallim* scholars as symbolic leaders. Scholars of the *sallim* group were called *sallim* after their surnames, namely, Kim *Sallim* and Song *Sallim*.

Many of the *sallim* scholars were the descendants of Song Chun-gil and Song Si-yŏl. Maech'ŏn explained:

> *Sallim* scholars belonged to the *Noron* group and member of the Ŭnjin Song clan alone dominated the *sallim* group generation after generation. The Ŭnjin Song family was comparable to the Chang family that domi-nated the Taoist group on Lunghu Mountain.[21]

In order to maintain their status, the *sallim* scholars had to compromise with people in power. Maech'ŏn said:

> *Sallim* scholars were closely associated with people in power without exception. When they had to deal with national protocol affairs, they had to consult people in power and followed their opinions. Song Tŏk-sang was regarded as a member of Hong Kuk-yŏng's *sadang* (blood pledge party), Hong Chik-p'il as a henchman of Kim Pyŏng-gi and Im Hŏn-hoe as a conficant of Min Kyu-ho.[22]

Song Tŏk-sang, Hong Chik-p'il and Im Hŏn-hoe were re-nowned Confucian scholars of the *sallim* group toward the close of the Yi dynasty. Song Tŏk-sang ended his life unhappily with the downfall of Hong Kuk-yŏng. But Hong Chik-p'il and Im Hŏn-hoe could survive as *sallim* by dint of their respective protectors, the Andong Kim family and the Yŏhŭng Min fami-ly. Hong Chik-p'il played an important role in the prince's suc-cession to the throne. When Hŏnjong died and Ch'ŏlchong was about to succeed him in 1849, the Andong Kim family made a plan to have Ch'ŏlchong succeed Sunjo in lineage in-stead of Hŏnjong for fear that the P'ungyang Cho family, who were Hŏnjong's relatives on the distaff side, might rise to power. In this regard, Kim T'aek-yŏng write:

> At the time of Ch'ŏlchong's enthronement, Kim Hong-
> gŭn insisted to Queen Sunwŏn (Wife of King Sunjo
> from the Kim family): 'The new king is an uncle of Hŏn-
> jong and he should therefore succeed Sunjo to respect the
> order in royal lineage.' Hong Chik-p'il supported Kim
> Hong-gŭn's idea to please him. Kwŏn Ton-in, then the
> prime minister, objected Kim Hong-gŭn's contention say-
> ing: 'The succession to the throne has little to do with
> seniority in blood relation and therefore Ch'ŏlchong
> should succeed Hŏnjong.' But Kwŏn Ton-in was exiled to
> Pukch'ŏng for having disagreed with Kim's opinion. Kim
> Chŏng-hŭi was also exiled to Pukch'ŏng on the pretext
> that Kwŏn's idea came from Kim Chŏng-hŭi.[23]

Hong Chik-p'il displayed his scholarly authority in such an
important matter of royal lineage, sending the prime minister
to an exile. Thus *sallim* became completely patronized scholars.

Meanwhile, the *sallim* scholars had complaints. Hong Chik-
p'il (1776-1852), who was calld Hong *Sallim* during the reign
of Ch'ŏlchong (1850-1863), said of the *sallim*'s degenerated
status wistfully: "When the dynasty was prosperous, important government affairs were dealt with by *sallim*. The fate of
the nation was dependent on *sallim*."[24] His words were recorded later by Im Hŏn-hoe (1811-1876), one of his disciples who
succeeded him as a *sallim* scholar:

> If *sa* were to survive in a troubled world, he should
> not be involved in a debate that might endanger himself.
> A man should read widely, cultivate himself, raise a
> family, cultivate a farm, serve his parents and worship his
> ancestors. There is little else to say about the conduct of a
> learned man.[25]

We can understand his state of mind by reading his memoir.

But both Hong *Sallim*, who was closely associated with the powerful Andong Kim family, and Im *Sallim*, who was likewise associated with the Yŏhŭng Min family, were not in a position to refuse to speak up and act as *sallim* in favor of their protectors.

REFERENCES

1. Yangban-jŏn, *Yŏnam-jip*.
2. *Jŭngbo Yŏyudang Jŏnsŏ*, Vol. 5, Kyŏngin Munhwa-sa. pp. 288-289.
3. *Maech'ŏn Yarok*, Vol. 1, National Historical Compilation Committee, p. 35.
4. *Jŭngbo Yŏyudang Jŏnsŏ*, Vol. 5, pp. 288-289.
5. *Maech'ŏn Yarok*, Vol. 1, p. 12.
6. *Tangŭi T'ongnyak*, Kwangmun-hoe, p. 18.
7. *ibid.*
8. *Jŭngbo Munhŏn Bigo*, Vol. 199, Kojŏn Kanhaeng-hoe, p. 313.
9. *Chosŏn Wangjo Sillok*, Vol. 34, p. 524.
10. *Jŭngbo Munhŏn Bigo*, Vol. 225, p. 621.
11. *Chosŏn Wangjo Sillok*, Vol. 35, p. 337.
12. *ibid.*, the chapter dealing with the year of Ŭlsa.
13. *Tangŭi T'ongnyak*, p. 18.
14. *ibid.*
15. *ibid.*
16. *Hansakye*, Vol. 4, *Sukchong-gi*, p. 6.
17. *ibid.*, pp. 14-15.
18. *Chosŏn Wangjo Sillok*, Vol. 42, p. 97.
19. *Jŭngbo Yŏyudang Jŏnsŏ*, Vol. 5, p. 50.
20. *Chŏng Tasan Jŏnsŏ*, Vol. 1, p. 227.
21. Hwang Hyŏn, *Ohakimun* 1, p. 2.
22. *ibid.*
23. *Hansakye*, Vol. 5, p. 18.
24. *Maesan-jip*, Vol. 52, p. 50.
25. *Kosan-jip*, Vol. 19, pp. 17-28, Chamnok Maesan Ŏrok.

Political Philosophy
of Korean Confucianism

HONG I-SŎP

Confucianism is essentially a political philosophy which originated in China. Following its introduction to Korea it has
been interpreted and promoted in various ways in close relation with the Korean political reality. Therefore, sooner or
later we come to know, when studying Korean politics or
Korean philosophy in terms of historical development, that
Confucianism constituted the basis of political ideal as well as
being the mainstream of pre-modern Korean philosophy. In
other words, to historically understand Korea it must be
realized Confucianism formed the backbone of all Korean
thought. The historical understanding of Korean politics or
the systematic study of Korean philosophy should be undertaken only after a substantial understanding of Confucianism
has been attained, and the result of understanding thus produced must be subjected to re-evaluation in light of present
reality.

Therefore, the question as to why Korea is a retarded nation
involves multiple factors from the past, i.e., the socio-
economic structure, legal system and political philosophy and
mental outlook. But the question primarily revolves around
Confucian political ideology which has long arbitrated the
ideals of the political power structure for the control of society.
The prejudiced and superficial criticism leveled against the
social functions of Confucianism merely revealed the distorted

aspects of the mentality of the Korean people, and hence, it seems, a distorted understanding of Korean society itself as a whole.

The Yi Period (1392-1910)

Confucian ideals were, of course, the political principles of the Yi period, and the difference of this era from the preceding one is that, in reorganizing government structure, the Yi dynasty attempted to change the then dual structure of Buddhism and Confucianism, which dictated the social conventions of the daily life of the people, into the monolithic unity of Confucian morality.

This phenomenon first became manifest in the land reform enforced during the dying days of the Koryŏ era. The land reform was not only advocated in order to revise what had proved unreasonable in the legal system in the course of social evolution, but was also proposed as a political ideal to promote the spirit of the Confucian royal road. Thus the land reform was urgently called for in the name of the king in order to relieve the people from living difficulties that resulted from the disintegration of public order. Capitalization of the Confucian spirit was the measure of the challenge to the ruling classes of Koryŏ, rather than of loyalty to Confucianism itself. In other words, Confucianism was promoted so as to oust the Buddhist king and ruling class of the Koryŏ dynasty who were in turn to be replaced by newly rising powers and ultimately by Confucian ideology.

It was Chŏng Do-jŏn (?-1398) who positively engaged in the promotion of Confucianism as a political ideal and as a practical code of ethics for the people at this point in the transition. His positive engagement was how to successfully accomplish the transition from Buddhist Koryŏ society to Confucian Yi.

His first attempt at reform in the Yi dynasty was a revision to the legal code according to Confucian ideals. His *Chosŏn*

Kyŏngguk-jŏn (Law Governing the State of Chosŏn) and *Kyŏngju Mun'gam* (Annals of Economy) made the supreme proposition that the legal code of the new kingdom should be so revised after the Chinese pattern based on Confucianism for the successful realization of Confucian political ideals at the time of transition from Koryŏ to Yi.

At the same time, in the training of bureaucrats the new kingdom of Yi made it the first rule to cultivate an entirely new Confucian personality by means of thorough education in Neo-Confucian ideals.

The Seeds of Conflict

Chu Hsi's *Sohak* (Small Learning) came to be emphasized as a rudimentary text in education along with a historical understanding of *Tonggam Kangmok* which formed the historical basis of the Chinese nation. Chŏng, on the assumption that success or failure in politics depends solely on Confucian education, emphasized the merits of school education. As Chu Hsi's political ideals and practical code of ethics were being firmly implanted, in the new kingdom a new pattern of thought with respect to politics and ethics emerged.

On the occasion of dynastic change the Confucian concept of loyalty to king forced many scholar-literati to reject obedience to the new government of Yi and harbor a longing for the old Koryŏ kingdom, and consequently they lost their object of loyalty. This state of spiritual vacuum was not confined to the early days of the kingdom but resulted in the split of Confucian bureaucrats into two opposing groups: the opposition escapists who steered clear of politics and the royalists who positively helped in the establishment of the new kingdom.

The causes of the split, which resulted in two groups that could not be reconciled nor perpetuated as a practical condition of the Confucian spirit, came to sow the seeds of conflict among the bureaucratic scholar-literati. Paradoxically, the split was the result of Korea's historical reality rather than of the Confucian spirit. The Yi dynasty in her earlier days re-evaluated the spiritual attitude of the scholar-literati who opposed obedience to the new kingdom and escaped from reality due to their loyalty to the former monarchy, and recruited them back into active society. The new monarchy praised their loyalty to the king and rewarded them accordingly reasoning that loyalty to the monarchy, either of Koryŏ or of Yi, was ultimately the same since the Yi government treated the Koryŏ people as her very own subject.

But the two Confucian factions not only claimed superiority over the other but also differed in their interpretation of Neo-Confucianism, thus creating an academic division. The two, of course, opposed each other in their political stands. On the other hand, the split was not deep enough for them to differ in their interpretation of the principal and common ideals of Confucianism. However, escapist opposition scholars such as Sŏ Kyŏng-dŏk (1498-1546) and Yi Hwang (1501-1570) contributed much to the academic development of Neo-Confucianism and Yi Hwang's disciples further contributed to the study of Confucian epistemology in actuality as detached from political reality. For example Yi I (1536-1584), while he was engaged as an important official in government administration, strongly advocated that contradictions and absurdities in the actual operation of politics must be eliminated or reformed. His contribution to the development of a new aspect of Confucian epistemology is noteworthy in the history of Korean Confucianism, and deserves close scrutiny along with his personal characteristics and the functions of his spirituality. Academic schooling other than Confucianism must also be credited to him.

Be that as it may, the issue of the Rites of Confucianism became a point of controversy and bloody struggles for political hegemony among bureaucrats from the end of the 17th century to early in the 18th century. Their controversy, however, lacked universal validity and centered around mourning apparel for the royalty. The controversy was, of course, waged on the basis of the Chinese Theory of Rites. But trouble rather derived from the fact that the verdict of victory or defeat in the controversy was arbitrated by the monarch himself who was not supposed to be an expert on the matter, and this abnormal controversy over the Theory of Rites was not primarily concerned with the realization of Confucian political ideals in actual politics. It was far removed from the positive practice of Confucianism and focused on the wrong goal.

The Real Learning School

Then a group of scholar-literati came to the fore later to become known as the "Real Learning School." They were realists who put forward a new political theory as a means of reaffirming Confucian political ideals. These scholar-literati, being aware of the fact that the practice of Confucian political ideals tended to become formal and superficial, attempted to recover the true Confucian spirit which had lost behind mere Confucian slogans. Therefore this school, in its ideological aspects, did not override Confucianism. Firmly founded on the realization of Confucian principles, the realist tried to analyze and overcome the incorrect points in the interpretation and realization of Confucianism. Therefore Korean realist scholars attempted to transform Chinese Confucianism into something like a system of thought, characteristic of and fit to Korean reality. Attempting a return to the essence of Confucianism, they did not cling to the Chu Hsi school of tradition but also assimilated the spirit of Wang Yang-ming. However, the reason, we presume, the realist, in general, failed to transcend the boundary of Neo-Confucianism is that instead of bringing Wang's spirit into the open, the realist amalgamated it and concealed it within the crust of Chu Hsi's learning. Although realist scholars put forward a new viewpoint differing from that of their predecessors who superficially observed and criticized Neo-Confucianism, what is more significant is the fact that the Wang Yang-ming elements colored their opinions.

Scholars of the Real Learning School freely criticized the state of affairs in the government and proposed reforms to government organization on the basis of the actual situation facing the country and of the promotion of the farm economy, as a means of overcoming political confusion, economic poverty and financial graft. However brief and cursory the above survey, we know that Confucianism took deep root for many centuries in Korean society as a political ideal.

As for the present-day influence of Confucianism on Korean society, it is necessary to consider the following two points: the traditional society still under the influence of Confucianism and in the process of modernization and the various forms of Confucianism still active in the less modernized aspects of Korean society.

Spiritual foundation of the modernization process: The process of the modernization of Chosŏn can be viewed from many angles but the conclusion inevitably leads us to economic problems. However, let us first consider here the spiritual foundation of this modernization. The start of Korea's modernization is generally timed when the Korean people began to consider to what extent, in comparision to neighboring Ch'ing China and Japan, her doors should be opened to the West upon her initial contact with Western capitalistic influence. The process of modernization should have hatched and developed within society itself, but under existing circumstances in the Korea of the time it was imposed on the masses from above, by the bureaucratic scholar-literati who attempted to clear away all social contradictions and absurdities, i.e., irregularities and graft, by means of organizational reforms. The Confucian concept of controlling the masses from above is also manifest in this campaign.

There were self-enlightenment mass campaigns among the

lower rural classes, and peasant uprisings, not against the monarch or the central government, but against provincial governors or against the economically powerful provincial elite, were a last means of economically preserving farmers' livelihood. These campaigns were, however, so conditioned by Confucianism that they were actually doomed to failure from the very outset. The principal parts of Confucian ethics were strictly observed. The monarch was taken for granted for an inviolable presence. The revolts were, in a word, not against the powers of the central government but against those of lesser provincial officials. There were, of course, times when they threatened the royalty in the capital, but still Confucian influence enabled them to uphold the inviolate nature of the king. Therefore, recorded peasant uprisings were rather against the graft of provincial officials than against the social absurdities of the times, and the rebels were not armed with any new ideological weapon with which to transform, on a Confucian basis, the existing society into a modern one. The fact that French enlightenment thinkers praised and capitalized upon Confucianism in creating a new pattern of thought reminds us of the fact that they had their own philosophical tradition, and other vital factors such as scientific, technological and historical conditions that worked hand in hand with that philosophy.

Korean modernization was actually the process of colonization by the aggressive forces of alien capitalism. So, the reasons by which Korea rejected foreign goods and the infiltration of Korea by foreigners in relatively modern times (1870-1910) were firmly based on Confucian principles. They took it for granted that "WE" were right (something orthodox and traditional) while aliens were heretics pitted against "WE," the right. Thus Korea rejected foreigners and foreign goods or those who brought foreign goods into Korea as heretics to "WE," to Korea (Chosŏn).

This reasoning still stands in the way of fully understanding the problems revolving around Korea. It was obviously a reactionary attitude, seen in the light of opening Korea to the international currents of the time, but it was to be so judged, on the other hand, in light of the nationalistic viewpoint. The group of scholar-literati which attempted the rejection of foreigners came to replace its principal spirit with that of combative action.

The Confucian scholars, who failed to formulate a basis on which not to commit their own country into the hands of the foreign aggressors and who failed to weigh the progressive forces of history and reaction against it in terms of reality, were forced to seek their own justification for rejecting foreigners in advance to a reform within their own society. Their justification could be found nowhere but in the Confucianism in which they were brought up.

In this period of the transition of the Confucian code of ethics, the fall of Korea did not take part with Confucianism but was bound more tightly with it. In the meantime, Korea endeavored to transplant the democratic ideas of modernized Japan, the United States and European nations, but it ended in falling victim to Japanese domination at the turn of this century, because at the time the independent spirit of Korean society began to stumble. This is, however, not to say that they wholly stopped to receive modern ideas. They rather continued to do so, but it was hardly possible for Korea to continue under the control of Japanese colonialists.

Here we must consider what Japanese colonial policy spiritually bequeathed to the Korean nation. Hosokawa Karoku of Japan observed the historical character of colonial Korea as "the process of colonial modernization." Korea apparently showed some aspects of modernization in appearance only, but actually fumbled under the colonial yoke and had no other way but spiritual resistance, compromise or tacit obedience. Such a phenomenon was, indeed, feasible under the conditions of an ordinary society, but it was perhaps more pronounced and distinctive in colonial society.

Therefore, all the positive forces of the national spirit were steered toward resistance since resistance against the colonialist preceded the understanding, transplanting and realization of the people's own philosophy, whatever it was, or system of thought. By compromise and by tacitly obeying colonial policy, they first compromised by means of self-betrayal and the latter category is viewed in two ways: negative compromise and resistance. But what counts here is the spiritual attitude of the obedient who caused the ruled to tacitly obey the colonialist. It deserves attention that Japanese colonial policy did not neglect to formulate protective measures for the preservation of Confucianism.. Under Japanese colonial rule the term "nationalism" was identified with, and no less shunned than, the term "democracy."

Japanese policy with respect to the protection of Korean Confucianism was to spiritually arrest the growth of the Korean nation and to subject her people to colonial bureaucratism. The Korean people more often than not compromised with this but generally, as mentioned above, rose up in resistance as early as from the end of the last century. It is needless to mention here again the tragedy of a nation put under alien rule. The modern tragedy of Korea, without regard to Confucian political ideals, came to characterize the Korean modernization movement.

To summarize modern Korean history, we know we stand where we are now because we were not subject to any kind of modernization. The reason we are so apt to bring up the modernization issue is that Korea lived her pre-modern times under the inhibition of Confucianistic political ideals, and we premise that a new point of view on Confucian ideals might have been obtained since then. In other words, that we were not once subjected to the process of modernization means we still live with the Confucian ideals which governed our lives in the pre-modern era.

Although Korean society has gone through 18 years of transition since 1945, and although efforts have been made since then to eliminate the spiritual remnants of pre-modern times in the field of education, Korean education, as a result of 40 years of colonial education which subjugated Koreans to Japanese imperialism, still retains the Confucian spirit. When we reached another turning point in 1945, we found ourselves still in a pre-modern atmosphere, socially as well as in respect to family life, because many who received a colonial education were still active and cries for democracy were drowned in that pre-modern atmosphere. And even though the younger generation of Koreans have received Korean education since 1945, few were immune to the ills of Japanese colonial education, while most of them were still bound to the old way of thinking and living.

The result was attested to in the first national assembly elections in 1948, Korea's first political attempt at democracy. Although the constitution the first National Assembly passed had some points giving rise to criticism and the nation was provided with the necessary articles legal basis on which to free itself from the restricted personal life inherited from a feudalistic and colonial society to take on modern liberalism, the point rather lay in that Korean society was devoid of the characteristics of a modern society the Constitution presupposed.

It was, in other words, inherent social ills rather than the Constitution itself that failed to get rid of backwardness. The poor management of the Constitution gave rise to repeated amendments over the past 15 years. Then what is the prime cause of all this? It is, of course, economic poverty and the management of law lacking the basis of economic power is practically unthinkable. If the law is formulated on a sound foundation, then the way of thinking of the person who operates that law has vital significance. The method of electing national assemblymen, although patterned, as far as the form or procedure is concerned, after that of advanced countries, counts less than the mode of thinking of the electors who actually cast the ballots.

It is a historical fact that what the Japanese left behind in

Korea in 1945 was not fit soil in which to sow the seeds of democracy. This is not to say that we are opposed to the transplanting and realization of democratic political ideals. Rather we must endeavor to pave reasonable way for the growth of democracy by ideologically overcoming the present state of confusion. Such endeavors, of course, should have come first. The reasonable and sound foundation should be more easily built, especially in times of chaos and absurdity, by means of democratic procedures. We must analyze and criticize the conditions of the past that still remain, that is, Confucian political ideas.

Before the realization of democratic political ideals, the Korean people had nothing for traditional political philosophy but their Confucianism. Therefore Confucianism eventually comes up for questioning whenever we take up the issue of Korean political ideals. Confucianism is, however, not the immediate question at issue, but its past functions when these show a responsive reaction on the current political surface.

A few of the important factors behind its social functions are: 1) Efforts to morally enhance the traditionally provincial autonomous character by means of community guidance and education, resulting in the stiffening of provincial powers, and 2) The solidarity of provincial powers centering around the *Sŏwŏn* (private school) and the *Hyanggyo* (state-run school), particularly from the 16th century onwards, and their development into factions, coupled with the manorial character of the *Sŏwŏn* further stimulated the proliferation of factions. These provincial powers were not only based on such an official foundation, but also 3) on villages made up of consanguineous marriage. Such amalgamated provincial powers, in cooperation with the aforesaid two factors, at times ignored, if not opposed, the central government by means of support from the individual powers of the central government and at other times rejected the representative of the central government. At still other times they even rejected all central government policies. But they never thought of ignoring or resisting royal decrees. They, in other words, conducted contradictory transactions while acknowledging the inviolability of kingship. These were the ill obstructing social development and they contributed hardly a thing to efforts aimed at social reform. This consanguineous organization was forced to proceed along the road to collapse in the pre-modern colonial period.

The Confucian formalized concept of filial piety and ancestor worship, and feudalistic longing for power was all the Korean people inherited from their past. The ideological confusion that followed 1945 resulted from this sentimental world. The election system, transplanted here from a democratic spirit, rapidly resuscitated the evil use of the system by collecting more ballots with only the longing for the power of feudal society. The blood and regional factions which developed under feudal society were reorganized this time under the new slogan of democracy. However perfect and sound any democratic principle imported from the West, Korea was not ready to receive and enjoy it. The contrary use of the traditional social basis was the most practical way to fulfill the immediate aim of winning more ballots without regard to what extent this would impinge upon the free development of future Korea. Paradoxically, without taking this fact into consideration, it is rather unrealistic to venture into the democratic political arena of present-day Korea. It is indeed very difficult to find a new organizational basis unless one aims to capitalize upon the traditional organization handed down from the feudal period. This organizational basis should have been reformed into a modern one in the process of modernization.

The Confucianism rooted in Korea was considerably misunderstood with respect to its basis spirit, and very much different from Western democratic political ideals. In other words, since it was affected by Confucian bureaucracy we must criticize it in its essence.

Political struggles raged during any change of government in Yi society and in such struggles it was not actual pros and cons concerning policy but roundabout things much as the royal mourning dress and unrelated or imaginary issues. The king was responsible for all things, including natural calamities and poor harvests. This attests to the fact that the people were faithfully subject to the spirit of the royal way as the Confucian political ideal. This restricting thought lasted until the end of the Yi period, and then the Japanese encouraged the Korean people to preserve this latent spirit. This is well reflected in the democratic politics we have had since 1945. Moreover, politicians who engage in state affairs must free themselves from blood or regional ties and demonstrate the spirit that they truly represent the will of the people. To do so, the old political ideals must first be criticized.

At present we find nothing meritorious in Confucian education, nor do we criticize any of the influences we were subject to under the old feudal system. In the process of transplanting and propagating the democratic spirit and way of living, the Korean people will sooner or later have to replace their spiritual foundation with that of Western democracy. But we simply cannot await the advent of such a day. We have to build such a spiritual basis necessary to modernize Korean society in its political as well as economic aspects. For this purpose we must first of all get rid of the way of thinking contradictory to democratic thought and replace it with the democratic way of thinking. The best way to effectively deal with the old way of thinking is simply to get rid of it.

By "old way of thinking" is implied: 1) Individual code of ethics in personal relations and social relations, and 2) Political understanding—the way to replace Confucian political ideals with those of democracy. The solution to the question revolves around freedom from the inhibited code of conduct stipulated in community-guild charter which inculcated the negative practice of ethics, and freedom from the bondage of blood and regional relations so as to establish individual independence, economically as well as spiritually, in a word, freedom from all restrictions.

Korea's present civil law is rapidly changing, although it is still not entirely free from its past bondage. Fortunately. the traditional, stagnant, Confucian family ethics are gradually fading away. If rapid development is to be achieved in this field so that civil law can stipulate the individual life more clearly and enable one to live with economic independence, then this phenomenon will be reflected in the political life of the country.

The fading sense of obligation is changing to favoritism and this trend must be wiped out by means of modernizing the organizational system. The problem is how to rapidly establish a modern organizational system. The hasty establishment of the system is most apt to overlook the basic conditions necessary to this end. The reasonable and sound management of a modern system requires corresponding modern spirit and economic support.

The perennial question of why Korea has failed to achieve modernization requires us first of all to seek conditions necessary for modernization rather than the causes that arrested Korean modernization. Another factor that obstructs the way to Korean democracy or modernization is the problem of language. The sycophantic spirit of the old Confucian bureaucrat longing for the Middle Kingdom China and the distorted understanding of the Confucian spirit produced two different languages, one for the ruling class and one for the ruled. This dual linguistic structure resulted in the present chaos and chasm, distinctive in the broader sense, between the two classes.

This is a matter completely different from our knowledge of Chinese characters necessary to understand Chinese culture. Contrary to King Sejong's (1397-1450) Confucian principle of the people and to the spirit of *Han'gŭl*, the language barrier still divides the two classes. And because of this barrier, there intervene many misunderstandings in communicating ideas among the Korean people. This is also the result of ill conduct of Confucian political ideas.

Whenever we speak of Confucianism in general, we take up three countries, Korea, China and Japan, which lived under the same Confucian political ideals and conclude that Korea failed to modernize, that China fell a prey to colonialism (although mainland China became a communist society) and that Japan developed into a capitalistic society. However, each has different social, historical and natural conditions and different backgrounds and their Confucianism functioned according to these differences.

The Confucian political ideals which steered pre-modern Korean society ultimately drove Korea to fall to colonial domination and made it fail to develop into a democratic society. The fact that China became a communist society requires us to re-evaluate the bureaucratic character of Confucianism. This subject must be brought into light not necessarily independently from the ideological corollary of the Chinese history of thought American scholars formulated.

Confucianism was rather soil cultivating an authoritative and bureaucratic spirit and contained elements hindering modernization. The same thing happened in former Korean society, and there was no room to display the stoic character of Confucianism.

The Life and Thought of Pak Che-ga

KIM YONG-DŎK

To all those who love their country and worry about its future, this writer would like to recommend *Pukhagŭi* (Treatises on Northern Studies). This is because the book is a valuable classic which typifies the spirit of the Practical Learning we have to inherit and further develop, is a culmination of the thought of the school, and is filled with modern rationalism. The most valuable feature of this classic can be found in its peerlessly progressive spirit, presenting measures to save the masses and the nation from poverty—our most urgent objective even now as it was in the past. These measures were proposed through the experiences and knowledge of Pak Che-ga, the author, learned in his life and employing a broad vision. Reading carefully this book written 192 years ago, one will be surprised to find out that the Yi society had many things common to ours, and the work is full of suggestions as to how to remedy the evils which plague our society. In other words, *Pukhagŭi* can serve us as a precious prescription if we read it with thorough discernment.

Pukhagŭi reminds us of the School of Northern Learning. It is a well known fact that a group of Practical scholars who were called the School of Northern Learning added further glory to the history of Korean culture and thought, and hence a prominent place is reserved for them in it. It was Pak's *Pukhagŭi* that represented the thought of Northern Learning most thoroughly and courageously, and so it can be easily imagined that the term Northern Learning had its origin in the work. Accordingly, no one may raise an objection to calling Pak Che-ga the summit of Northern Learning. It was in resistance to its times and society, as well as a reform attempt. What Northern Learning aspired to achieve should be inherited and further developed by us, because its objectives correspond to ours.

We will look at the background of the times in which Northern Learning grew up. The tendency prevalent in the mid-18th century during the reign of King Chŏngjo was that the evil aspects of Neo-Confucianism still held sway over the society. Despite the fact that the Yi kingdom actually maintained tributary relations to Ch'ing, the Koreans despised Ch'ing as barbaric, and regarded their country as the land of civilization, in the belief that the tradition of Chinese civilization had already ceased to exist in China itself. In short, the attitude of being rebellious to Ch'ing still formed the dominant current in the minds of Koreans as a byproduct of the Manchurian invasion. As a result of their falling victim to futile self-conceit, although Korea had nothing better than Ch'ing in any respect, our vision became narrower in scope, and production withered, resulting in growing social stagnation and poverty.

It was Northern Learning that advocated correction and overcoming of the situation. The term Northern Learning, originating in Mencius, implies the will to devote oneself to learning with a humble mind. Why this very reasonable assertion was considered resistance and an ideology of reform can be explained by the fact that the trend had taken so firm root that antagonism to Ch'ing was our moral obligation and just cause, and persecution was severe against any attempt at criticism or dissension. It was considered wise for one's self-protection to flatter, appease and even yield to this trend of darkness.

Northern Learning was directly related to national life and the masses. Pak Che-ga stressed the only way to save the people is to develop methods of utilizing vehicles and bricks.

Korea had no ox- or horse-driven carts worth mentioning at that time. Though vehicles were already in use in the Koguryŏ kingdom, the technique of their manufacturing retrogressed, and their use gradually declined on account of Korea's rough mountain paths and hilly roads. Shortage of vehicles prevented smooth exchange of commodities. Whereas eels were so abundant in seaside towns as to be used as fertilizer, they were quite rare in Seoul. Likewise dates were abundant in Poŭn, hemp cloth in Yukchin, and honey in the Kwandong district, but they were rarely found in other places. Such a deplorable state in regional exchange of goods entailed greater poverty.

Most of the scholars who were regarded as belonging to the Northern School had visited Ch'ing, witnessing what a great role vehicles played in China's economic life. Naturally they asserted that it was most urgent to learn the technique of making vehicles from China and propagate it.

As we have seen, the Northern School advocated absorption of the Chinese system of utilizing vehicles and implements for improving the nation's economic life. They deplored the fact that whereas bricks were produced in abundance in China and solid houses, warehouses, and castle walls could be constructed, most Korean buildings were flimsy and inconvenient because Koreans did not know how to use properly earth, water, and timber which they had plentifully. Emphasizing the benefit that might result from utilizing bricks, the Northern School scholars studied the technique of making bricks and personally demonstrated it. Turning to agriculture, they also emphasized import of various farm implements from China, and their domestic production as a means of revising the primitive and inconvenient Korean tools and farming method for achievement of greater productivity.

Pak Che-ga placed stress especially on the use of irrigation facilities and fertilizer. Even though water was too abundant on one side of a dike, he observed, the other side parched for want of water, and this kind of phenomenon was caused by the lack of irrigation facilities. Korea lacked irrigation facilities, Pak explained, due to her backwardness in the skill of their installations, as in the case of vehicles and bricks. This backwardness entailed an unnecessarily high cost in installation, and the facilities, even if installed, turned out to be inefficient. He again emphasized absorption of these techniques from Ch'ing China. These of his assertions were closely interrelated in an organic system and synthesis.

When fertilizer is administered to the soil, its effect is beyond doubt. Though there was a huge amount of night soil in Seoul, its utilization as fertilizer was blocked on account of the lack of vehicles to carry it to the field, and this was the same as losing a harvest of one million *sŏk* of rice, Pak said. Besides paying keen interest to farming, he introduced a unique theory of commerce, which can be considered the best thing in his scholarship. Whereas most Northern School scholars, being of the opinion that the restraint of commerce was recommendable for physiocratic policy, advocated similar restraint on currency circulation, consumption, and luxury by regarding the relation between agriculture and commerce as that between the main business and a side work, Pak fully recognized the significance and necessity of commerce, and stressed positive encouragement of commerce and enhancement of productivity as its basis.

"Economy can be likened to a well. It will dry up unless it is used constantly." "If people do not know how to use tools, they naturally do not know how to make them, and the lack of knowledge will result in further impoverishment," Pak said.

In this manner he stressed that consumption of what is produced stimulates production. He saw that restraint of consumption was not wise, and advocated that all efforts be focused on the encouragement of production. Here we notice that Pak's theory resembles modern economics. He further saw that the main factor which discouraged the will to production on the part of farmers and handicraftsmen and exhausted production itself was the excessive number of idle *yangbans* (aristocrats). The *yangban* class who could earn their livelihoods only when they obtained government positions, inherited their status and often remained unemployed. Such aristocrats grew in number continuously, and they indulged in exploiting commoners as a means of eking out their living. Under these circumstances, farmers and handicraftsmen could hardly subsist.

Pak Che-ga asserted that all idle *yangbans* be encouraged to engage in commerce with the aid of capital and shops to be provided by the government. This assertion was aimed at destroying the feudal caste system, as well as being a revolutionary proposal which might have overthrown the very basis of the feudal Korean society, even though he did not mean to include any but those idle *yangbans* in commerce.

Of his numerous seniors, Pak admired most and studied under Yi Chi-ham (T'ojŏng by pen name), Cho Hŏn (Chungbong), and Yu Hyŏng-wŏn (Pangye). His amazingly far-sighted view and modern thought had their sources in the learning of these teachers of his. T'ojŏng once asserted active trade with foreign countries as a means of rescuing the people of Chŏlla Province from impoverishment which he personally witnessed. This assertion found a passionate supporter in Pangye. Pak also praised T'ojŏng's assertion highly by referring to it twice in his books. He emphasized sea trade with Ch'ing and commerce with many other foreign countries after building up the national power. This assertion that Korea should be opened to foreigners—for voluntary opening of the nation's ports was made 98 years before the signing of the Kanghwa treaty in 1876 marking the formal opening of Korea.

His far-sighted vision and patriotism which led him to propose the opening of Korean ports to foreign commerce failed to win support not only from the public but even from such conservative Northern School scholars as Pak Chi-wŏn (Yŏnam) and Yi Tŏk-mu (Ajŏng). His proposal was criticized by his fellow scholars as being "too lofty" and "too radical." However, this only suggests that Pak was the greatest among Northern School scholars in conviction and progressiveness. The modern significance of this theory can be found in his view of national defense, too.

"Military preparation can be made with little cost only

when made within the bounds of popular living." In his military theory, military preparation, technology, and productivity are combined into one. Employment of vehicles in the army makes transportation convenient even though they do not become weapons at once, and use of bricks gives rise to formidable fortresses, he said. Various techniques, handicraftsmanship, and animal husbandry, when they prosper, can naturally serve as military preparedness at less or no cost. This is the principal in military affairs, and weaponry and military training are but the subsidiaries.

This view is akin to the modern concept of production war or total war.

Pak Che-ga, the most modern Practical scholar in the premodern era, was born an illegitimate son of Pak Pyŏng, a royal secretary, on November 5, 1750. He spent his childhood on the slopes of Mount Namsan in Seoul. He lost his father at the age of 11. His family made a living by his mother's needlework, and the difficult living forced his family to move from place to place frequently. Illegitimate children at that time were doomed to an unfortunate life under the feudal system, not being treated properly as humans. Feverish and talented, Pak found it a great agony that his birth as an illegitimate child was combined with another misfortune—poverty at home. These adversities, however, prompted the development of his spiritual self.

In finding good friends and teachers, he was very fortunate, as he himself boasted. Since he was 11 years of age he made friends with Yi Tŏk-mu, Yu Tūk-kong, and Yi Hūi-gyŏng. They spent a fruitful youth by sharing food and shelter together. Their mutual stimulation and joint study enabled them to grow into the group of great Northern School scholars.

At first they came to fame as precocious poets. Their poems won fame first in Peking as "poems of the four great masters." They displayed their genius in poetry. Since early in his life, Pak was ardent for a trip to Peking. He wanted to experiment with what he had learned and studied. His wish was finally fulfilled when he turned 29 years of age in the second year of King Chŏngjo's reign. Ch'ae Che-gong, a great statesman and a leader of the *Namin* (Southern Faction), provided a special favor for Pak and Yi Tŏk-mu.

Their trip to China lasted for three months, and they stayed in Peking for 30 days. The book he finished in September that year, three months after his return from China, was *Pukhagŭi*. The work contains his excellent proposals for national salvation, as well as his frank and valuable opinions for the improvement of Korea's rural and urban life. *Pukhagŭi*, which he authored at the age of 29, was submitted to the throne 20 years later in the 22nd year of King Chŏngjo's reign at the monarch's request for agricultural works. Pak was then the magistrate of a local county. That version of *Pukhagŭi* which was submitted to the king was a summary of the original text, exactly one-third of its length, in which revision was made and the order was changed in the contents.

This writer is of the opinion that distinction should be made among its "Inner and Outer" departments and the memorial part when discussing *Pukhagŭi*. Though an immortal work *Pukhagŭi* was never reprinted before the liberation. Immediately after the liberation, the memorial part was translated into modern Korean and published. The publication of *Pukhagŭi* in its entirety was not undertaken until 1962, when the National History Compilation Committee of the Education Ministry published a collection of writings of Pak Che-ga, together with *Pukhagŭi*. It is regretful, however, that its full translation is yet to be undertaken.

Pak was appointed a librarian at the newly established Kyujanggak Royal Archives in 1779, and after that he had devoted most of his career to the post, playing a leading role in the compilation which brought glory to the literary activity in King Chŏngjo's era. Most outstanding among the compilation achievements at Kyujanggak were *Muye Tobo T'ongji* (an encyclopaedia on military arts with illustrations) and *Kyujang Chŏnun* (a book of Korean phonetics). Engaged in the position, Pak received a special favor from the king and was be-friended by such prominent scholars as Ajŏng and Chŏng Yak-yong (Tasan by pen name).

He visited Peking four times—once in the second year and twice in the 14th year of King Chŏngjo's reign, and finally in the first year of King Sunjo's reign—and associated himself with leading Chinese scholars and men of letters.

His lofty personality, broad scope of vision, and great endowment in poetry, calligraphy, and painting won him a higher reputation in China than in his home country, and his fame in China exceeded that of any Korean court official. A collection of his writings (*Chŏngyu Koryak*) was published in Peking in two volumes.

The sudden demise of King Chŏngjo who had patronized him brought misery to Pak for the rest of his life. The political upheaval in which the Southern Faction collapsed gave those who had detested Pak's progressive ideas a golden opportunity to inflict persecution on him. He barely escaped death at the hands of his enemies who tried to blame him with a lethal charge—he had thoroughly advocated Northern Learning—a false one, indeed. He was instead exiled to Chongsŏng in Hamgyŏng Province. Three years later he was freed, but we do not know what he did after that.

Chŏng Yak-yong:
The Man and His Thought

HAN YŎNG-U

The period from the 17th to the 19th century marked a great
turning point in Yi dynasty society, as well as an age of epoch-
making changes in ideology. A group of scholars who were
generally called the Real Learning school or reform-minded
Confucianists emerged to conduct deep and highly professional research on all such fields as politics, economy, society,
and culture, thereby bequeathing voluminous works presenting fresh measures for reform.

Characteristics by which the Real Learning thought can be
basically distinguished from the Confucianism of the preceding ages, namely, the Neo-Confucianism of Chu Hsi, may be
summarized under the following two points.

The first characteristic is modern consciousness. The practical scholars demanded respect for civil rights and equality of
all people both in economy and in social standing; adopted a
scientific and empirical epistemology and view of the universe,
a rational view of ethics, and a positivistic methodology in
their academic research; and keenly recognized the importance of natural sciences, technology, and research.

The second characteristic is their national consciousness and
their dedication to autonomous spirit. Discarding the traditional China-centered view of the world, they asserted the
uniqueness and independent aspects of Korean history, and on
this basis, they conducted research into our traditional culture

185

systematically, on a broad scale, thereby laying the foundation for Koreanology.

Despite the fact that the Real Learning was equipped with eminent critical spirit and progressiveness, it harbored too lofty ideals, and most of the scholars who belonged to the school were secluded in retirement under adverse conditions. For these reasons they failed to make their thought reflect the existing political reality. Nevertheless, the Real Learning thought exerted profound influence on a group of reformists, who advocated independence and modernization in and after the 1870s, when the penetration of Japanese and Western influence was about to encroach on Korea's sovereignty and force her to Westernize herself. Its significance newly discovered by these leaders, the Real Learning thought had great influence on subsequent nationalist and modernization movements.

Given birth in the 17th century, Real Learning blossomed in the 18th century and attained the zenith of its development in the 19th century. It was Chŏng Yak-yong (Tasan by pen name) who completed the system of the Real Learning and elevated it to such a height. The domain of his research was broad, embracing virtually all academic fields, such as philosophy, political science, economics, military affairs, law, literature, mathematics, dynamics, physiology, medicine, astronomy, and geography; and he bequeathed enormous amounts of work consisting of more than 500 volumes, all of which remain to date as *Yŏyudang Chŏnsŏ.*

His Life

Chŏng Yak-yong was born in scenic Mahyŏn in the vicinity of Seoul (presently Nŭngnae-ri, Wabu-myŏn, Yangju-gun, Kyŏnggi Province) in 1762. Like most Real Learning scholars, Chŏng was born to an aristocratic family belonging to the Southern Faction. His father, Chŏng Chae-wŏn, entered government service in his youth and was appointed to the post of local magistrate. With the tragic death of Prince Changhŏn on order of his father, King Yŏngjo, as a turning point, Chŏng retired from government appointment and engaged in farming.

Yak-yong was brought to Seoul at the age of 14 when his father was again appointed by the government. By the time he turned 16 years of age, he had already become engrossed in the Real Learning by reading the works of Yi Ik (1681-1763). Befriended by Yi's disciples such as Kwŏn Ch'ŏl-sin and Ch'ae Che-gong, and other Real Learning scholars such as Pak Chi-wŏn, Yi Tŏk-mu, and Pak Che-ga, Yak-yong was deeply influenced by them. At the age of 23, in 1785, he was first introduced to the Christian doctrine by Yi Pyŏk, and learned about the Western world from him. Later Chŏng had opportunities to read and examine books on Christianity, modern European astronomy, mathematics, maps, clocks, telescopes, books on European customs, and European utensils.

These experiences enabled Tasan to realize the evil effect of Chu Hsi's Neo-Confucianism which indulged in empty theories and talk. He could also revise his hitherto narrow China-centered view of the world, shifting his interest to new scientific and technological knowledge. This conversion provided an important momentum for enriching the content of his progressive thought and elevating it to a higher level. Though he first believed in Catholicism, he soon abandoned it after realizing the falsity of its tenets. It seems that the intrigue plotted against him by his political opponents further prompted his decision to digress from Catholicism.

Passing the Civil Service Examination in 1780 at the age of 28, Chŏng started his government service. Fully displaying the scientific knowledge he had already acquired, as well as his great endowment, Tasan made notable achievements in projects aimed at promoting national interest and public welfare. He distinguished himself especially in designing the Han River bridge, by his theory of architecture, and his invention of a crane which he submitted to the government for utilization at the time of constructing the Suwŏn fortifications.

Tasan was appointed a secret royal inspector for Kyŏnggi Province when he turned 33 years of age. The appointment enabled him to witness the distress of the extremely impoverished farmers, and the corruption and disorder of local administration, by inspecting every corner of the province. The theoretical foundation was laid firmly at that time for the progressive political and economic reform measures Tasan later made public with a view to improving rural life. In realistic poems he depicted the miserable conditions of farming villages which he witnessed during the inspection.

A man of upright character, Tasan brought to strict punishment all corrupt officials he discovered, regardless of their ranks. This won him affection and respect from the people, but he also incurred jealousy and complaints from his political foes. His later demotions were connected with their jealousy and machinations—he was demoted from the position of a bureau director of the Ministry of War (senior third rank) to that of a provincial official (junior sixth rank) at the age of 34, and again from the position of an assistant secretary to the king (senior third rank) to that of the Koksan magistrate (junior third rank) at the age of 36. While serving as a magistrate in Koksan, he exerted himself to put into practice his aspirations and ideals. In fact, he made notable administrative achievements.

In 1801 King Chŏngjo, who favored Chŏng Yak-yong, died, and his son, King Sunjo, acceded to the throne. Upon this opportunity, Chŏng's political opponents (the Old Faction) accused the officials belonging to the Southern Faction as believers in an evil religion, and they were suppressed and persecuted in the so-called Sinyu Catholic Persecution of 1801. Chŏng was arrested and banished to Changgi, Kyŏngsang Province, and later removed to Kangjin, Chŏlla Province. In Kangjin, Chŏng lived in a hut on the slope of Mount Tasan (presently in Kyultong, Tosam-myŏn, Kangjin County), devoting himself to reading and writing. His 19 years of exile until 1818 when he was released at the age of 57 years enabled him to emerge as an all-embracing authority of the Real Learning.

Although his long, secluded life in a remote mountain village was really an unfortunate one, it nevertheless was a good opportunity for him to deepen and develop his scholarship and thought. Like many other Real Learning scholars, he authored immortal works in very unfortunate circumstances. Refusing to compromise with political power, he poured all of his zeal and effort into completing the Real Learning. At that time he conducted historical research on the voluminous Confucian classics from the angle of the Real Learning, and attached new and rational annotations to these classics. His representative essays written at that time include: *Chuyŏk Simjam, Yŏkhak Sŏŏn, Nonŏ Kogŭmju, Maengja Yoŭi, Taehak Kongŭi, Sogyuron,* and *Ohaknon.*

Tasan showed unreserved sympathy with farmers who were moaning in sore plight through daily contact with them, while analyzing and criticizing the feudal system in which corrupt officials could exploit farmers to the marrow. He formulated ideal reform measures covering the land system, taxation, the government personnel system, laws, the educational, military, and political systems. The most eminent essays embodying these ideals were "*Wŏnjŏng*" (discussing the rightful form of government), "*Wŏnmok*" (expounding the rightful posture of rulers), "*T'angnon*" (an essay on King T'ang of the Chinese Yin dynasty), "*Chŏnnon*" (an essay on the land system), and "*Kamsaron*" (explaining the duty of governors).

Released in 1818, as mentioned above, Chŏng Yak-yong returned to his home in Yangju. For 18 years, until his death in 1836 at the age of 75, he gave up appointment to the government and devoted himself to research and writing with a view to improving national life.

Mongmin Simsŏ (48 volumes) which he completed in 1818 when he was paroled from exile and *Kyŏngse Yup'yo* (40 volumes, also known as *Pongnye Ch'obon*), which he made public in the preceding year in unfinished form, are his two greatest works, representing Tasan's thought most comprehensively. Whereas the former advocates the reform of local administration which is closely connected with the living of farmers, ethical awakening of provincial officials, and the stabilization of agricultural economy, the latter presents his own plans for the reform of the central administrative structure. The ideal he aspired to realize in reforming the central administrative structure was the system of the ancient Chinese Chou dynasty (the so-called Chou civility).

His Thought

His view of the world, his view of nature, and his epistemology

The first thing we should examine in discussing Tasan's thought is his view of the world. Discarding the biased, narrow traditional view that the globe is four-cornered, static, and China occupies its center, Tasan correctly recognized the fact that it is round, revolves on its own axis, and there are a number of countries in addition to China scattered around its surface, thereby rejecting the attitude of being subservient to China. This progressive view of the world was based on his correct and thorough recognition of natural sciences and technology.

He tried to rectify the traditional common practice of despising and slighting technology by correctly recognizing the important position and role it played in man's life. He thought that man can be distinguished from animals only because he has techniques and is able to develop them. He wrote as follows in his *Kiyeron* (an essay on techniques and crafts):

The more our agricultural techniques are developed, the more we shall be able to produce in the same acres and the greater productivity we shall achieve even with the mobilization of little labor. . . . The higher our spinning and weaving techniques are elevated, the larger quantity of yarn we shall produce even with little raw material, and the more beautiful cloth we shall weave even with the utilization of labor for a short duration. . . . The development of our military techniques will make our soldiers more courageous in offense, defense, transportation, and constructing encampments, and also make them more invincible to danger. . . . The development of our handicraft techniques will make our houses, utensils, castles, ships, and vessels more solid and convenient. If we truly learn excellent techniques and encourage their utilization, our country will become rich, our armed forces stronger, the living of our people will be improved, and their health will be promoted.

With the conviction that techniques are the motive power for developing human society, Tasan criticized the then society which was backward in terms of technology, and stressed the need of promptly introducing advanced Western technology through China.

He not only recognized the importance of, and studied, natural sciences and technology, but he himself possessed the knowledge and technique of how to construct a castle and make rifles, cannons, and military vehicles. In addition, he himself designed a crane and produced printing types. He was also the first Korean to study and experiment with vaccination.

In epistemology, Chŏng Yak-yong took a progressive position, too. In recognizing the origin of nature and all matter, he rejected mysterious and speculative elements and took an empirical position. He did not recognize the existence of things except visible ones. He regarded *T'aegŭk* centering in the materialistic *chi* as the substance of all materials. He thought that the four cardinal elements—heaven, earth, water, and fire—deriving their origin in *T'aegŭk* interact with each other to give form to all various matter, such as lightning, wind, mountains, marshes, the sun, the moon, and the stars.

He saw in *li* the rule governing all matter. Based on the notion that *li* permeates each aspect of matter, Tasan rejected Mencius' subjective idealism that the rule governing all nature's creations resides in man's mind. He also criticized the theory on *li* advanced by followers of Chu Hsi.

Just as mind, as the organ of thinking, is reliant on organs of perception, such as the ear, eye, mouth, and nose, Tasan reasoned, perception is formed only when concrete objects impinge upon the sense organs. According to him, man's physical activity, his sensation, and his thinking are possible with the aid of blood and *chi*, and his mind must be stirred to become will before joy, anger, sorrow, or awe is generated; will commands *chi*, which, in turn, commands blood, changing his complexion and stimulating his limbs. On the basis of his empirical epistemology, Tasan rejected Chu Hsi's theory that knowledge precedes conduct and, in its stead, proposed the theory that conduct brings about knowledge. He implied unity between learning and thinking by saying, "Being engrossed in thinking without learning is as harmful as devotion to learning without thinking."

His theory of human nature; view of ethics

Chu Hsi's followers interpret that man by nature possesses the four moral norms of benevolence, righteousness, civility, and wisdom, which are rather feudalistic in nature, thereby drawing a limit to his moral cultivation in his lifetime. Chŏng Yak-yong rejects the possession of ethical or moral norms *a priori*, and asserts that morality can be formed through practice and self-training in life. He explained:

> Benevolence, righteousness, civility, and wisdom are formed after corresponding conduct. Therefore, benev

olence can be achieved only when one loves others; before this love, benevolence does not exist. After one does a good act, one can recognize righteousness. Before he so acts, righteousness does not exist. . . . How can it be asserted that benevolence, righteousness, civility, and wisdom are inherent in human mind, like seeds in a peach or apricot?

Concerning human nature, Chŏng also criticized the view of traditional Confucianists and advocated a new, reasonable view. By critically synthesizing Mencius' theory that human nature is good, Hsun Tzu's theory that human nature is bad, and Yang Hsiung's theory that human nature is a blend of both good and bad, Chŏng developed a new theory which runs as follows:

Man receives from Heaven talent, force, and nature. Talent is his ability. . . . both to do good and to do wrong. It is difficult for force to make him do good, but it is easy for force to make him do wrong. Therefore, it is hard to do good as long as he follows only his talent and force. His inborn nature has the propensity to love what is good and hate what is wrong. Therefore, when one is faced with what is good and what is wrong, he will not commit a mistake if he acts according to the dictates of his nature. It is called the Way to act according to nature.

According to Tasan, man is by birth neither good nor bad. Only according to whether he follows his nature or not, he becomes either good or bad. There are no gradations in the quality of innate human nature, and all are equal in this regard. On the basis of this interpretation of human nature, Chŏng Yak-yong classified men into two types: "*Sang-ji*" (innately wise men) and "*ha-u*" (innately stupid men) and assailed the generally accepted Confucian view that the latter cannot become the former, asserting that all can become sages if they exert themselves for self-training. Chŏng's advocacy of equality of human nature and the importance of self-training after birth has a deep relation to his democratic political and economic thought, which also advocates equality.

Based on his empirical epistemology and scientific rational thought, Chŏng bitterly criticized all irrational moral doctrines and unscientific religions, supersititions, mysticism, and fatalism by exposing their falsehood and harmful effects. He vehemently assailed the practice that the government honors as chaste a woman who commits suicide upon the death of her husband, who died a natural death. He criticized such a woman as committing the sin of suicide and, being narrow-minded by nature, neglecting her duty to her children and parents-in-law. A truly chaste woman, according to Chŏng, is one who defends her husband under attack from a fierce animal and is killed together with him, who resists to the death a lecher who tries to defame her honor, or who, when her husband is executed on a false charge, exposes the irregularity involved in the incident and is executed together with him.

In the same fashion, Chŏng also criticized the traditional wrong view of values concerning filial sons and loyal subjects. He also pointed out harmful effects arising from belief in geomancy, which holds that good or bad geographical positions determine men's rise or fall; the practice of selecting auspicious dates for large or small occasions; and onomancy, which teaches that man's name controls his destiny. He also exposed the falsity of physiognomy, which holds that one's appearance determines his material welfare and social standing. He asserted, to the contrary, that one's occupation changes his character which, in turn, changes his appearance. From this viewpoint, he exposed the harm of physiognomy as follows:

> . . . . A change in man's abode and nutrition will, without fail, bring about a change in his mood and body. Wealth and honor or worry and calamity will also generate an easy-going psychology and grief. We can find

a man who looked bright in the morning but depressed in the evening, or a man who looked pale yesterday but bright today. How can a man's looks remain static? If a farmer believes in physiognomy, he will lose his profession, and if a government official believes in it, he will lose friends, and if the king believes in it, he will lose subjects.

This view was a great blow against the fatalism which justified the innate superiority of the feudal ruling class and the inferiority of the ruled. His was an eminent view which rightly recognized the importance of environment for both the rich and the poor, and for both the high and the low.

His political, economic thought

Most prominent in Chŏng's system was the part that dealt with political and economic thought. Rejecting the orthodox Confucianism of Chu Hsi, which indulged in empty theories and talk, and which made no actual contribution to daily life, Chŏng bitterly exposed and accused its falsehood and corruption, and asserted that the main emphasis in learning should be shifted from problems of ethics and morality to practical problems designed to elevate people's welfare, such as politics and economy. He believed that a true Confucianist is one who is a master of both scholarship and military arts, is familiar with current affairs, is able to take charge of anything he is required to do, and is determined to devote himself to the cause of good government for the promotion of public welfare. He regarded the traditional Confucianists as not true Confucianists, for they were engrossed in empty theories and talk while remaining quite unfamiliar with current affairs. His attitude of research was thoroughly realistic and practical, and it was natural for him that politics and economics were the fields to which he devoted himself with most emphasis.

Although he was born to a *yangban* (nobility) family, the

experience he gained from his government career and long years of exile, the influence received from senior Real Learning scholars, and his knowledge of modern European thought made him side with poor farmers and small landowners. Big landlords and corrupt government officials were his greatest enemies. His political and economic thought is characterized by its devotion to the enhancement of the interests of small landowners and impoverished farmers. From this viewpoint of his sympathy with the lower classes, he developed a philosophical system which, based on democracy and the principle of equality, is progressive.

He raised an objection to the traditional Confucian theory of government which, seeking the origin of the ruler's power and that of a state from metaphysical Providence, asserted their sacredness and inviolability. According to Chŏng, only farmers existed in a classless society in ancient times, without being governed by a ruler. According to necessity in their daily life, however, they selected their village chiefs, heads of their *myŏns*, their magistrates, and finally their king. In this manner rulers came into being, along with their power. Chŏng's view is quite similar to the European theory of the social contract.

Having denied the sacred and inviolable dignity of ruling power, Chŏng made it clear that sovereignty rests not with the king or a ruler but with the people. He thought that since sovereignty rests with the people, it is just that they change their ruler. As the king is not a sacred proxy of Heaven's decree, but a ruler invested with his position by the will of the people, Chŏng concluded, it is just that they replace their ruler if he neglects their will or acts disadvantageous to their interests. In his eminent political essay, "On King T'ang," Chŏng wrote:

> How was the king born? Did he descend from heaven like the rain? Did he gush forth from beneath the earth like a spring? No. Installed by five households, a man

becomes the chief of a *lin*; installed by five *lins*, a man becomes the chief of a *li*, and installed by five *lis*, a man becomes the chief of a *hyŏn*. Nominated jointly by these chiefs of *hyŏns*, a lord is born. It is the king who is chosen by these lords. Therefore, it can be said that the king is appointed by the will of the people.... Therefore, if the five households do not like the chief of their *lin*, they hold a conference and elect a new chief.... if the lords do not like their king, they hold a conference and elect a new king.... How can it be called a chastisement of the king?

Tasan likened the replacement of kings to that of the conductors of dance troupes. He continued:

When a troupe of 64 dancers performs a dance, they select one from among themselves and let him conduct them with the baton. If he commands the dance well, in good harmony with the musical accompaniment, he wins respect from members of the troupe and is called 'our great conductor.' On the contrary, if he is inharmonious with the music while conducting his dancer, he is demoted to member's status, and another more talented conductor is selected and respected as 'our great conductor.' It is the people who demote their leader or promote him to leadership and respect him. If to select a leader or to replace him with another is accused as wrong, is the accusation just?

Chŏng defined politics after the Han dynasty in China as "politics from above" in allusion to his rejection, while calling the politics before Han "politics from below" of which he expressed his approval. By "politics from above" he meant autocracy, and by "politics from below" democratic politics which is contrary to the former. In other words, the basic tone of his political philosophy can be found in his rejection of autocracy and his support of democracy.

Concerning the process of legislation and the purpose of law, Chŏng also voiced his views based on democracy and the principle of popular sovereignty. He asserted that laws should be enacted according to the will of the people, and so should be profitable to the people. He exposed the irrationality of the feudal autocratic politics in which laws are enacted according to the arbitrary aims and interests of the ruler, in complete disregard of popular wishes or interests. Chŏng's democratic ideology led him to the clarification of the host-guest relation between the ruled and the ruler. He asked himself: "Does the ruler exist for the sake of people, or do the people exist for the sake of the ruler?" Then he answered his own question: "The ruler exists for the sake of the people." He bitterly criticized the dilemma of the then social system in which it was generally held that the people properly existed for the sake of the ruler.

Although Chŏng's political ideology amply contained elements of democracy and civil rights, he was still unable to dream of modern democracy or a modern form of republican government. He did not totally negate the existence of an autocratic monarch, nor did he positively assert the position of the people as responsible for politics. Rather, he regarded a monarchy based on virtue and civility as the most ideal form of government. His monarchy, needless to say, was based on democratic consensus, and so it can be distinguished from autocratic monarchialism.

Trying to realize various democratic purposes within the framework of monarchy, Chŏng advocated the prevention of various atrocities by the ruler, which are apt to arise from monarchy, by means of his voluntary good government. For this reason he proposed the ethics of the ruler be summarized in the phrase "virtuous government." Contrary to "legal government," which attempts to subjugate the people with threat and coercion, "virtuous government" tries to comply with the law of nature and humanity in governing the people.

"Virtuous government," which is an indispensable element of Chŏng's political ideology, requires cooperation from local magistrates and officials. It is because they are in the forefront of government, dealing directly with the people. However, they looked to Chŏng quite contrary to the image of his ideal ruler. Instead of being desirable rulers who defend the people like their own children and govern them like fathers, they wielded power to exploit helpless farmers at will. These rulers looked to Chŏng like hungry beasts or publically recognized robbers.

In his "On Magistrates," Chŏng plainly and satirically described how magistrates and other high and low local officials exploited farmers. Defining these officials as authorized robbers, Chŏng said that the provincial magistrates were the biggest robbers. "Unless these biggest robbers are eliminated, all the farmers will starve." He also described how cruelly petty local officials exploited farmers: "Like hungry tigers which have caught a boar, or hawks which have caught a pheasant, they nimbly and fiercely pounce upon farmers."

Showing his boundless sympathy with powerless farmers who were gasping under the agony of feudal exploitation and oppression, Chŏng sharply analyzed and criticized all aspects of state administration with the earnest desire to stabilize their living and insure the promotion of national wealth. He exposed the corruption of dishonest government officials, the disorder impairing the administration and the judiciary, and the misery of the populace. Chŏng proposed a series of progressive reform measures—the abolition of the feudal caste system and *yangban* system, appointment of able persons to government posts by discarding partisan and regional factionalism and in disregard of their social standing, the abolition of the grain loan system which had already been degraded into usurious exploitation (the system was originally designed to release government grain to farmers as loans in the season of spring poverty and recover it in the autumn harvest season with some interest), and the consolidation of military duty and farming.

Most illustrious among his reform measures is his farm

reform measure represented by his *"yŏjŏn"* system, the like of which cannot be found among other measures proposed by Real Learning scholars. Like his senior Real Learning scholars, Chŏng realized that the fundamental key to the solution of public welfare lay in the reform of the land system. Like the *"hanjŏn"* system proposed by other Real Learning scholars, with the aim of fixing the maximum and minimum land ownership; or the *"kyunjŏn"* system proposed by other scholars, with a view to distributing land evenly, Chŏng's *"yŏjŏn"* system was basically aimed at achieving economic equality by readjusting land ownership. Chŏng believed that his system embodied the spirit manifested in the *"chŏngjŏn"* system of ancient China. In particular, Chŏng's *"yŏjŏn"* system had many differences from the *"chŏngjŏn,"* *"hanjŏn,"* and *"kyun-jŏn"* systems. In quality, the *"yŏjŏn"* system was something more meaningful than a mere land system.

We shall examine the contents of his land reform measure which centered around the *"yŏjŏn"* system. First, he advocated the principle that only those who farm themselves should be entitled to ownership of land, and those who do not farm should be denied ownership. The principle was aimed at rectifying the situation under which the tenant system thrived, so that a small number of wealthy landlords occupied the bulk of land and an increasing number of farmers were degraded into tenants, so that the gap between the rich and the poor was widening, and the state tax revenue was dwindling. Once the principle was applied, Chŏng believed, all landless farmers could possess their own land, and all the above stated dilemmas would be eased. The *"yŏjŏn"* system was devised in order to translate the principle into action. In the system, about 30 households would be combined into one *"yŏ,"* would jointly possess the land in their *"yŏ,"* and harvest jointly. This is the second characteristic of Chŏng's land reform measure. Third, Chŏng proposed that the harvest would be divided among the households according to the number of work days each provided. Therefore, farmers who worked more would get a larger share, and those who did not work at all would be omitted from the distribution.

What can be done for those who are not engaged in farming, such as merchants, artisans, *yangban literati*, etc.? Chŏng answers: Merchants can get food grain in exchange for their commodities, artisans can also exchange their products for grain, and concerning *literati*, only those who conduct research on agriculture and make a contribution to farmers should be entitled to provision of grain, and they should be treated 10 times better than physical workers. He asserted that those *literati* who lead an ivory tower life should change their profession to commerce or handicraft.

Even though Chŏng's land reform proposal may remind us of the socialist collective farm system, his basic spirit was not socialism but "economic equality." The principle of economic equality was not Chŏng's monopoly, but it was the long tradition consistently characterizing the economic ideology of China and Korea since ancient times. A group of officials who advocated a land reform toward the close of the Koryŏ dynasty also harbored the same ideal.

It may not be too much to say that Chŏng's ideology of land reform symbolized by his *"yŏjŏn"* system was an overall summation of his reform measures for politics, economy, culture, and all other fields. The democratic ideology which permeates his political thought and the principle of equality which runs through his economic thought constitute the foundation of his philosophy.

The Limit of His Thought

We have so far examined the outline of Tasan's thought. We discovered that his thought richly contains elements which are empirical, based on the principle of universal equality, democracy, and rationality. In this respect, his thought, like that of other Real Learning scholars, had its roots in modernism. His autonomy and national consciousness is thorough, another characteristic common to all Real Learning scholars.

One thing we should be careful about in summing up his thought is that the modernism contained in it is much different from the "modern thought" of the Western world which is described as "bourgeois thought," though there are many similarities between the two. His democracy is different from bourgeois democracy, and his principle of equality is also different from bourgeois equality. He was not basically a bourgeois thinker, nor did he concern himself with bourgeois society. Tasan's fundamental ideal was, in all respects, to construct a powerful, centralized kingdom which, based on the traditional agricultural society, was filled with democracy and the principle of equality. His ideal truly embodied the basic spirit of ancient Confucianism, especially that of Mencius and the ideals of the Chou dynasty. Tasan's thought, like that of other Real Learning scholars, was basically in ideology which, inheriting Confucian philosophy, underwent improvement so as to include elements of democracy and equality. The strong "classicism" manifested by Chŏng and other Real Learning scholars was not "reactionary" but "reform-minded" classicism. Herein lies the reason why a reform advocating classicism is often progressive in nature, as history shows.

Chŏng's reform measures were too idealistic and too revolutionary to be accepted by the feudal rulers. There was no political force strong enough to put his thought and ideals into practice. However, his great ideology, aspiring after democracy, equality, and freedom, provided a strong spiritual prop for Korean national leaders who devoted themselves to the cause of defending our national sovereignty and modernizing our country in the period of national crisis in the latter years of the Yi dynasty and during the Japanese rule. Still today, his thought is our priceless inheritance which can fill up our spiritual sterility.

REFERENCES

Hong I-sŏp: *A Study of Chŏng Yak-yong's Political and Economic Thought*, 1959.

Chŏng In-bo: "The Life and Achievements of Tasan" contained in *Ch'omwŏn's Scattered Essays on Koreanology*, 1955.

Ch'ŏn Kwan-u: *A History of the Real Learning Thought in Korea*, 1970.

Tonghak Thought:
The Roots of Revolution

SUSAN S. SHIN

Tonghak was an indigenous Korean religion founded in 1860 by Ch'oe Che-u. After the Founder's execution by the Korean government four years later, the sect survived underground and, in 1894 dissident *Tonghak* activists led the first nationwide peasant uprising in Yi dynasty history. The *Tonghak* Movement, with its martyrs, revelations, nationalism and organizational skills has fascinated Korean and Western scholars alike. It has inspired at least two historical novels in Korean and innumerable scholarly works. In view of these previous efforts the reader may well wonder how another attempt may be justified. My original intention was to study the organization of the *Tonghak* Movement to determine how it was possible for this originally religious and apolitical movement to mount a serious challenge to the dynasty. As I became more familiar with the rites and written works devised by the *Tonghak* Founder, I came to disagree with some previous English language interpretations and felt the need for a more thorough examination of *Tonghak* thought itself.

Although the *Tonghak* message to believers changed drastically between 1864 and 1894, it was essential to the movement throughout the period. It is therefore important to avoid the reductionist argument which interprets ideas merely as a function of socio-economic grievances. It is also

204

clear that *Tonghak* was a genuine, not a pseudo-religion.

I also concluded that Ch'oe Che-u's written works were heavily indebted to the neo-Confucian tradition that still prevailed in nineteenth century Korea. This was not the orthodox Chu Hsi school with its emphasis on statecraft and social relations, but rather the tradition of neo-Confucian spirituality with its religious and even mystical vision of man's essential unity with all creation. One can find echoes of *Tonghak* thought in Wang Yang-ming and, in Japan, in the writings of the seventeenth century scholar Nakae Toju.

Although *Tonghak* is a syncretic religion whose elements can easily be traced to indigenous and borrowed traditions, the *Tonghak* Movement was surely unique in Yi dynasty history. It is the only known instance of an indegenous religion with its own scripture, and surely the only one to threaten the monarchy with a massive popular uprising.

Revelation and Martyrdom

What sort of man was the *Tonghak* founder? To the Korean state, threatened by foreign penetration and domestic unrest, Ch'oe Che-u, whose pen name was Su-un, was a heretic, at once of a fortune-teller and crypto-Catholic. To his followers on the other hand he was the Founder, whose divine calling was confirmed by miraculous powers of healing and prophecy. From these conflicting viewpoints and, above all from Su-un's own writings, the outlines of a life may be discerned.

Ch'oe Che-u was born into an ancient and well respected clan that counted among its numbers Ch'oe Ch'i-wŏn, the noted scholar of the Silla period, and Ch'oe Chin-ip, who led troops during the Manchu invasion of Korea, and who died defending the town of Homch'ŏn. Su-un's father Ok (Kunam) was, by Su-un's account, a man of enough means to devote himself to scholarship and literature. The elder Ch'oe was childless, or at least sonless, and, at the age of sixty took a young widow, Madame Han, as a second wife. A son, Che-sŏn, was born of this union in 1824. About Che-sŏn's childhood, we know only that his mother died when he was six. As was customary, he was married in his early teens to a Madame Pak of Ulsan. When Che-sŏn was but fifteen his elderly father died leaving him head of a household and heir to his father's land.

Che-sŏn left no comment on his childhood, or on his ambiguous position as son of a remarried widow.[1] His father had given him a conventional education in the Chinese classics, but his mother's remarriage barred him from using this education to seek office through the examination system. By temperament restless and moody, he was ill-suited for a life of rustic gentility. He tried his hand at teaching neighborhood children, but according to the anonymous author of the *Su-un Haengnok*, "could not reconcile himself to common place existence, and began to hate it... so he set off as a peddler traveling around from place to place."[2] During his wanderings, he is said to have studied the texts of Buddhism, Taoism and Catholicism, as well as books of divination.[3]

Although he had little to say about external details, Ch'oe documented his inner life in such a vivid and colorful manner that he should be left to speak for himself. The following is a fragment from his autobiographical essay "On Cultivating Virtue" written during the summer of 1862.

> The flow of months and years cannot be arrested. Unfortunately my father died suddenly and left me orphaned when I was only sixteen. What did I know? I was like a child. My father's life work was consumed by fire. His descendent, grieving because he could not fulfil his duty, lost heart and could not go on. I was familiar with household affairs, but knew nothing of farming. I could not work faithfully at my studies, nor could I hope for an office. My patrimony was gradually dissipated, and my future was insecure.... As I grew older, my body became

too weak that I could not separate the two strokes of the character "eight" and I feared hunger and cold. At the thought of approaching forty, how could I not sigh at my failure? Without a home, shall I say that heaven and earth are wide? Everything I did went awry, and I had no place to rest.[4]

This is the account of a man who saw in his past only bereavement and failure, and in his future, nothing but poverty and hopelessness. Without denying his misfortune, this essay should, I believe, be taken as symptom rather than as history. His vague sense of guilt toward his father, his anxiety about his health, his sense of bereavement and pessimism indicate depression. Later he was to write to his sons and nephews that "of all the sufferings I have endured during my lifetime, I most regret having failed in my occupation."[5] But what exactly was his failure? As the son of a remarried widow he was excluded from the civil bureaucracy. But office holding was, in any case, the prerogative of very few and during Ch'oe's lifetime high offices were concentrated in the hands of the so-called in-law clans. Outside of an official career, the only traditionally sanctioned source of wealth and power was land holding. Che-sŏn had inherited his father's holdings, but preferred the life of an itinerant scholar to that of landlord cum-entrepreneur. With the exception of his penchant for travel and the study of religion, Su-un's objective situation was by no means uncommon in the Korea of his day, and efforts to portray him as the object of personal discrimination are unconvincing. Whatever one's interpretation of Su-un's condition, there is no doubt but that by middle age, his prospects were bleak indeed. Unable to support his wife and children, he was further humiliated by his wife's departure for her natal home in Ulsan. He himself was either ill or anxious about his health, and he had recently sold the last of his father's fields. Then, inexplicably, came relief in the form of prophethood.

In the tenth lunar month of 1859, he had taken his family to his native place Yongdam near Kumi Mountain west of Kyŏng-ju. There he vowed not to leave the mountain and changed his name from Che-sŏn to Che-u meaning "to save the ignorant." The retreat to Yongdam and the change of name are clearly a metaphor for the rebirth that conversion is said to provide. The following year at the height of spring, God revealed himself to Su-un and commanded him to disseminate the Heavenly Way. Su-un left several accounts of this experience, one of which is notable for the swing from deep depression to euphoria upon receiving the revelation.

Pitiful, pitiful, my family's fate was pitiful. I failed to bring honor to my parents. Unfilial as I was, resentment and rancor piled up. A son born in unfavorable times, I idled the years away. Living my life, I was suddenly for-ty. Is this all for a lifetime of forty years? There was no way out. Here in Yongdam I heard the sound of flowing water and saw the high mountains. When I turn to see the mountain streams on either side and the water flow-ing as it always did, and the trees and grasses that I treasure, my unfilial heart laments. Crows and magpies seem to mock me, and the pine trees are melancholy. I was faithful, but my unfilial heart feels sadness and remorse. My poor father received no recompense. I sum-moned my wife and children and instructed them: There is no end to Heaven's benevolence. On the fifth day of the fourth month of 1860—how can I record it? How can I express it? In my sleep or while awake, the limitless Great Way came to me. How wonderful! My fate was wonder-ful! God said to me, "You are the first in the fifty thou-sand years since creation. Since creation I too have labored without success, but I succeeded after meeting you. I succeeded and you received my will. That is your fate." Hearing this I felt great joy and pride. Mankind! Did you know that limitless fate approached? Marvelous, marvelous, this fate is marvelous. Amidst the beauty of

Kumi, cultivating the limitless Great Way, the destiny that comes once in fifty thousand years. The only one chosen in ten thousand years rejoices. Amidst the beauty of Kumi, made of things with form, my fate met its time.[6]

By Su-un's own account, the revelation was the turning point in his life. Born in "unfavorable times," his fate, nevertheless, met its right time in its second birth. Where the first life had brought only grief, the second brought a meaningful mission. The contrast between the two could not be more clearly drawn. The revelation lifted Su-un from depression to exhaltation, from obscurity to renown, from self-deprecation to self-respect as Founder and Master, from poverty to sufficiency (his followers provided for his family), from bereavement to the protection of God, from dependency and helplessness to authority as the possessor of magical techniques.

To be called upon by God is a form of self-transcendance. While Su-un's goal before the revelation had been to bring honor to his family's name in the form of individual success, his mission now became the salvation of mankind. It is surely significant that Su-un, so preoccupied with his health, should single out the talisman that cured illness as the visible sign of his calling.[7] The talisman, called the elixir of immortality (*sŏnyak*) was to be written on a sheet of white paper. The paper was then burned, the ashes dissolved in a cup of water and drunk. Su-un experimented first upon himself, consuming "several hundred" such potions until, after several months he had the "appearance of an immortal and the physique of an adept (*sŏnp'ung togol*)."[8]

Apart from experimenting with the talisman, Su-un apparently spent the next several months cultivating the Way, that is, meditating and interpreting the incantations that were to form the essence of his teachings. For the rest of his life, he devoted himself to spreading his way, renouncing his former hopes of material success. While loss of his patrimony had formerly evoked feelings of guilt and remorse, he now praised poverty as a sign of virtue, and counseled resignation to it.[9] Just when Su-un began to preach is not clear, but by the summer of 1861, he had devised the rudiments of *Tonghak*: the talisman, the incantation in which followers professed their faith, and according to some interpretations, made the divine spirit descend, and the simple rituals of initiation and congregational worship. Word of his "supernatural powers" circulated and "intelligent scholars" began to seek him out. One of these early followers was Ch'oe Si-hyŏng, his successor as leader of the *Tonghak* Movement.

Then suddenly and without explanation, he left his village and made his way to Chŏllanamdo. One account claims that Su-un left because he failed to win converts.[10] According to another, he was forced into hiding because the authorities believed he was practicing Catholicism.[11] He traveled alone staying in private homes, curing sickness with the talisman or preaching the Way. Around the end of the year he reached Namwŏn and took up residence in a Buddhist temple. Here he wrote his Chinese language essay "A Discussion of Learning." In the third month of 1862 he left his "hermitage" and returned to Kyŏngju. In the several months that remained to him, he continued to expound the Way and lay the foundation for a simple organizational network of district leaders (*chŏpchu*). In December of 1863 he was arrested and, after a most perfunctory hearing, was executed for heresy.

One of the official charges against Ch'oe Che-u was that he took his "artifices" from Catholicism, then circulating clandestinely in Korea. Yet the most cursory study of Su-un's thought leads to the conclusion that the dominant influence on his thought was, without question, the neo-Confucian tradition in which he was raised. His works are full of admiring references to "former masters" and he respectfully mentions Confucius by name. His concern with spiritual cultivation and his belief that every human being is capable of enlightenment indicate an affinity with the idealistic philosophy of Wang Yang-ming and his followers. Even when striving to convey his unique experience of revelation and rebirth, Su-un could not avoid the vocabulary of neo-Confucianism. For him, neo-Confucianism was not the empty formalism that is appeared to twentieth century intellectuals. It was rather a living, viable tradition that affected, albeit differently, all social classes.

I have already mentioned the talisman that cured illness as a sign of Su-un's calling. The other manifestation was the *Tonghak* incantation. These incantations resemble the prayers of the world religions in that they express faith in God and devotion to a divinely inspired teaching. The incantation fuses worship and magic as it unites the believer with divine creativity and leads him to an intuitive grasp of truth.[12] Although many *Tonghak* practices were modified or fell into disuse after the Founder's death, the ritual of reciting incantations remained at the heart of *Tonghak* at least until the uprising of 1894. Large groups of believers would assemble in the home of a leader where their chanting resembled "singing in unison."[13] Later when *Tonghak* believers mobilized to petition the King, they would gather in large numbers on a broad plain where their chanting "echoed through the neighborhood."[14] These assemblies of believers dressed in white, reciting in unison left potential converts with an impression of dignity and high purpose. Believers may have gained a sense of solidarity while, to Korean authorities the incomprehensible chanting could only be taken as a sign of subversive intent.

The Tonghak Incantation

Su-un gives two accounts of the origin of these incantations. In "On Propagating Virtue," he writes that he received the incantation from God. "Take this incantation and teach mankind about the Lord, then you too will experience fullness of life and will propagate virtue throughout the world." In his later work, "A Discussion about Learning," Su-un says only that God instructed him to express the Way in writing. When after several months of study, he came to understand the Way completely, he "composed incantations and perfected the technique of making the divine spirit descend." Though the incantations vary slightly in working and nuance, they all express the essence of Su-un's teachings. In the earliest extant version, the believer in effect, asks for God's favor: "I pray to God to look to me. If one remembers God forever, all will be realized." The last phrase "all will be realized" has been interpreted, rightly, I believe, as a prayer for material benefit.[15] Su-un later revised the first phrase and recast it as a declaration of faith in the divine origin of nature: "Serve God and creation (*chohwa*) will be tranquil (*chŏng*). If one remembers God throughout one's life all will be realized." The revised incantation omits any reference to material benefit and holds out to the believer the promise of enlightenment, here conceived as intuitive insight into the workings of nature. To express nature, the totality of creation, Su-un uses the Taoist term *chohwa* rather than the more usual Sino-Korean word *kaebyŏk*. He must have been familiar with its usage—it occurs in the *Lieh-tzu* for he glosses it in the "Discussion of Learning" as "all will be realized of itself" or "taking no unnatural action" (*muwi ihwa*). Here Su-un echoes both the ancient Chinese faith and the Korean animistic belief in propitiating nature through the worship of Heaven. But by the time Su-un explicated his incantation in December 1861, he seems to have moved away from the belief that individual communion with the divine might lead to natural stability. The conception of the divine similarly changed as Su-un reinterpreted his incantation in the vocabulary of neo-Confucian ethics. In his earlier work "On Propagating Virtue" written in the spring of 1861, Su-un had claimed to have been called by the Ruler of Heaven (*ch'ŏnju*), also called the Lord on High (*sangje*), the anthropomorphic deity of ancient Chinese provenance. In the "Discussion of Learning" of December 1861, Su-un avoids mention of the source of his revelation. He does call the incantation a verse showing respect for God (*ch'ŏnju*), but he assigns supernatural powers to the vital force (*ki*) of neo-Confucian philosophy. When Su-un prayed that "ultimate creativity" (*chigi*) or vital force may descend he was referring, he said, to "the mysterious and remote which encompasses all things and rules all things. Although it has form, it cannot be described. Although it can be heard, it cannot be seen. It is the vital force of the undifferentiated universe."[16] The believer who enters the Way tries, through self-cultivation, to "bring his mind into correspondence with vital force and save himself."[17]

In a commentary that echoes Su-un's Taoist-like mysticism, the Ch'ŏndogyo leader Yi Ton-hwa interpreted "limitless creativity" as "the autonomous creative principle made by God," a creative potentiality that can be grasped by intuition alone: "Ultimate creativity is a miracle which cannot be grasped by human consciousness. Not only can it not be expressed by words and writings, it cannot be perceived by the senses. It can only be felt intuitively."[18]

What originated as a simple prayer for divine help was thus recast as a quest for enlightenment. The "basic" or "thirteen word incantation" had assumed a link between individual worship and natural harmony as the believer declared his faith in the Ruler of Heaven. The "Discussion of Learning" in effect transfers supernatural power to "ultimate creativity" while still calling upon the believer to revere Heaven. This is accomplished by taking the word *ch'ŏnju* in the incantation and dividing it into its components, so that the believer declares his willingness to serve Heaven. The *ju* of *ch'ŏnju* is reinterpreted as the verb "to respect. . . just as one respects parents. . . . Thus understanding virtue, bearing it in mind without forgetting, one succeeds in transforming infinite creativity and succeeds in attaining sagehood."

The Neo-Confucian Incantation

This quest for enlightenment is in keeping with the neo-Confucian faith that through study and self-cultivation, one can attain the Way and live in harmony with the principles of Heaven. Echoing the *Doctrine of the Mean,* Su-un wrote, "According to our Way, if one follows God's principles, all will follow of its own accord. If each cultivates his heart, rectifies his vital force and follows his own nature, God's Way will be revealed of itself."[19]

In prescribing this course of spiritual exercises, Su-un clearly distinguished his Way from the faith sects of Buddhism in which salvation could be achieved by chanting mantra or, even more simply, by invoking the name of Buddha. Attaining the Way required time and active moral effort. "If it takes ten years of practice (*kongbu*) to realize the Way and establish virtue," Su-un wrote in Korean, "one may say that he achieved it rapidly." This is not to say, however, that only a small elite could be expected to achieve it. Su-un excluded no one. *Tonghak* sources stress that his first convert was his own life, and that only after instructing members of his immediate family, did Su-un seek disciples outside. These included persons of humble birth without formal education, though Su-un was clearly elated when "distinguished scholars came to inquire about the Way." On the possibility of universal enlightenment, Su-un wrote, "Even the most ignorant hears the word. . . and reads the prayers. . . . In this insubstantial world, are those who appear ignorant really so?"[20]

As one who had been transformed by a mystical experience, and who sought to guide others to the same end, Su-un left guidelines rather than detailed instructions. One who committed himself to the Way first vowed to serve God forever. Then he or she embarked upon a course of self-cultivation. Called cultivating the mind and rectifying one's vital force, Su-un believed this method (*pŏp*) or practice (*su*) to be his orignial contribution, but it clearly owes a great deal to neo-

Confucian spirituality. Compare this phrase to Ch'eng I's description of the enlightened man as one who "rectifies his mind and nourishes his nature," Ch'eng I was describing the enlightened man's pursuit of sagehood, a process that did not necessarily depend upon devotion to an anthropomorphic deity. Yet Su-un's formulation and this phrase from the *Reflections on Things at Hand*, with which Su-un was undoubtedly familiar, both assume that by individual effort one can achieve enlightenment expressed as sagehood. For both, sincerity, construed as a kind of praxis, is the key to spiritual advancement. When Su-un writes that "the great Way consists of holding fast to sincerity (*sŏng*) and seriousness (*kyŏng*) and cultivating them little by little," he seems to have used sincerity synonymously with faith in God. In "On Propagating Virtue," he writes of having received from God a talisman that cured illness and bestowed fullness of life (*changsaeng*). After experimenting successfully upon himself, Su-un applied it to a number of patients, only some of whom recovered. He explained the uneven results as a difference in degree of sincerity. Those who practiced sincerity "and believed in God improved without fail, but the talisman had no effect upon those who ignored the Way and its Virtue. Did it not then depend upon the patient's sincerity and reverence?"[21]

Motivated by faith and sincerity, the convert "practiced the Way" through spiritual exercises that again have Chinese precedents. Although Su-un himself does not use the term, the editor of *Ch'ŏndogyo Ch'anggŏnsa*, Yi Ton-hwa, mentions that Su-un and his successor Ch'oe Si-hyŏng practiced "quiet sitting," (*chŏngjwa*), a form of meditation in which the convert was to exclude extraneous thoughts from his mind in order to concentrate upon his essential nature.[22] More dynamic than "quiet sitting," though not incompatible with it, was *kongbu*, understood as "effort" or "practice" rather than its contemporary meaning "study". "Effort" included meditation, reciting the incantations, and compliance with Su-un's prescriptions for daily life.

It is characteristic of Su-un's eclectic teaching that his rules of behavior, most of which merely affirmed Korean concep- tions of propriety, are listed after the classical Chinese virtues of benevolence, righteousness, decorum, and knowledge.

> The gentleman dresses correctly: the vulgar (*ch'ŏn*) eats on the road and folds his hands behind his back. In the home of believers, the meat of bad animals [i.e. dogs] is not eaten. Sitting in a gushing cold spring is harmful to the health. For men and women to associate is forbidden by our National Code. To recite an incantation in a loud voice is to neglect our Way. To propagate these rules is to practice the Way.[23]

The Indigenous Background

To point out Su-un's debt to Chinese predecessors is not to imply that *Tonghak* thought had no indigenous roots. The use of talismans to cure illness, and the practice of reciting incantations aloud are found in Korean Shamanism. The con- tent of the *Tonghak* talisman itself may be traced to the Korean book of prophecy, the *Chŏnggamnok* (Record of Chŏnggam) which predicted that the Yi dynasty would fall after five hundred years and be replaced by the Chŏng dynasty. During the disorder of the interregnum one could "wisely protect one's body between 弓弓 and 乙乙." Su-un believed that the Western powers, which had invaded China, would soon reach Korea, and that the same characters would protect one from harm during the inevitable conflict. Accord- ing to the testimony of believers collected by the Governor of Kyŏngsangdo after Su-un's arrest, Su-un had predicted an invasion from the north "between the second and fifth months of 1863."[24] (Another account gives the nineteenth day of the twelfth month of 1863 as the invasion date.) When this date passed without incident, Su-un revised his prediction instructing his believers that the disaster would occur on the eleventh day of the twelfth month of 1864. Each year had its beneficial characters which, when written on paper, burned and the ashes drunk in water, would protect the believer. Su-un had taught his believers that "during the *imjin* and *imsin* years, the characters 松松 and 家家 are beneficial, but that during the year *kapcha* (1864) the characters 弓弓 are beneficial."[25] The reason for the special efficacy of these characters remains obscure. At one point in his report to the throne the Governor of Kyŏngsangdo wrote that the talisman consisted of 弱 meaning the character 弓 with two dots below it.[26] Elsewhere Su-un is said to have testified that 弓 was "half the character 穹 (sky) and that its power lay in naming the Great Ultimate which is also called 弓弓."[27]

Another *Tonghak* practice that recalls the shamanist tradition is Su-un's sword dance and song which cured illness and also protected the believer from Western invaders. The sword dance stems from the traditional Korean belief that illness is caused by an evil spirit invading the body. When the *Tonghak* believer Yi Chong-hwa testified that Su-un's talisman "made the pest demon flee and the illness spirit leave," he was expressing this belief. Yi's description of the *Tonghak* seance contains the essentials of the shamanist healing rite *salp'uri* in which the spirit which intrudded into the body and caused the illness is expelled by stabbing it with a sword and spear.[28] The *Tonghak* practice of burning a paper talisman and drinking the ashes in water is also practiced in shamanist rites, in the P'yŏngyang area and probably elsewhere, the *Chesŏk kut* or "ritual of the heavenly spirit," included burning a piece of white paper that had covered a water jar and mixing its ashes with the water in the jar. Family members holding the *kut* would drink the water to fulfil their wishes.[29]

While the specific content of *Tonghak* beliefs and rituals may be traced to Korean and Chinese precedents, the emergence of *Tonghak* as a popular religion cannot be understood without reference to contemporary events. *Tonghak* was in part a response to Western imperialism and the arrival of Christianity in Korea. Koreans were aware of the Opium War by which the British compelled China to open its ports to trade and Christianity, and of the Second Anglo-Chinese War in which England and France attacked Peking. This is the war to which Su-un refers in his discussion of Western Learning:

> Now in the fourth month of 1860, the world was in disarray and people's minds were confused, and no one knew where to turn. Strange news spread over the world. The Westerners established a doctrine through whose efficacy they could accomplish all things. In war no one could withstand them, and China was burned. Won't we perish as well? The reason for this is none other than that their way is called the Western Way, their learning is called Western Learning or the Teaching of the Lord of Heaven [i.e. Catholicism] that is, the Holy Teaching. Isn't it that they know the Heavenly order and receive the Heavenly mandate?[30]

What is striking to the twentieth century reader is the view that Catholicism was somehow responsible for Western military supremacy. To attribute this to mindless xenophobia would be to overlook an enduring aspect of the Neo-Confucian tradition in which the sacred penetrated every experience and every realm of thought. Confucian education stressed the primacy of correct principles, from which proper action was to follow. When even the Catholic missionaries eased resistance to their teachings with the wonders of European technology, it was not unreasonable to conclude that ships and firearms also derived from this correct spiritual orientation. Toward the awesome unity of Western belief and power, Su-un felt the ambivalence common to East Asians of his generation: Hatred for Western power, but grudging respect for the technology on which it was based. Su-un did not deal concretely with the problems of integrating Korea into the international order. His vision was religious, and his mission was to remind his countrymen that strength lay in reviving traditional values. During the Founder's lifetime, *Tonghak* thought was overwhelmingly conservative in that it appealed to tradition to-ward off disaster. A passage from the "Song on Encouraging Learning" links the eclipse of traditional religion to the foreign incursions.

> In 1860, in this decadent time, the vicious Western bandits invaded China, built their cathedral, and spread their way throughout the world. . . . I thought over what I had recently heard and realized that the simple people of our country have abandoned propriety and the five relationships. Men and women, old and young, children and servants, gather in groups and heed idle talk. They secretly pray to God day and night that when they die they might go to the Jade Palace in the Thirty-three Heavens. Those stupid people didn't even pray when their parents died, didn't carry out a memorial service, and abandoned the five relationships.[31]

Here Su-un criticizes the popular Taoist belief in an afterlife in the "Thirty-three Heavens," but his strongest comdemnation is reserved for Korean Catholics who omitted the Confucian memorial service for deceased parents. This breach of traditional morality was so scandalous to the State that it provoked the first arrests and executions of Korean Catholics in 1791.[32] To the orthodox Confucian, this failure to show respect to one's parent was a violation of the most important virtue, filial piety. To Su-un, already burdened by a sense of guilt toward his father for failing to "continue the family's honor" this must have been all the more outrageous.

Millenarian Hope

If, as I believe, Su-un's teaching were ostensibly conservative and called for the restoration of traditional Confucian values, why was the first nationwide uprising in Korean history carried out in the name of his Way? This question cannot be answered without reference to the movement that emerged after his death, but an account of Su-un's thought would be incomplete without some mention of those ideas that spurred resistance to traditional authority. Buried in his hymns and essays, and neglected during his lifetime are scattered phrases that could be reinterpreted to suggest a coherent ideology of resistance.

As I have mentioned, Su-un's attitude toward authority was conventionally respectful. He accepted the supremacy of age over youth, men over women, and ruler over subject. Only once in his Korean language poems does he venture a veiled criticism of corrupt officials and yamen clerks: When those above cannot be trusted, those below entertain doubts. When those above cannot be respected, those below become arrogant.[33] Even this mild rebuke may have been within the Sino-Korean tradition of remonstrance.

Like many prophets before him, Su-un gave the humble a new sense of dignity as God's creation. "Having been born under the same heaven," he wrote, "we are all alike whether immortal or man."[34] If man as man was the noblest manifestation of God's creative power, and if each had the capacity to become an immortal (*sŏnbun*), then social differences might seem less important. If faith, not book learning, was the key to enlightenment, and intuition, not orthodoxy, was the way to truth, then the poor and lowly were raised, and the wealthy, with their leisure for study were demeaned. But as in other teachings, the doctrine of man's equality in the eyes of God could cut both ways. It could have subversive implications, or it could reconcile the humble to their station with the consolation of other worldly rewards. During Su-un's lifetime and, indeed, until shortly before the *Tonghak* Rebellion, the latter side dominated. Su-un's writings were not only silent on the subject of social equality, they even counseled acquiesence to one's Heaven sent fate. Faith in Heaven and the *Tonghak* talisman might ward off illness. Sincerity and reverence bestowed harmony upon the household. Enlightenment might make one an immortal, but individual or collective efforts to improve one's material lot were not recommended. Sudden wealth and honors were "inauspicion" and subject to equally sudden loss. Better to content oneself with "honorable poverty" from the outset and await a better time. For if each one followed the Way, a "sagely era of great peace will return, and the nation will flourish and the people will be secure. . . ."[35] To his followers Su-un promised the end of the "decadent age" and the coming of the "beneficient flourishing age." But though peace and disorder, security and want had alternated in the past, the coming era would never end. The limitless great Way would endure "forever without limit."[36]

NOTES

1. Yi dynasty law did not prohibit the remarriage of widows as such, but discriminated against the sons and grandsons of remarried women by forbidding them from competing in the lower and higher civil service examinations, and banning them from office. This law was first published in the revised edition of the *Kyŏngguk Taejŏn* of 1485. For a discussion of women's status in the Yi dynasty, see Martina Deuchler, "The Tradition; Women during the Yi dynasty," in *Virtues in Conflict*, ed. by Sandra Mattielli.

2. Anonymous, *Su-un Haengnok* (A Biography of Su-un) reprinted in Kim Sang-gi, *"Tonghak gwa Tonghaknan."*

3. Yi Ton-hwa, *Ch'ŏndogyo Ch'anggŏnsa* (A History of the Founding of Ch'ŏndogyo), p. 3.

4. *"Sudŏngmun"* (On Cultivating Virtue), Su-un's works were originally published in 1880 as the *Tonggyŏng Taejŏn* (Collection of Eastern Scriptures) and the *Yongdam Yusa* (Posthumous Songs of Yongdam). I have used the versions reprinted in the *Tonghak Kyŏng-*

jŏn by Ch'oe Tong-hŭi.

5. *Kyohun'ga* (Song of Instruction)
6. *Yongdamga* (Song of Yongdam)
7. The ability to cure illness was commonly taken as a sign of supernatural power in China and Korea, and has been reported as early as the first century A.D. in China. See Muramatsu Yuji, "Same Themes in Chinese Rebel Ideologies," in A.F. Wright, ed., *The Confucian Persuasion*, p. 244.
8. *Ansimga* (Song of Comfort)
9. *ibid.*
10. Ch'oe Chin-yŏng, *The Rule of the Taewŏngun*, p. 28.
11. Yi Ton-hwa, *Ch'ŏndogyo Ch'anggŏnsa*, p. 19.
12. Yi Ton-hwa, "*Ch'ŏndogyo Kyŏngjŏn Sogŭi*" (Interpretation of the Ch'ŏndogyo Scriptures), *Asea Yŏn'gu*, Vol. 6, No. 2, (Dec. 1963), p. 249.
13. Kim Ku, *Paekbŏm Ilchi* (The Autobiography of Kim Ku), p. 26.
14. O Chi-yŏng, *Tonghaksa* (The History of Tonghak), p. 96.
15. Ch'oe Tong-hŭi, "*Tonghak sasang ŭi chosa yŏn'gu*" (A Survey of Tonghak Thought), *Asea Yŏn'gu*, Vol. 35, (Sept. 1969), p. 119.
16. *Nonhangmun* (A Discussion of Learning)
17. Yi Ton-hwa, "*Kyŏngjŏn Sogŭi*," p. 250.
18. Yi Ton-hwa, "*Kyŏngjŏn Sogŭi*," p. 249.
19. *Nonhangmun*
20. *Tosunsa* (Song of Cultivating the Way)
21. *P'odŏkmun* (On Propagating Virtue) Ch'eng I's more secular formulation is "The way to make the self sincere lies in having firm faith in the Way," *Reflections on Things at Hand*, compiled by Chu Hsi and Lu Tsu-ch'ien, trans. Wing-tsit Chan, p. 37.
22. For a description of quiet sitting in the Neo-Confucian tradition and of the range of situations in which it was employed, see Theodore de Bary, *The Unfolding of Neo-Confucianism*, p. 175.
23. *Sudŏngmun* (On Cultivating Virtue)
24. *Ilsŏngnok*, 1864, 2nd month, 29th day.
25. *ibid.*
26. *ibid.*
27. *ibid.*
28. Kim Kwang-il, "Traditional Concept of Disease in Korea," *Korea Journal*, Vol. 13, No. 1, (1973) p. 43. According to Dr. Kim, the *salp'uri* was still performed in Seoul in the early 1970's.
29. Yi Jŏng-yŏng, "Divination in Korean Shamanistic Thought," *Korea Journal*, Vol. 16, No. 11, (1976), p. 8.
30. *Kyohunmun*
31. *ibid.*

32. This incident was provoked by Bishop Alexander de Govea's condemnation of the Korean memorial service for ancestors (*chesa*). As a result, when his mother died in 1791, Yun Chi-ch'ung, a maternal cousin of Chŏng Yak-yong, refused to prepare the customary ancestor tablets, or hold a memorial service at her funeral. The outraged relatives reported him to the throne, and Yun was arrested and executed.

33. *Tosunsa*

34. *Ansimga*

35. *Mongjung Noso Mundapka* (Talks with Young and Old While Dreaming)

36. *ibid.*

GLOSSARY OF CHINESE CHARACTERS

Tonghak (東學)

Ch'oe Che-u (Su-un) (崔済愚 — 水雲)

sŏnyak (仙藥)

sŏnp'ung togol (仙風道骨)

Ch'oe Si-hyŏng (崔時亨)

chŏpchu (接主)

chohwa (造化)

chŏng (定)

kaebyŏk (開闢)

muwi ihwa (無爲而化)

ch'ŏnju (天主)

sangje (上帝)

ki (氣)

chigi (至氣)

Ch'ŏndogyo (天道教)

kongbu (工夫)

pŏp (法)

su (修)

sŏng (誠)

kyŏng (敬)

changsaeng (長生)

chŏngjwa (靜坐)

ch'ŏn (賤)

Chŏnggamnok (鄭鑑錄)

imjin (壬辰)

imsin (壬申)

kapcha (甲子)

sŏnbun (仙分)

chesa (祭祀)

Yun Chi-ch'ung (尹持忠)

Chŏng Yak-yong (丁若鏞)

the thirteen word incantation

(侍天主造定永世不忘萬事知)

An Ch'ang-ho:
The Man and His Thought

An Pyŏng-uk

Any nation has a historic task to resolve. A great man clearly recognizes what the task is, shows the method of settling it, and displays to the people his courage and confidence that they can solve it.

A national leader is one who exemplifies the national vision, and teaches a method of national dedication to it.

An Ch'ang-ho (Tosan by pen name), whom this writer is going to explain, was one of Korea's most eminent national leaders. The historic task facing Korea at the time when Tosan lived was the recovery of her national sovereignty. The task called for the liberation of the Korean people from 'the aggression of Japanese imperialism, the restoration of their political sovereignty, and the establishment of a foundation for their national independence and prosperity. An devoted his life of 59 years and four months to the achievement of this historic task. Tosan was a patriotic revolutionary who devoted his whole life to the Korean independence movement, a great thinker who possessed the philosophy of national salvation, and a prominent educator who exerted his utmost to improve national education.

In 1876, Japan forced Korea to accept an unequal treaty, thereby taking the first step toward aggression against Korea. In 1910, Japan finally succeeded in occupying Korea by forceful means, annexing her as a colony. For the succeeding

36 years, Japan enforced colonial rule on Korea, perhaps without parallel elsewhere in severity. On August 15, 1945, Korea was liberated from political subjugation to Japan on account of the latter's defeat in World War II.

Korean history during the period from 1876 to 1945 was dotted with tragedies as a Japanese colony and with gallant movements dedicated to the cause of national liberation from the status of a Japanese colony.

It was in 1878 that Tosan was born, two years after Korea was forced into the unequal treaty. It was in 1938 that he died a martyr to patriotism. The agonies he had undergone while serving his prison term became critical, seven years before the liberation. His life coincided with the period when the Korean people were enslaved by Japan and when they struggled hard to regain their independence. In understanding the life, the man, and the thought of a person, it is decisively important to know the nature of the period in which he was born.

What Korean history commanded to achieve at the time An Ch'ang-ho lived was the restoration of national independence. He could hear the historic command, and remained loyal to it until his last moment. He was a statesman and an educator, as well as a prominent thinker. He was both an educational thinker and a political thinker. He was a thinker who possessed the vision of national independence, a program of social reform, and the philosophy of character innovation. The three formed an inseparable relation in him. His system of thought, whose gist comprised his theories on the "four greatest spirits," character innovation, reform of racial characteristics, and accumulation of the "three greatest treasures of national capital," not only gave a national vision to the Korean people at that time, but showed the future direction they must follow. His philosophy has universal validity applicable to any nation.

Having imprisoned him, the Japanese police asked him if he would give up his independence struggle. In a self-possessed manner, Tosan replied:

"No, I cannot. When I eat, I eat for Korean independence. When I sleep, I sleep for Korean independence. This will not change as long as I live. As all the Korean people want their independence, Korean independence will become reality; as world opinion favors Korean independence, it will become reality; and as Heaven orders Korean independence, Korea will surely become independent.

"I don't want to see Japan perish. Rather I want to see Japan become a good nation. Infringing upon Korea, your neighbor, will never prove profitable to you. Japan will profit by having 30 million Koreans as her friendly neighbors and not by annexing 30 million spiteful people into her nation. Therefore, to assert Korean independence is tantamount to desiring peace in East Asia and the well-being of Japan."

It is easy to understand with the above statement how defiant Tosan's national spirit was, and how firm a posture and vision he had as a national leader. We shall first examine his manhood, then his life, and finally his thought.

His Manhood

First of all, Tosan was a man who lived up to sincerity. What he hated most was a lie and what he loved most was truth. His character was based on sincerity and his philosophy on truth.

His ideal was to inculcate all with sincerity, so that the Korean people as a whole could grow into a sincere nation. At the *Taesŏng Hakkyo* (Taesŏng School) he established in P'yŏngyang to educate young boys and girls, the prime precept was "sincerity."

"Keep away from deceit even at the cost of your life. Don't tell a lie even for a joke. Repent bitterly if you lost sincerity even in a dream."

These maxims Tosan demanded his pupils to bear in mind. "Let all of us study sincerity. Let all of our people make a strenuous effort to become a sincere nation. This is the only means of saving our country." Tosan believed this and put it into practice.

"Oh, you, the lie! You are my enemy as you have destroyed my country. I won't tell a lie in all my life as you are our sworn enemy who killed our lords.

"Let us pledge again and again that we will discard all the lies hidden beneath our skin and fill the gap with sincerity.

"State affairs are sacred, and it is not right to attend to sacred affairs by profane means.

"Let each individual harbor sincerity and honesty in his heart."

Thus Tosan appealed to the whole nation. This was his conviction. With devotion to sincerity, he lived a life dedicated to truth.

Second, Tosan was a man of love. His desire for the nation was to see all the people study how to love—how to love each other, their country, their compatriots, and their jobs. He once wrote on the theme of "A Sentient Society and a Merciless Society." Defining Korean society as merciless, he appealed to his people to devote all their efforts to constructing a sentient society.

"Let all of us, men and women, study love. Let all of our 20 million Koreans study love and become a people who love each other.

"Why is our society so cold and why does it lack warmth? We should create a society in which all smile with tenderness.

"Let us follow the principle of non-resistance in dealing with our compatriots, though it may sound feeble. If our compatriot beats us, let us be beaten. If he abuses us, let us be abused. Let us not pay evil with evil among ourselves, but let love guide us.

"If we love each other, we shall survive; if we fight each other, we shall perish.

"Is there anything happier than to have comrades whom one can trust entirely?"

His ardent desire for the nation was to convert a world of strife into a world of mutual love, a merciless society into a sentient society, and a society of distrust into a society of fidelity. Tosan emphasized *chŏngŭi tonsu*, which is one of pivotal points in his philosophy.

Chŏngŭi means mutual love and *tonsu* cultivation with depth, thus, the phrase means cultivation of the spirit to love each other more firmly. He believed that the Korean people should cultivate the virtue of *chŏngŭi tonsu* so that they would create a harmonious and sentient society in their land. In his late years, he built a small retreat on Mount Taebo about 30 *ri* away from P'yŏngyang, naming it *Songt'ae Sanjang* (Pine Moss Mountain Villa). He also erected a gate at the entrance to his villa, planning to put a signboard on the gate with the letters—SMILE, meaning that all who entered the gate were asked to smile.

He believed that a smile movement should be launched throughout the country with the aid of posters to be put up in places which people frequented, and of statues and paintings showing a smiling face. How beautiful it is to receive others with a smiling countenance, he thought, for a clear smile symbolizes happiness and expresses harmony.

He earnestly wanted to see all the Korean people form the habit of smiling, a smile always lingering in their eyes and mouths. He liked the English word "smile" very much. A smile of an infant, a smile of an old man, a smile of a young man—all these attracted his great admiration. A new image of the nation Tosan envisioned was that all the people smiled at each other with warmth. In him we can find religious devotion to love and peace.

Third, Tosan was a serious man devoted to self-control and moral training. He was serious in thinking, speaking, and conduct. He hated "casually," "an indifferent attitude," and "do as one pleases." "A gentleman behaves himself," as taught in the Chinese classics. Tosan was a man who always behaved himself.

He constantly reflected on himself and submitted himself to self-training in morality, while advancing toward the summit of perfect personality. In receiving others, he always held himself upright, never letting himself lose his posture. He always sat straight when he took a seat. While walking, his gait was always upright. Even when he was alone, he behaved with prudence. He never deviated from the right path in both speech and deed. He never acted against etiquette. He observed modesty and order in whatever deed.

Tosan was firmly determined to become a great man himself first, and, through constant efforts and moral training, he could finally elevated himself to the height of a great personality whom all the people admire.

People are in the habit of lamenting the lack of great leaders in Korea. "Why is it that we have no great men?" they used to ask. Tosan once made the reply:

"That we lack great men is ascribable to our lack of persons who are determined to become great men and make an effort to that end. Why are the people who lament for the lack of great men not making an effort to become great men themselves?

"It is rather easy to crush a horde of cavalry, but it is difficult to correct one's bad habit. So we must make an effort for life," he taught.

As a result of his constant self-control and moral training and his effort to become a great man, Tosan eventually became one of Korea's greatest leaders.

It was only a few years that he could spend with his wife because of his busy activity in the independence movement. He lived almost a bachelor's life. However, he left no scandal involving women. As clean as he was in pecuniary matters, so puritanically ascetic a life did he lead. His conscience did not permit him to love or enter an intimate relation with any woman other than his wife. He was a man who almost attained the state of a sage.

Tosan was also an example of a democratic leader. Though

he was a man of conviction, he was not a man of bigotry. He never forced others to accept his view.

"If I have one rightness, others may have one rightness. If we refrain from hating others because they have a view different from ours, and from finding a vent for our intolerance, harmony will reign over our society.

"Since ancient times our people have had no tolerance to accept views different from theirs, but asserted only their view to be right, so that severe partisan strife ensued. It is as likely that I make a mistake as that others may do right. Having found that others had a view different from theirs, our ancestors branded them as villains who violated the teachings of the sages and massacred all of their clansmen, unleashing purges of scholars and partisan feuding. This evil practice still persists today. Therefore, we must recognize and hold in high esteem the freedom of thought and the press. It should be the basic nature of a civilized people that they maintain friendly relations with and respect for others, even though they have different views.

"Both an angular stone and a round stone can find their usefulness. We should not try to find fault with others for the reason that they have a different character." In these sayings we can find Tosan's democratic way of thinking and personality.

He devoted his 60 years of life to national salvation. He was so heavily engrossed in the independence struggle that he could not manage to buy a skirt for his wife or a pencil for his children. Without considering his own happiness or the well-being of his family, he busied himself with the independence movement. He had no defect for which we can ever blame him, either in his private or public life.

Being an example of a great leader, he had an excellent personality. He will remain the source of our everlasting admiration as the beacon torch of our people, and as a teacher of all.

His Life

An Ch'ang-ho was born the second son in a farming family on Torong ait along the downstream River Taedong on November 9, 1978. Tosan was his pen name. The ordeals during his imprisonment caused him to die a martyr to the cause of national survival at the present Seoul National University Hospital on March 10, 1938. He was 61.

The Sino-Japanese War (1894-1895) broke out when he was 16 years of age. Witnessing a fight between Chinese and Japanese troops in P'yŏngyang, the boy asked the question: "Why are they fighting not elsewhere but in Korea?" He reached the conclusion:

"The alien forces are fighting on our soil at will because we are powerless. Korea is powerless and exists only in name! Now let us build up our strength. First of all we must strengthen ourselves."

First and foremost Tosan's philosophy demanded the reinforcement of national power. How can we build up our strength? This was his lifelong task. The conclusion he reached was to build up strength through character innovation and renovate our national character through unity and training. Born as a child of this realization was *Hŭngsadan*, which was aimed at building up our true national might.

In order to strengthen his own ability, Tosan came to Seoul at the age of 17 and entered *Kuse Hakdang*, where he learned the Christian doctrine and was converted to Christianity. Korea, being so powerless, started to become the target of political aggression and economic domination by world powers at that time. Japan, Russia, and China, vied with each other in seeking an opportunity to engulf Korea. Faced with the extreme national crisis, the Korean people were awakened to the need of self-realization and modernization, emphasizing the strengthening of their power. Taking the van in the enlightenment movement was the *Tongnip Hyŏphoe* (Independence Association) led by Sŏ Chae-p'il (Philip Jaison).

So, who returned home from the United States where he exiled himself after the failure of the *Kapsin* Political Upheaval in 1884, in which he had taken part with Kim Ok-kyun and Pak Yŏng-ho, founded the newspaper *Tongnip Sinmun* (The Independent) in April 1896, and established the *Tongnip Hyŏphoe* in July the same year. Centering around the association, a modernization movement was launched with the aim of opposing the tributary attitude toward Ch'ing China, promoting the cause of national autonomy, awakening the people, and reforming the domestic administration. As a result, a public lecture meeting was held for the first time in our country and the word "freedom" came in vogue.

The establishment of the Independence Association was a historic event which heralded the advent of the modern age for the Korean people, and it was in 1897, the year after the association was created, that Tosan was admitted into its membership at the age of 20. The association was later expanded into *Manmin Kongdong-hoe* (Association of Universal Fraternity). In 1897, the 20-year-old man convened a meeting designed to organize a local chapter of the association in P'yŏngyang.

Addressing an audience of hundreds of ranking officials, including P'yŏngan Governor Cho Min-hŭi, at the Kwoejae-jong Pavilion in the city, the young man with close-cropped head spoke with great eloquence. That was his famous speech known as the Kwoejae-jong speech, which made him renowned in the whole of P'yŏngan Province. Listening to him, all were rejoiced firmly believing that a great leader had emerged.

Returning to his native village, he founded *Chŏmjin Hakkyo* (School of Gradual Progress). He devoted all his zeal and sincerity to education. His great endowment started to manifest itself at that time.

Though at the primary level, the school was the first private and coeducational institute established by a Korean. The name of the school, "*Chŏmjin*," has special meaning, for it signifies constant forward progress. Therefore, the school was the first expression of Tosan's motto: "Let us build up our national power."

Pledging that he would become an exemplary patriot, Tosan continued the study how to make new progress every day throughout his 60 years of life. Tosan, who steadily progressed toward the height of sincere personality, could finally bring himself up into a great national leader. His attitude of making steady progress in achieving anything must be regarded as a sound and sure method of attaining success.

It was in 1902, when he turned 25, that Tosan arrived at San Francisco with his newly-wed wife. While earning his livelihood by working as a hired man with an American family, he entered an American institute to learn English. However, the misery Korean immigrants were suffering in the United States did not permit him to devote himself solely to study. He resolutely suspended his schooling in order to organize and train Korean immigrants. One day on a San Francisco street, Tosan witnessed a scene—two Koreans were fighting, each grabbing the other's topknot, while a group of Americans watched them with amusement. Tosan instantly forced the two apart and asked why they were quarreling. He found out that the two, both ginseng retailers, each claimed that the other had violated their previously agreed sales area.

Witnessing the scene of two Koreans fighting each other was a turning point, and Tosan was resolved that he would exert his utmost to elevate Korean immigrants in the United States to the due level of civilized people. Pledging that he would do his best to improve the living of Koreans resident in America, Tosan started personal visits to their homes at the rate of 10 households a day, sweeping their gardens, cleaning their toilets, polishing the window panes, wiping the floor, hanging up curtains, and planting flowers in their gardens. In this manner, he taught them sanitation, orderliness, and beautification of their environments. Though they first mistook him for an insane man, they were finally deeply impressed by his sincerity and lofty ideals, and readily submitted themselves to his leadership.

So wonderful was his power of influence. Soon the Koreans formed the habit of shaving often, and changed their skirts and dresses frequently, so as not to show stains on the collars. They also learned to speak in a low voice, not to cause annoyance to others, and made an effort not to emit disgusting odors. In this way a complete change occurred in their life. The effort made by Tosan finally led them to a spiritual revolution in their daily life.

He especially emphasized to Korean immigrants in the United States the need to cultivate the virtue of following truth, cooperation, and law-abiding spirit. He established a fraternity society and a work camp for Koreans. By founding *Tongnip Hyŏphoe* and the *Tongnip Sinmun* newspaper, he exerted himself in organizing and leading the Koreans. As a result, their life was improved and their economy become more prosperous day by day.

He was in the habit of admonishing Koreans picking oranges in an American orchard:

"To pick even one orange with sincerity in an American orchard will make a contribution to our country."

Teaching that when one picks even an orange, one should attend to it as if it were his own business, Tosan inspired them greatly with an earnest attitude of life. His image as he exerted his utmost to provide adequate leadership for Koreans in California reminds us of young Gandhi as he led the movement of non-violence and truth-finding for Indian settlers in South Africa. It is not without reason that Tosan was called a Gandhi of Korea.

In 1906, when Tosan turned 29 years of age, he returned home after four years of stay in the United States to take part in a national salvation movement, after Japan won the war against Russia (1904-1905) and forced Korea to sign a protectorate treaty in 1905. His imposing appearance, his grandiloquence, his ardent personality, his resolute conviction, and his careful ability at organization fascinated people in Korea. He soon became the pivotal leader in national movements.

Four months before his fatherland was finally annexed by Japan in 1910, Tosan again left for the United States. During the three-year period before his second departure for America, he took a very active part in all sorts of movements, freely displaying his ability in all directions. While launching a national salvation movement by organizing *Sinmin-hoe,* a secret political association of the most celebrated patriotic leaders, he enlightened the people with his eloquent lectures, touring every nook and cranny of the country. He also founded *Taesŏng Hakkyo* in P'yŏngyang, organized *Ch'ŏngnyŏn Haguhoe* (Young Students Association), and set up the *T'aegŭk* Publishing Company and a ceramics company, thereby making an effort not only for education but for industrial development.

Although the period of his activity was relatively short, the seeds of patriotism and national spirit he had sown achieved continuous growth, coming into bloom in the form of the March 1 movement ten years later. Especially Tosan emphasized guidance of the populace through education, mass enlightenment, and the development of national capital through expanding industries. Concrete expressions of the realization were Taesŏng School, the Young Students Association, and the ceramics company in Masan. The name Taesŏng most eloquently shows his characteristics. Taesŏng, great accomplishment, is suggestive of his ambition to build up the leading force for independence by producing the type of men who could achieve greatness by a method gradual progress.

Admiring his personality and thought, a large number of ambitious young men came to his school, where they received profound influence and teaching from him. Although Taesŏng School was ordered to close after only two years of existence, on account of the annexation, it has a significant historic importance as a hotbed of nationalism and spirit of independence, due to its teaching that a man should not tell a lie even at the cost of his life and its attempt to cultivate a sound and patriotic personality.

Tosan went into exile in the spring of 1910 when the nation was about to suffer the tragedy of deprivation of its sovereignty. He planned to establish a bastion of the independence struggle in Manchuria, but the plan met frustration on account of lack of funds. He arrived in the United States in 1911 by way of Siberia, Europe, and the Atlantic. Tosan planned to form *Taehan Kungmin-hoe* (Korean People's Association) in California in 1912, with branches in Hawaii, Siberia, and Manchuria, for the purpose of uniting Koreans abroad into a single organization so that they would be able to serve as the basis for future independence movements. However, provincial factionalism and the existing political situation prevented the plan from materialization. Be that as it may, the plan reflected a grand vision worthy of Tosan.

One of the most noteworthy achievements of Tosan was the creation of *Hŭngsadan* in 1913. An organization dedicated to the undertaking of ground-leveling work for independence movements, *Hŭngsadan* was a movement designed to help the nation build up its ability for independence, as well as a crystallization of Tosan's thought. It was a movement dedicated to the training of leaders for national independence. Tosan's guiding principle was to do all the work but return the merits to others. Although *Hŭngsadan* was his brain child, he did not brandish his name in its organization. He was never a demagogue who was greedy for honor and vanity.

That *Hŭngsadan* was in existence for more than 50 years in spite of Japanese suppression and persecution is truly a rare success in a land like Korea, which often witnesses severe partisan strife and disunity. This success can be attributed to Tosan's extraordinarily prudent planning when he laid out its basic ideology and organization principles.

Immediately after the outbreak of the March 1, 1919, independence movement in Korea, Tosan went to Shanghai.

The diary recording his activity under the provisional Korean government in exile in Shanghai describes his impressive dedication to the cause of national affairs, while exerting his whole sincerity and zeal in order to bring success to the independence movement. He served the provisional government as Director-general of Internal Affairs and Deputy Prime Minster in succession. Resigning from the government position, he asserted the need for formation of a National Representative Assembly, but the plan was frustrated on account of Communist tactics.

In 1932 when Tosan was 55 years old, the incident involving patriot Yun Bong-gil broke out at Hong-gu Park in Shanghai. Tosan was arrested by Japanese police and imprisoned at Taejŏn, where he served four years. After his release from prison, he toured all parts of the country, but interference by Japanese police deprived him of the freedom of speech. He confined himself to Songt'ae villa on Mount Taebo near his native village, after designing the retreat himself.

One month before the outbreak of the Sino-Japanese War (1937-1945), Japanese police arrested all Korean nationalist leaders. Tosan was again imprisoned, together with his comrades who held membership in *Suyang Tongji-hoe,* a Korean branch of *Hŭngsadan.* He was released on bail on account of stomach and liver disorders. While receiving medical treatment at the present Seoul National University Hospital, he died. In 1938 the great national leader ended his 59 years and four months of life. His achievements as a patriot, a revolutionary, and a moralist will shine forever.

His Thought for Statecraft

One of the writings he bequeathed is "To My Dear Comrades." This is an open letter he sent to the comrades of *Hŭngsadan* in America, Mexico, and Hawaii on July 7, 1921. The letter contains the nucleus of his thought. Let us examine its gist. The letter, in short, pointed out that the Koreans had not yet built up enough strength for the recovery of their sovereignty, emphasized that they must develop such strength, and discussed what should be the sources of the strength and how they could build it up. The following is what Tosan actually said to his comrades. A gist of his nationalist thought, it reminds us of Fichte's "Rede an die deutsche Nation."

"What I earnestly want to ask you is this: 'Build up your strength. Build up your strength.'"

In other words, Tosan believed that the Korean people had the national task of restoring their independence, and that the task could be achieved only when they built up the strength to attain it.

"What we can trust is nothing but our own strength. Independence originally means to acquire one's own strength and rely on it. On the contrary, to trust others' strength and live by relying on it constitutes enslavement. If you profess dedication to the cause of our independence but, in fact, rely on the development of relations among other countries, it would become contradictory to our independence movement."

As a man cannot run more than his strength permits him, a race cannot attain development more than its ability permits. Greater projects require greater strength, and smaller ones smaller strength. With smaller strength one cannot achieve a great work. If his strength is greater, he can do greater work, and if it is smaller, he cannot but do smaller work. Only if one has strength, can one survive; if not, one perishes. This is the rigorous law of nature and history. There is no luck or miracles in this world. Strength determines all. Therefore, we must believe in our own strength and build it up. In this way, Tosan emphasized the philosophy of strength.

"Pears grow on a pear tree, and wild pears on a wild pear tree. The fruit of independence will grow on a race which is entitled to independence, and the fruit of national ruin will grow on a race which is destined to enslavement. Success in small or large matters is a fruit of one's strength. It is the heavenly way and principle that if one has but small strength, one will make small success; if one has great strength, one can make great success; if one has no strength, one will die, and if one has strength, one will survive. No matter how repeatedly I think it over, I reach nothing but the conclusion that what we can rely on for our independence is but our own strength. Therefore, members of our *Hŭngsadan* are those from the start who believe in their own strength and lament our insufficient strength."

After emphasizing the necessity of strength and its expansion, the letter discussed what kind of strength we must build up. He first emphasized the strength of unity and moral strength. Then he mentioned the strength of knowledge, pecuniary strength, and the strength of personality. To explain him in another way, he stressed the capital of trust, the capital of knowledge, and pecuniary capital. Of savings he emphasized "alliance savings."

In order for an individual to make his living in society, he needs capital such as health, knowledge, and skill. In order for a race to establish an independent country, it needs various kinds of strength and capital.

"We all know what great strength we shall be able to display when we unite our pecuniary strength, our strength of knowledge, and our strength of solidarity, and when we further elevate the capacity of persons who consider themselves humanitarians and the strength of personality of those who belong to the middle and upper classes. Let us deposit in alliance our capital of fidelity by not telling a lie and by living up to sincerity. Let us deposit in alliance the capital of knowledge by cultivating the ability of engaging in one profession after learning one or more aspects of knowledge and technique. Let each of our households have a deposit of at least 1,000 *wŏn*, saving more than one-fifth of its income."

At present everybody emphasizes the need of forming national capital in order to accelerate modernization and economic growth of a developing country. One of Tosan's most salient features can be found in his emphasis, in addition to pecuniary capital, on the capital of fidelity and knowledge. This is also the reason why he is regarded as a forerunner in forming the ideology of modernization.

Tosan explained that factors conducive to expanding our national strength are the cultivation of sound personality and sacred unity of those who possess such personality. He observed that Korea confronted three bankruptcies at that time: The first economic bankruptcy, the second the bankruptcy of knowledge, and the third moral bankruptcy. What would be the means of saving the nation from these bankruptcies? Who would be able to accomplish the job? And what were the causes of the bankruptcies? According to Tosan, the nation was faced with the danger of these bankruptcies on account of its lack of sufficient strength.

Therefore, it was most important to reinforce national strength. What is national strength? According to him, national strength, which also steers the destiny of the nation, is the sum total of all individuals' strength of virtue, knowledge, and physical might. Political and economic power and military might are found in organization, and a result of all individuals' strength. Therefore, in order to build up the nation's basic ability, the only means to resort to is to nurture and unite individual strength.

National strength springs from individual strength and from its organization on a nationwide scale. For this reason, Tosan emphasized training in character building and unity above anything else.

The way to patriotism for each individual is to cultivate in him a sound personality. When each individual transforms himself into a sound personality, our nation as a whole will become stronger. Self-reform will bring about national reform, and character innovation will results in national innovation.

Herein originates Tosan's belief that "moral self-training equals independence." Before fighting, one has to strengthen one's fighting ability. He again explained:

"Since the national humiliation of 1910, we have always repeated the slogan 'Let's fight,' but we have neglected the task of building up our strength to fight. So we always shouted to fight without actually engaging in fighting.

"The only means of making our nation sound is to cultivate in ourselves a sound personality.

"Do you love your country? If so, you should first transform yourself into a sound personality. If you feel sympathy with the ailing populace, you should become a doctor. Unable to become a doctor, you should first cure your own ailment and become a healthy man.

"I call man a self-reforming animal.

"If you love Korea as I do, let us reform Korea in cooperation. We must reform her education and religion, her agriculture and industry, and her customs and conventions. We must also reform her food, clothing, and housing, her cities and rural communities, her rivers and mountains."

He stressed national reform through individual self-reform, and national revival through personal self-revival. He also asserted that moral self-training would bring about national independence, and that to achieve individual transformation into a sound personality was the means of loving one's country. Self-revival is a task assigned to each individual. The task cannot be entrusted to others. There is no other means for each individual than to reform himself all alone. This is the surest way and a shortcut to national reform, he taught.

Tosan observed that man is a self-reforming animal.

He taught: Reform yourself first, starting with the easiest thing, the nearest thing. Reform yourself gradually, without pause, and with sincerity. Reform yourselves in groups, for that gives you courage and encouragement. Through your self-reform, become a sound personality. This constituted his philosophy and principle of reform.

"To reform the Korean nation as a whole, we must start

from individual reform. Individual reform requires each of us to reform himself, which we cannot ask others to fulfill.

"All great tasks can be achieved when one starts with smallest things. The most difficult tasks can be resolved when one starts with the easiest thing."

His national reform movement called for individual renovation and reform as a start. *Hŭngsadan* was an organization created for just that purpose. As its name suggests, it was an organization aimed at producing gentlemen, namely, leaders for nationalist movements. The gentleman Tosan envisioned is a man who possesses sound personality, who can provide great leadership for society. He taught that a sound personality must contain three elements:

First, a sound moral character that can make for others to follow in thought, speech, and deed. A sound character must be based on virtue. Necessary for the cultivation of virtue, according to Tosan, are devotion to substantiality, practice, loyalty, and bravery, which we may call his four great qualities.

Second, acquisition of more than one professional skill or productive ability. This Tosan emphasized with particular stress. According to him, our first duty is to earn our livelihood by ourselves, without relying on our parents or relatives. This requires our own ability, namely, professional knowledge or productive skill. Our people, as Tosan observed, have regarded technicians and productive skill as base, while cherishing idling without work. No national prosperity and wealth can be expected from such evil customs of shunning labor. He stressed one skill to each and work to all. "Individuals can perform their duty to Heaven and mankind by working for their nation." This constitutes the nucleus of Tosan's view of life.

Third, a strong body as a prerequisite for a sound character. He emphasized "three great educations"—moral education, physical education, and intellectual education. To him, moral education is more important than intellectual education. Intelligence without virtue is apt to become a source of vice, while intelligence without physical health may give rise to complaints.

He saw that national independence and prosperity could not be expected without reform of the national character and strengthening of the people's might. With sharp judgment, he analyzed the shortcomings of our national character. According to him, the first and foremost factor which prompted the decline of our nation was deceit, which he considered the source of all vices.

He urged that deceit be eliminated in our thought and deed. As long as we fail in this task, national prosperity and wealth cannot be attained. When we rid ourselves of lies, the day will come liberating us from the tragedy of decline. When we all become sincere, the day will come promising us a happy life.

"Let us base the great and sacred task we are going to achieve not on the foundation of void and deceit but on that of truth and justice."

This was Tosan's philosophy of enterprise. The second defect of our national character, according to him, was fondness for empty theory and futile argument, devoid of practice and actual deed. Tosan went to such an extreme as to assert that the 500-year history of the Yi dynasty was a history of empty theories. Doctrinarianism and futile arguments are liable to give birth to slander, defamation, and intrigue. According to him, our mouths destroyed us. In argument, one is apt to blame others without committing himself to any responsibility. An evil habit is to reproach others while trying to dodge any responsibility.

Tosan also distinguishes the host's spirit and the guest's spirit. The former is readiness to take all responsibility, not only for what turns out good but for what turns out bad. The guest's spirit is an attitude of a bystander who is irresponsible, thinking that he has nothing to do with anything.

"I ask you, how many are there among Koreans who act as

hosts? Those who have the sense of responsibility for their nation are hosts and those who do not feel any responsibility are guests. A true host has no criticism to make and no difficulty to encounter. He is only filled with thought of the responsibility for how he can best serve his society. . . . The basic problem of any society lies in how many hosts it can have.

"We see many reproach others for their failure to join forces, for their forming factions, and for their internal strife. But if these very persons who make the reproach are united themselves, we can have a force of several millions."

Emphasizing a strong host's spirit and sense of responsibility, Tosan pointed out that the indifferent guest's spirit is a product of empty theory and futile argument. Distrust and disruption leading to factional strife and flunkeyism originate in deceit, doctrinarianism and futile argument, and inertia. Realizing that deceit and futile argument were the most serious defects of our national character, Tosan was resolved to eliminate these evils in his own mind and life.

As mentioned above, Tosan upheld his "four greatest qualities" as a means of achieving individual reform—a prerequisite for national reform.

The first one is devotion to substantiality, to something that is true, concrete, fruitful, and devoid of falsehood. In other words, it meant to put truth into practice. Gandhi urged *satyagraha*, grasp of truth. Tosan's devotion to substantiality is similar to Gandhi's teaching. Its aim was exertion for truth and self-training to become a sincere man.

The second called for practice with diligence. In other words, it urged actual practice by rejecting empty theories and futile argument. Tosan believed that one deed is more persuasive and effective than one hundred written articles. His philosophy was based on deed and practice, urging all the people to act. He himself showed an example of true patriotism, leadership, truth, and love through his own actions. That he pushed ahead with his plan to construct a utopian community throughout his life was an expression of his desire to show an example in this respect. He taught harmony between learning and practice.

The third was loyalty and righteousness. Man should always be righteous, trustworthy, and loyal. He should exert sincerity and maintain confidence from others once he has started an undertaking, even though he foresees it would bring him a drawback. Betrayal and mistrust were what Tosan hated most. He taught exertion for an enterprise and fidelity to people.

The fourth is bravery. Man must be courageous if he is ever to succeed in any undertaking. Hesitation and cowardice are apt to lead one to evil. If one can strictly distinguish right and wrong, and sides with righteousness, one always needs bravery.

Tosan believed that all should live up to the spirit of devotion to substantiality, practice with diligence, loyalty and fidelity, and bravery, and that this would lead one to patriotism and national prosperity. Together with character building, Tosan also urged training for unity. The Korean people lacked opportunities for a group life, they needed self-training for unity. They needed to learn how to unite themselves. Tosan was fond of using the phrase "sacred unity," by which he meant everlasting and inviolable unity. Comrades who share the same beliefs ideals must establish sacred unity. What is the basic purpose of cultivating a sound personality, learning the method of deepening mutual love in a gradual and steady process, and promoting firm unity? It is nothing but to lay the foundation for the nation's prosperity in the future. It aims at devoting and even sacrificing ourselves for the country and regaining our national sovereignty on the basis of nationwide solidarity. Tosan once used the phrase, "loyal men and women who live up to the ideal of devotion to substantiality and practice with diligence." The type of man *Hŭngsadan* aspired to produce was a leader who, being loyal and trustworthy, regards devotion to substantiality and practice as more precious than his own life itself.

The purport of *Hŭngsadan* was officially proclaimed as: ". . . to establish the foundation for our nation's future prosperity by uniting loyal men and women who are resolved to devote themselves to substantiality and practice with diligence, by helping them develop mutual love in a steady process of self-training, by providing them with moral education, physical education, and intellectual education so that they can cultivate sound personality in themselves through training themselves in alliance, and by creating a sacred organization."

This succinct but meaningful expression contains Tosan's most profound philosophy. The expression is also a crystallization of his tears, blood, and sweat. His 60 years of life which he lived with sincerity and zeal, as well as his personality and philosophy, are well expressed in this declaration.

To sum up, Tosan's unshakable conviction was: The nation's prosperity and happiness cannot be expected without individual moral reform and national reform, in which all should put into practice the ideal of devotion to substantiality in a steady process, materialize character innovation, learn the method of uniting themselves with mutual love, and become a people who are sincere, diligent, and brave. Tosan lived in order to put this ideal into practice. The great human image, the noble life, and the immortal achievements he left behind will remain glorious in our history as an everlasting example for our nation's statecraft and statesmanship.

Social Philosophy
of Tongnip Hyŏphoe

SHIN YONG-HA

Social Basis

The social philosophy of *Tongnip Hyŏphoe* (The Independence Association, hereinafter to be referred to in abbreviation as TH) represents a system of social awareness created to preserve the independence of the nation through spontaneous strengthening of the power of the Korean people toward the end of 19th century when the great powers were out to colonize Korea in search of mining, railroad, forestry and fishery interests.

The prevailing concept of the philosophy of the TH seems in need of modification in some respects.

First, the philosophical lineage of the TH can hardly be traced back to the heritage of Western bourgeois thought. Two streams of thought are noticeable; one stems from the influence of Western bourgeois thought as introduced by Sŏ Chae-p'il and Yun Ch'i-ho; the other is the stream of indigenous thought of reform Confucianist tradition as represented by Namgung Ŏk, Chŏng Kyo, Chang Chi-yŏn and Pak Ŭn-sik. These two streams combine to form the social philosophy of the TH. Yi Sang-jae played a most important role in amalgamating the two streams during the existence of the TH and later came under the influence of Christianity in prison following the dissolution of the TH.

247

The first stream was predominant on account of its sophisticated theory and the level perception of its advocates; mainly by means of the *Tongnip Sinmun* (The Independent) they criticized the premodern social institutions and awareness, and propagated nationalistic and bourgeois ideas.

The second stream accounted for the majority opinion which was held by the middle stratum of the TH membership. But the first stream was largely reinforced by the second stream. The second stream reflected the growth of national philosophy and helped in selective introduction of bourgeois thought, thus constituting the backbone of the social philosophy of the TH. The association began publishing *Hwangsŏng Sinmun* as its organ.

Those who regarded *The Independent* as the only organ of the TH failed to notice the second stream. Thus, the TH had two more organs in the *Tongnip Sinmun* and *Hwangsŏng Sinmun* for the duration of its existence. Secondly, the social philosophy of the TH mirrored the socio-economic state of Korea at the time, rather than the influence of foreign ideas. Characteristics of the three socio-economic changes were:

1. Rise of bourgeoisie—Reorganization of market and the coming into being of various stores and modern joint-stock companies gave rise to a bourgeoisie.
2. Growth of farmer class—The *Tonghak* rebellion and its 12-article program evidenced the growth of the farming populace.
3. Emergence of miners and longshoremen—Mining industry and opening of ports for foreign trade created a class of wage earners.
4. Emancipation of "untouchables"—The Reform of 1894 recognized previous outcasts such as butchers and slaves.
5. Formation of a new intellectual class—Introduction and expansion of modern school system contributed to the rise and growth of a new educated class.

In the face of the mounting threat of aggression by big powers the emerging bourgeoisie, farming and wage earning classes and liberated outcasts were all gripped by crisis feelings and concerned about the future of the country.

The new intellectual class could be divided into several categories, of which the TH members represented the most progressive wing, comprising the two streams as mentioned above.

The social philosophy of the TH was the philosophy of this emerging social force, deriving its inspiration from the native *Silhak* (Practical Learning) school and the Western bourgeois thought.

The social philosophy of the TH has three aspects that should be looked into from three angles. They are the idea of independence, the idea of civil liberty, and the idea of self-help reforms. These components could be likened to the three sides of a triangle. Formerly, the philosophy of the TH was identified with the Western bourgeois philosophy of civil rights, but this was an overestimation of Western influence on the thought of the TH. The social structure and the tasks of 19th century Korea were different from the nature and goal of 18th century Western bourgeois society.

Idea of Independence

Concept of Sovereignty

The thought of the TH is based on the theory of independence and sovereignty. The basic principles of the TH were declared to be "the consolidation of the foundation of independence and strengthening of sovereignty." It was a reaction against a conservative segment of the bureaucracy which tended to rely upon a certain power for national survival.

The country was in a crisis, according to their belief. Since sovereignty is an essential quality of nationhood, their main interest was in maintaining the nation's integrity under the pressure of foreign powers.

By *Chajujipkwŏn* (sovereignty) they meant no dependence upon foreign powers, and the spontaneous spreading of justice throughout the country. This is to exercise sovereignty over the nation through independence.

In the midst of rivalries among colonial powers, the country could not rely upon one big power to prevent the inroad of others. We could count on no one except our own countrymen, and the surest way to retain independence and sovereignty was not to depend upon any outside powers.

The TH thought that upholding civil rights was necessary for independence. A nation is made up of individuals; therefore, an independent and strong nation must have independent and strong individuals whose rights should be respected and promoted. This is how the concept of independence espoused by the TH led to the idea of civil liberties.

The conservative faction maintained that establishment of royal prerogatives should necessarily involve infringement upon civil rights; on the other hand, the TH held that respect for civil rights was the basis of national strength and reinforced the power of the king.

On May 8,1898, the TH sought to dissuade the conservative faction from the old line of thinking by organizing a public debate on the theme that higher status of the people results in stronger royalty and more prosperous nationhood. In a petition to King Kojong on Oct. 25, 1898, the TH made a strongly-worded and lucid criticism of the old-guard prejudice against civil rights.

All this implies that the old guard adhered to authoritarian monarchy, while the TH came out in support of constitutional monarchy.

It was the conviction of the TH that independence is hard to maintain under authoritarian monarchy, but that it could be better maintained under constitutional monarchy based on popular consensus born of respect for civil rights. The crowning of King Kojong as Emperor was merely a symbolic change meant for external independence.

Accordingly, the assertion that the TH did not embrace the old-line group was not true. Rather, constitutional monarchy was thought to be the way to preserve independence, bringing the conservative faction into the same fold.

The TH felt the need for greater sense of dignity and patriotism among the people for the sake of national independence. A prolonged period of suppression by the Yi government misled the people to think that loss of independence was not so much loss of the nation as demise of the Yi dynasty. Under the circumstances, the TH emphasized the fact that the crisis involved not only a dynasty but the entire nation. This is why the TH concentrated on advocating love of the nation.

The TH contended that solid patriotism is generated by the participation of the people in government and enlarged civil rights. The ordinary people can love the nation only when they consider the country their own. This shows the democratic nature of the patriotism the TH advocated. The TH believed patriotism was inherent in man's nature and formed the primary spiritual defense of independence.

Protection of Economic Interests

Natural extension of the spirit of independence held up by the TH was in opposition to the concession of economic interests to foreign powers. It insisted on recovering interests already yielded to foreigners.

Independence must be backed by economic independence, and could only be preserved by the development of one's own national resources and industries. The TH likened government and finance to the body and blood vessels which have to be protected and nurtured for oneself.

Conceding resources, territory or other economic interests to foreign powers, therefore, is tantamount to yielding independence. The TH would neither rely on foreign powers nor exclude them; friendly relations with them should be sought, but economic interests should not be given away.

"If there was gold, silver and coal deposits within the country, we should explore them, not foreigners enrich themselves by exploiting these resources, thereby impoverishing the population. Conceding railroad, electric and mining rights to foreigners was like selling the country out to them," the TH said, "The land of Korea is the great inheritance from our past kings and the abode of 12 million people; giving up an inch of it to foreigners is an act betraying the kings and millions of compatriots."

The TH considered the already conceded interests as irrecoverable by compulsion, but demanded that they be restored through diplomatic negotiation or purchase.

Opposition to foreign concessions was the main target of the TH in 1898, and was instrumental in discouraging big powers from rending additional interests away from Korea.

Neutral Diplomacy

First, in order to gain time for achieving self-help after having checked the immediate exploitation of economic interests by foreigners, the TH viewed maintenance of the then prevailing balance of power as necessary. It thought independence could be consolidated for the duration of such balance of power.

Secondly, the TH called for fair and self-reliant diplomacy for the retention of the balance of power. The secret diplomacy of conceding interests to foreign powers that had been conducted by the conservative faction was denounced for its disservice to the nation, intensifying bickerings among big powers and foreign intervention in the internal affairs of Korea.

Thirdly, the TH maintained that neutral diplomacy should be practiced, without favor or prejudice to any country. For this, two reasons were given. Independent and neutral diplomacy would keep foreign governments from attempting intervention and changes in the Korean government; moreover, partial diplomacy was likely to touch off a Russo-Japanese war, bringing hostilities and destruction to the Korean peninsula.

Fourth, the TH was of the opinion that Korea's diplomacy, most befitting a weak country caught between big powers, should not embitter or provoke these powers. Unfavorable treaties ought not to be concluded, and the nation's economic and military prowess had to be strengthened to recover rights yielded through such treaties already entered into.

The TH aimed at promoting independence and neutral diplomacy to maintain balance of power among big nations and to increase internal strength in the midst of intense conflicts, suspicions and aggressive designs. From this arises the idea of enlightened self-help.

Enlightened Self-help

The TH thought independence at that time was only nominal, and we lacked the internal strength and foundation to sustain it. "Independence in name will not be complete independence if it does not become independence in deed." Being based on the prevailing balance of power, independence might be lost whenever the balance tips. Therefore, the importance of self-reliance was brought to the fore, so that independence could be preserved even when the balance of power collapses.

The TH contended that such self-help (or reliance) must be enlightened. In this respect the philosophy of the TH reached out in a different direction from the concept of *wijŏngch'ŏksa* (uphold justice, reject injustice) or *Tonghak* thought.

By enlightenment the TH meant formation of a system by means of refining the ideas and customs to suit reason and the tide of the time, adopting the merits and discarding the demerits after comparing those of this country with others.

The principle of enlightened self-help encompasses a wide range of sweeping reforms in all aspects of national government. Such reforms and changes in laws were to be carried out on the strength of national consensus. This line of thinking was similar to the consensus theory of Kang Yu-wei of China, but anticipated the latter by one year.

The TH claimed that enlightened self-help cannot be achieved without knowing two things—the "tide of the time and the world" and "one's self." The TH thus endeavored to stimulate national consciousness and self-discovery, out of which its theory of national culture developed.

Theory of National Culture

The interest of the TH in discovery of self evolved into a theory of national culture. It ascribed the spiritual weakness of the nation to preoccupation with Chinese history in ignorance of Korean history.

Coming from a background predominantly of reformed Confucianism, members of the TH, including Chŏng Kyo, Namkung Ŏk, Ch'oe Kyŏng-hwan, Ch'oe Pyŏng-hŏn, Hyŏn Chae, Yang Chi-yŏn, Pak Ŭn-sik, Sin Ch'ae-ho, Kwŏn Pyŏng-hun, Han Paeg-wŏn, Kim Yŏng-jin and Yu Ho-sik, tried to formulate Korean history from a nationalistic standpoint. The initial fruits of such effort appeared in *Taedong Yŏksa* (History of the Great East). The five-volume work was written by Ch'oe Kyŏng-hwan in 1896, but could not come off the press until after 1905 because of the official ban placed on its publication by Education Minister Sin Ki-son for its allegedly excessive nationalism.

The book was a systematic reformulation of Korea's ancient history. It developed the theme of the orthodoxy of the Three Kingdoms, drawing upon Sŏ Kŏ-jŏng's *Tongguk T'onggam* (Survey of the Eastern Country) and *Tongsagang-mok* (Outline History of the East). It thus clarified the fact that ancient Korea was a strong and civilized country equal

to China. In the book, China is not called the Middle Kingdom; the author intended to replace the China-oriented historical interpretation by a nationalistic Korean viewpoint—
a remarkable change at that time.

Taedong Yŏksa left a great impact on many TH members
and later historians, providing a point of departure for modern historical studies of Korea. Especially noticeable was the
fact that the philosophy of *Silhak* embodied in An's *Tong-
sagangmok* had been carried over and further expanded by
Taedong Yŏksa.

The TH also insisted on using the national script, *Han'gŭl*;
such TH members as Chu Si-gyŏng, Chu Sang-ho, Chi Sŏg-
yŏng, Ch'oe Kwang-ok and Sin Hae-yong took the lead in
full-fledged and modern research on the Korean language,
calling for the following programs:

1. Formulation of unified Korean grammar;
2. Adoption of spacing formula;
3. Compilation of a Korean dictionary;
4. Exclusive use of *Han'gŭl*;
5. Horizontal transcription in *Han'gŭl*.

All of these programs were considered revolutionary at the
time and achieved considerable progress. These studies of the
Korean language were all promoted as means of bringing
about independence, civil rights and self-help.

The TH adopted the first national anthem of Korea. In
September 1896, it proposed a national anthem and in December proposed that it be sung at a gathering of the TH; the
ceremonial program of the Independence Festival of 1898 included the national anthem (Yun Ch'i-ho was the probable
author of its lyrics, but data are insufficient to ascertain the
fact). Moreover, the TH organized nationwide campaigns to
write patriotic lyrics for popular singing.

The TH rediscovered the *Silhak* philosophy of the late Yi
dynasty period and introduced it to the people. At first, the
TH used the term *Silhak* to mean experimental social or
natural sciences of the West, but later reformulated its con-

cept as being unique to the Korean tradition of learning from practical things.

Usually, rediscovering and conceptualization of *Silhak* is attributed to the scholarly work of Ch'oe Nam-sŏn, Yi Nyong-ha and Chŏng In-bo between 1916 and 1917, but actually it was done by members of the TH toward the close of the 19th century, 20 years earlier than the aforementioned historians.

The results were first printed in the April 17, 1899 issue of the *Hwangsŏng Sinmun* under the title "Outlining the exposition of Korea's foremost economist, Chŏng Yak-yong." The August 3 and 4 editions of the same newspaper also carried article on *Silhak* and its protagonist, Chŏng Yak-yong.

It is undeniable that these articles were the major intellectual sources of rediscovered *Silhak*. The national awareness of the TH was advanced by its ideas about civil rights and self-help.

Concept of Civil Liberties

Rights to Popular Freedom

The TH developed its concept of rights to popular freedom in the belief that independence and prosperity of a nation are predicated on the civil rights and prosperity of its constituent individual members.

In the first place, the TH insists on the rights to life and property, by which the common people could be protected against premodern exploitation by the privileged and the bureaucracy.

Worthy of note was the fact that some of the TH leaders espoused popular rights to life and property prior to their exposure to Western bourgeois ideology. Inspired by *Silhak* philosophy, they developed their own conception of the people's rights to life and property for the protection of the farming and lowly populace from arbitrary exactions by the gentry and bureaucrats.

Treatment of criminals posed a serious problem. Opinions were still divided as to whether corporal punishment or forfeiture of property inflicted upon criminals should be regarded in the same light as the rights of ordinary people. Under the influence of Western civil philosophy, some thought that they should be treated on an equal footing.

Such ideas as "government must protect the life and property of the people," or "not a penny should be taken in tax except by law" had not been alien to Koreans. This line of thinking was long established; only the growth of the people was required to put the thinking into effect. Western bourgeois philosophy exerted more influence upon technical and criminals.

The TH also advanced the cause of freedom of the press and of assembly. This was intended not only to protect the people from exploitation by the gentry and bureaucratic class, but positively to nurture civil rights, thus enabling the common people to defend their own rights. Two trends are discernable in TH's advocacy of the rights to freedom of the press and assembly. In Korea, freedom of the press on the part of the gentry was deeply rooted, and popular assemblies were rather prevalent, as was the case with the *Tonghak* groups. On this native base the Western bourgeois ideas of freedom of the press and assembly were transplanted and amplified by the TH. Available data indicate that the resolutions and procedures of the TH and the *Manmin'gong-dong-hoe* (a mass fraternity) combined the content and form of both East and West.

The concept of freedom of the press and assembly advocated by the TH was a merger of the native stream and the current of Western bourgeois thought, and was strengthened, instead of weakened, by the latter. The press and assembly of the *Manmin'gongdong-hoe* since the autumn of 1898 were led by the bourgeois stratum and its philosophy, but their persistent demand for freedom could not last long without the adamant tradition of the freedom of the gentry, press and the growth and vigor of the farming population.

The petition submitted by the TH on October 23, 1898 stated that criticizing and denouncing cabinet ministers belong among the rights of the people, and a nation can hardly be sustained in the absence of a popular press, which erodes politics and law.

Right to Popular Equality

The TH went beyond the advocacy of freedom and pressed for the right to equality. Stating that all men are born equal, it demanded the abolition of the caste system, and the equality of the sexes.

Criticisms were made against the remnants of slavery; such criticisms had been anticipated by *Silhak* thinkers, and the institution was formally brought to an end with the emancipation of public slaves in 1801 and private slaves in 1894. Denunciation of the remnants of slavery was a typical example of the effective synthesis of Western bourgeois philosophy and the indigenous *Silhak* tradition. Editorials in *The Independent* written by Sŏ Chae-p'il represented the same synthesis of the two currents.

The *Silhak* school of Chŏng Yak-yong was in favor of the complete elimination of the slave system, and out of it grew the idea of equality. *Silhak* scholars took issue with treating fellow men as property that could be bought and sold.

The concept of the equality of the sexes promoted by the TH was most heavily influenced by Western bourgeois ideology. Korea's reformed Confucianism had no established idea about feminine rights. Under heavy influence of Western philosophy, the TH—especially Sŏ Chae-p'il and Yun Ch'i-ho—made many contributions to the enhancement of the rights of women.

Popular Sovereignty

The TH advanced the theory of popular sovereignty that sovereignty rests with the people who are the masters of the nation; this is based on concepts of the rights to freedom and equality. Describing office holders as servants of the people as well as the king's subjects. The TH criticized the fact that officials did not regard people as the masters of the nation.

Sŏ Chae-p'il said, "For centuries, the Korean people, believing that officials are all sages and respectable personalities, entrusted them with the life and property of themselves and their families; they paid taxes for the upkeep of these officials for them to take care of public affairs; the people delegated their role of master to those paid officials, but the servants soon turned out to be the masters, and the real master was reduced to servant, placing his life and property at the mercy of the former servant; for this the master has only himself to thank, because his inability caused such aberrance of the servant."

This version of popular sovereignty theory was explained along the line of traditional philosophy that the people are the foundation of the nation, and must be strong to make the country secure. The idea "for the people (*Wimin*)" and "of the people (*Minbon*)" was firmly rooted in reformed Confucianism, and merged with the impact of Western bourgeois thought to constitute the popular sovereignty theory of the TH.

The influence of Western philosophy becomes more manifest with the following ideas, beginning with universal franchise.

Popular Franchise

The development of Korea's native philosophy that proceeded from the theory of popular sovereignty to universal franchise failed to institutionalize the participation of the citizenry and farmers in government.

The TH leadership headed by Sŏ Chae-p'il and Yun Ch'i-ho broke through the failure to demand direct and institutionalized popular participation in government. In particular, Sŏ suggested that universal franchise be given the local people, so that they could elect local magistrates; this, he said, would be a solution to the problem of local maladministration and restive farm population.

When the local magistrate is chosen by popular vote, he argued:

1. The magistrate will be loved, not resented by the constituents.
2. Capable and conscientious persons will be elected.
3. They will be well informed of local conditions.
4. They will be more concerned about and interested in promoting the welfare of people who elected them.
5. Better administration to meet the popular trust is certain to improve the lot of the citizenry and people.

To have administrators elected by popular vote was a revolutionary idea at the time.

The concept of universal franchise was further broadened by the TH to call for the inauguration of a legislature at the national level.

Formation of a Parliament

On April 3, 1898, the TH called a forum on the political urgency of forming a parliament. Many TH members and other participants attending the debate put forward a proposal for the establishment of a parliament.

Later, *The Independent* elaborated in its editorial on the advantages of inaugurating a parliament based on the principle of separation of powers. On July 3, a petition demanding the formation of a parliament was submitted to the king.

The campaign of the TH for a parliament actually meant

the reorganization of Chungch'uwŏn (privy council), which was an advisory organ for administration and a depository of careerists, into a legislative body. It met with fierce opposition from conservative bureaucrats, but was supported by such reform-minded officials as Pak Chŏng-yang, Han Kyu-sŏl and Min Yŏng-hwan. After a series of revisions, agreement was reached between representatives of the government and the TH to adopt a new privy council system. This marked the beginning of a parliament in this country.

1. Under the new system the council had the power to:
   a) make laws,
   b) approve the decisions of cabinet,
   c) consent to cabinet recommendations, subject to royal sanction,
   d) advise on provisional recommendations of cabinet,
   e) decide on popular suggestions and petitions.
2. The council chairman would be appointed by the King and its vice chairman chosen by council members.
3. The council consisted of 50 members, of which 25 were recommended by the government from among those who had rendered meritorious service to the state, and the remaining 25 chosen from among the members of the *Inmin Hyŏphoe* (People's Association) above 27 years of age and well versed in politics and jurisprudence.
4. The term of office of the council members was 12 months; new elections were to take place one month prior to the expiration of the term of the outgoing council.
5. When the government and the council was in disagreement, a joint conference of the two was to be called to arriving at concurrence; the government could not act unilaterally.
6. In the interim, the TH would choose the 25 members who would be popularly elected.

These organizational rules were amended again by an intrigue of the old-guard faction to allow the participation of the *Hwangguk Hyŏphoe* (Imperial Association) in the new privy council. Thus the first Korean parliament came into being on December 16, 1898 with four government officials, 17 TH members and 29 members of *Hwangguk Hyŏphoe* taking part.

The parliament was dissolved in only 40-odd days. However, it represented the first institutional realization, albeit imperfect, of the concept of popular franchise presented by the TH, and as such the first translation of the ideas of freedom and civil rights into parliamentary democracy.

It must be pointed out here that the TH's preoccupation with the formation of a parliament by reorganizing the privy council was motivated not only by respect for popular freedom and civil rights, but also by a far-reaching aspiration for the preservation of national independence. The TH feared that the King and the conservative factions might give away economic interests to foreign powers and this might pave the way for eventual surrender of the nation's independence under pressure. The TH intended to install a parliament capable of preventing such irresponsible and weak-kneed decisions. The TH sought to safeguard the national independence and integrity by means of a popularly-elected, responsive parliamentary body.

If the TH and the embryonic parliament continued to exist for long, imposition of Japan's protectorate treaty upon Korea and the subsequent usurpation of the nation's sovereignty would not have been so easily attained. The combined forces of the TH and the people could have either frustrated the takeover attempt or at least delayed it.

Concept of Self-Help and Reform

Constitutional Government

The TH dwelt on specific self-help programs based on civil rights for the maintenance of independence.

First, authoritarian monarchy would be reformed and separation of powers introduced; the cabinet would be strengthened to enforce a policy of enlightenment and self-help. The TH conceived of a cabinet that would include Pak Chŏng-yang, Han Kyu-sŏl, Min Yŏng-hwan and Yi Sang-jae.

Second, the parliament would be directly and popularly elected eventually, after a period of tutelage by the TH. Yun Ch'i-ho would be named to lead the parliament.

Third, when the cabinet and the parliament became capable of executing self-help reforms, strict rule of law would be established in accordance with constitutional and other laws.

Fourth, upon the establishment of constitutional government, "nation-saving" self-help policies would be undertaken with the consent and support of the people. They reckoned five years would be required to achieve self-reliance and self-help sufficient to maintain independence in case international balance of power was affected.

Reform of Public Finance

The TH asserted that overall modernization of the public finance system was necessary in preparation for self-help.

Important features of the reform plan were:

1. Overall modernization of the system of appointing central government officials.
2. Direct selection of local officials.
3. Increased professionalism and efficiency of administration.
4. Balanced development of regions.
5. Open management of administration and finance.
6. Unified control of finance by the Finance Ministry and budgeting in the black.
7. Repayment of Japanese loans.
8. Reform of taxation system and elimination of miscellaneous levies.

9. Conduct of agricultural survey and population census.

10. Taxation on foreign merchants.

The TH planned to have the "budget in the black" spend one third in administrative expenditure and two-thirds on carrying out self-help programs. According to its blueprint, such programs would be pushed jointly by the government and the people, but financing was to be provided by the government.

New Educational Philosophy

The TH gave priority in government spending to "new education, and manufacturing plants."

It considered the education of the rising generation and the masses as most essential to achieving national strength.

Establishment of schools devoted to new education was viewed as most urgent; plans were formulated to bring into being, stage by stage, 1) elementary schools, 2) girls' schools 3) secondary schools or colleges, 4) vocational and professional schools; and private schools.

Especially elementary schools ought to be established for each community to expose all school-age children to new education. It was likened to sowing of seeds in spring. The need for schools for girls where prospective wives and mothers could be taught and trained was pointed up with emphasis almost equal to that given to schools for men, on the grounds that women account for half of the entire population. The plan was presented in defiance of strong opposition from conservative groups.

It was also proposed that the duration of elementary, secondary and college education be equally three years. The proposal was conceived to suit the prevailing practice of starting elementary education at a late age.

The TH proposed an overhaul of curriculum, putting greater stress on engineering, agronomy, medicine, military science, mathematics, chemistry, meteorology, astronomy, geography, physics, political science and economics, linguistics and athletics (Reformed Confucian schools included literature and Chinese classics as primary subjects). This was a remarkable departure from the existing curriculum centered on Oriental classics and Chinese history. Members of the TH also insisted that in all school education: 1. *Han'gŭl* be used as the primary national writing system; 2. Arabic, instead of Chinese, numerals, be introduced in teaching mathematics; 3. History of the West as well as of Korea be taught.

Fourth, the TH requested and planned the publishing of textbooks for schools and books for the general public.

Fifth, for the sake of introducing natural science, technology and other new knowledge of the West, translation of foreign books, expansion of foreign-language institutes, and sending of students abroad were strongly urged.

Industrial Development

As part of self-help programs, the TH emphasized industrial development next to education.

First, the TH said that Korea should diversify from an agricultural economy in pursuit of mercantile and industrial advancement. The modern economic structure it envisaged had the following breakdown in terms of population: 50% in agriculture, 30% in commerce and industry; 20% in public service and professions.

Second, industrialization received top priority in the economic growth scheme of the TH. Pointing out that Western powers had accomplished prosperity and military might through industrialization, it suggested that we must do likewise. The order of priority the TH set was: 1. spinning industry; 2. iron mills; 3. timber industry; 4. paper making; 5. glass manufacture; 6. leather industry. The TH showed most active interest in the spinning industry, for which it worked out a very concrete blueprint.

Third, the TH proposed that industrial growth be attained

by means of *Changguk* (manufacturing plants) equipped with steam engines and other machinery. Members of the TH were well aware of the potential and effectiveness of steam engines and modern machinery, and they made many efforts toward enlightening the people on the scientific value and utility of the new energy and tools.

For the financing of these industrialization projects the TH contemplated a combination of private capitalization through encouraging the formation of joint stock companies and financial investment by government. The government was advised to set up model plants where technical training could be given, while the creation of private industrial plants was liberally encouraged.

Fourth, introduction of modern technical know-how from Great Britain was sought. The TH was interested in bringing about an industrial revolution by building major industrial plants with steam-powered engines and mechanical equipment.

Fifth, the TH emphasized the need for exploring such mineral resources as gold, silver, copper, iron and coal. It urged that development of mining be encouraged to serve the goal of national prosperity by producing raw materials and helping industrialization; it criticized mining concessions to foreign powers and the practice of dispatching official mining agents as reckless and damaging to the property rights of the people.

Sixth, the TH made the following specific recommendations on agricultural, forestry and fishery development:
1. Reclamation of idle land and irrigation;
2. Diversified farming and development of commercial agriculture;
3. Introduction of new livestock breeds;
4. Forestry development and timber export plan;
5. Establishment of agricultural experimental stations, and development of new species and new farm implements;
6. Development of coastal fishing and export of marine

products.

Seventh, the TH proposed the following reforms for the growth of commerce:

1. Expropriation of commercial rights granted to foreigners and guarantee of complete freedom of commercial activity;
2. Inauguration of modern banks;
3. Uniform weights and measures, and introduction of the metric system;
4. Currency reform and double gold-silver standards;
5. Improvement of international payments position.

Eighth, the TH claimed that railroad construction was essential to industrial growth, and urged the return of the Seoul-Inch'ŏn, Seoul-Pusan and Seoul-Sinŭiju lines from foreign management to Korean; it also planned the construction of a Seoul-Wŏnsan rail line. Purchase of engine-propelled coastal ferries and improvement of highways were also suggested.

Concept of Modern National Defense

Fearing a change in the balance of power in the Far East might bring military clashes between Japan and Russia on the Korean peninsula, the TH advocated strong and self-reliant military preparedness to defend the nation against external invasion. It called for:

1. Creation of a navy to support the army;
2. Repair and expansion of arsenals;
3. Intensive training by Continental drill techniques;
4. Establishment of a military academy;
5. Building up of military power strong enough to deter aggression by Japanese or Russians.

Reform of Social Customs

The TH conceived of a sweeping reform of the nation's

social customs. Important changes it proposed included;
1. Elimination of early marriage;
2. Liberation of women, and eradication of concubines and *kisaeng* entertainers;
3. Introduction of scientific sanitation and hospitals, and ban on opium smuggling from China;
4. Elimination of superstition and divination;
5. End of geomancy;
6. Elimination of nepotism and factionalism;
7. Prohibition of gambling and speculative activities.

The TH declared self-help reforms could only be carried out on the basis of articulate assertion of national independence and popular participation in government.

In retrospect, the balance of power around Korea existed for seven years between 1897 and 1904. The TH sought to take advantage of the period to insure independence on the strength of the combined energies of the people. Its social philosophy was embodied in the principles of spontaneity, civil rights, self-help and of freedom and independence-reform, which embraced the concepts of independence, civil rights, self-help, and reforms.

With the dissolution of the TH, a major philosophy and movement to save the nation from the danger of aggression by foreign powers came to an end. During the period 1881-1893, when Japan had the desire but not the capacity for aggression, Korea wasted valuable time under the pressure of Chinese intervention, failing to achieve national self-reliance. During the seven years 1897-1904, when Japan had the capacity for aggression, but could not defy the prevailing international balance of power, the TH was suppressed and could not prove effective in the face of the increasing collusion of the conservative ruling circles with the Japanese, depriving the nation of its second chance for survival.

However, the philosophy of independence, civil rights and self-help advocated by the TH continued to provide inspiration and momentum to the subsequent anti-Japanese independence movement. Inside the country, Yun Ch'i-ho organized the *Taehan Chagang-hoe* (Korea Self-help Society) to undertake public enlightenment campaigns; it formed a base for the later 1919 independence uprising; outside the country, such leading members of the TH as Yi Tong-nyŏng and Yi Sang-sŏl created the *Taehan Kungmin-hoe* and an independence army which was active in the Russian maritime provinces and neighboring Manchuria; Pak Yong-man and An Ch'ang-ho organized their independence movement in Hawaii and the mainland United States; and Pak Ŭn-sik organized a provisional Korean government in Shanghai and published the newspaper *Tongnip Sinmun*.

The social philosophy of the TH marked a milestone in the evolution of modern social philosophy in Korea.

Re-evaluation of the Samil Independence Movement

SHIN YONG-HA

Many papers and books have been published on the March 1 Movement, a popular uprising against Japanese rule on March 1, 1919. In this paper, I will comment on some of the points of this independence movement just 60 years ago which have been, in my opinion, misunderstood or misinterpreted.

March 1 Movement and Self-Determination

One of the important misinterpretations of this anti-Japanese movement which I would like to point to is that the movement was launched under the influence of U. S. President Woodrow Wilson's self-determination doctrine. But this point of view is far from the historical facts, thereby requiring modification. To understand correctly the cause of the movement, we must review the nationalism and "the Taking-chance Strategy" that prevailed in Korea during the declining days of the Yi dynasty.

Nationalism was very strong in those days when the dynastic rule of the country was about to fall. Demanding absolute independence of the country, nationalists called for constructing a modern strong nation state. After 1905, this nationalism was so strong among young people that they organized even guerilla war against the Japanese forces stationed in the coun-

270

try. Between 1905 and 1910, nationalists launched a movement to save the nation by education and enlightenment, and many youths were infused with the thought of absolute independence and patriotism. This patriotic enlightenment movement and the youths educated in this movement were to provide the driving force for the March 1 Movement in 1919.

In 1910, the Korean people underwent the most inhuman colonial rule of Japan in history, and came to feel how precious national independence was to their life. Under Japanese rule, their human rights were mercilessly trampled on and their economy was unlimitedly exploited. Under the circumstances, they craved more for the absolute independence of a sovereign state.

On the other hand, the Wilson doctrine of self-determination was for the colonies of the defeated powers of World War I (Germany, Austria, Turkey and Bulgaria), and it called for independence, autonomy and even mandatory rule of these colonies. So the doctrine was a weak concept of self-government intended to solve international problems after the war.

But the thought of national independence which provided the motive power for the March 1 Movement was based on a strong and developed doctrine of independence which was far more specific and appropriate to the situation of Korea at the time than the mandatory rule-included Wilson doctrine. Thus, the March 1 Movement had no ideological relation with the Wilson doctrine.

What relationship, then was between the March 1 Movement and the Wilson doctrine? In short, the answer to this question is that "the Taking-chance Strategy" in the nationalist movement at the turn of the century related the Wilson doctrine to their struggle for national independence in an attempt to make the most of change in the international situation of the time for this struggle.

These chance-seekers in the nationalist movement wanted to build a strong power first and then to launch an independence movement on the basis of this power when change in international situation provided an opportune time for such a movement. In other words, they hoped to make use of change in the international situation for their independence movement ("Chance and Power," *Taehan Maeil Sinbo*, Jan. 13, 1910). This "Chance-strategy" characterized the nationalist movement at the turn of the century and the independence movements thereafter.

Independence fighters thought that the chance would come in the form of war. So when World War I broke out in 1914, they tried to make the most of this change in the international situation for their movement against Japanese rule. This was before the announcement of the Wilson doctrine. When Japan joined the Allied side, Koreans wished Germany to win the war, and when Germany turned the tide of war in her favor in the early part of the war, independence fighters prepared in 1917 an anti-Japanese movement plan similar in scale to the March 1 Movement. But the war ended in Germany's defeat and the victory of the Allied Powers, including Japan, and Korean independence fighters, greatly disappointed, decided to give up their 1917 independence movement plan.[1]

On January 8, 1918, President Wilson of the United States, the strongest of the Allied Powers, announed a 14-point peace plan, including the self-determination doctrine for the colonies of the defeated powers of the war, and in November of that year an armistice was signed with Germany accepting Wilson's 14-point peace plan. This encouraged Korean independence fighters, and they thought that the international situation was not necessarily in disfavor of their anti-Japanese movement, though Japan was a victorious power in the war. They considered the armistice as a chance for them to rise against Japan.

But the independence fighters were well aware of the fact that the Wilson doctrine of self-determination was applioable to the colonies of the defeated powers and not to those of Japan, like Korea, because Japan was a member of the victorious Allied Powers. This was proved by the Japanese investigation records on the March 1 Movement leaders. In spite of their knowledge of this, they wanted to make use of the Wilson doctrine and the New Korean Youth Party, located in Shanghai, dispatched its representative to the Paris peace talks and secretly informed the independence fighters at home of its plan to rise against Japan. In other words, this party in exile wanted to make the most of the Wilson doctrine, demanding that the Allied Powers apply the Wilson doctrine not only to the colonies of the defeated powers but also to the colonies of Japan. This was included in the independence declaration issued on February 8, 1919.

> III. We demand that the Paris peace conference decide on application of the self-determination doctrine to Korea. We have already presented this demand to the legations stationed in Tokyo for delivery to their governments and dispatched three representatives to Paris. The representatives dispatched to Paris have joined other representatives of Korea who had earlier arrived in Paris for a united movement.

In the course of preparing the March 1 Movement, its leaders over-publicized the meaning of the Wilson doctrine, but they well knew in the early stage of the preparation that the doctrine was not applicable to Korea. They understood the doctrine as a means of settling the problems of the colonies of the defeated powers. But some independence fighters who were seeking the opportunity of an anti-Japanese movement considered that had the Paris peace conference decided on application of the Wilson doctrine to the colonies of the defeated powers, they could make use of such a decision in turning world opinion in favor of their demand for application of the doctrine to the colonies of the victorious powers, including the independence movement in Korea.[2] In view of "the Taking-chance Strategy" developed toward the end of the 19th century, this can be considered as an attempt to make a small chance a big chance for the independence movement.

Lying herein is the relationship between the March 1 Movement and the Wilson doctrine. The movement was not under any ideological influence of the Wilson doctrine. Its leaders did not start it with the hope that the doctrine would bring about independence for Korea. They knew that the doctrine was for the colonies of the defeated powers, but they nevertheless tried to make use of it in their independence movement, hoping that world opinion would move toward the application of this doctrine to the colonies of the victorious powers. In other words, they wanted to make a positive use of change in the international situation for the independence of Korea.

To repeat, the March 1 Movement was not ideologically influenced by the Wilson doctrine of self-determination. It was a movement developed from the nationalistic power built through the nationalist and enlightenment movements, such as the 1884 coup d'etat, the 1894 agrarian revolution, the movements of the Independence Society and the United People's Association 1896–1898, the enlightenment movements and guerilla wars 1905–1910 and various independence movements in and after 1910, making use of change in the international situation of the time.

In asserting this opinion, I do not mean that I disregard the international situation of the time, while considering the domestic situation only. If there had been a similar independence movement in Manchuria, China, Vietnam or in India in those days and if such a movement had had a spill-over effect on other countries, I would willingly stress the influence of the Wilson doctrine on the March 1 Movement in Korea.

But the Wilson doctrine of self-determination was not of such a nature; it was related to the policy of the Big Powers for redivision of colonies among themselves. In Korea "the Taking-chance Strategy" was developed as a strategy for national independence toward the end of the last century when the Yi dynasty was on the decline, and under this strategy independence fighters wanted to make a small chance provided by the Wilson doctrine for their independence movement a big chance.

Nearly all the independence fighters of the time knew the nature and limits of the Wilson doctrine. Yet, they over-publicized it, making the small chance a big chance in an attempt to make the most of it for their anti-Japanese movement. Only a few people had an illusionary hope in this doctrine. What I want to stress here is that nearly all the two million people who took part in the March 1 Movement did not know anything about the Wilson doctrine. They voluntarily participated in the movement, considering it one of the many such movements being promoted in the country at the time. So I can conclude that the established theory that the March 1 Movement was under the influence of the Wilson Doctrine must be fundamentally revised or thrown away.

Non-Violence and Violence

Another established theory on the March 1 Movement that I must revise here is that the movement was more meaningful because it did not use violence, or that the movement failed because it used no force. This theory is, I think, based on the observation of only the style or method of the movement. In other words, this theory fails to see the nature of the independence movement in those days.

The independence fighters of the time attached importance to both violence and non-violence. Violence and non-violence are but a style or method of such a popular struggle even today, and therefore with only the style or method of a popular struggle, we cannot correctly understand the nature of such a struggle. So the effectiveness and appropriateness of non-violence as a method of the March 1 Movement should be measured by both the objective and subjective conditions of the independence movement in those days. To understand this problem correctly, we must understand the independence war strategy which was adopted in the early 20th century when the Yi dynasty was falling to Japan and which afterwards supported the independence movement until 1945 when Korea was liberated from Japan at the end of World War II.

This strategy for independence was adopted by the New People's Society in 1909 when national representatives of the society held a meeting at the home of Yang Ki-t'ak, president of the society. The gist of the strategy follows:[3]

1. To organize and develop an army strong enough to defeat the Japanese in a modern war. The army should be based in areas not under Japanese control, such as Manchuria and the Maritime Provinces of Siberia.

2. To educate and train youths of the country to infuse them with a strong spirit of nationalism as a means of building the power for independence.

3. To make a war that Japan would wage against China, Russia or the United States under her expansionist policy a chance for an independence war against Japan.

4. To win independence in the war against Japan, the independence army based in Manchuria and the Maritime Provinces will march into the country to form a united front with domestic independence fighters trained and organized by the New People's Society.

As seen in the above, under this independence war strategy violence was adopted as the main approach and non-violence as the secondary approach. And this strategy tells that the independence fighters of the time attached great importance to violence as an approach to independence.

But this approach was not considered appropriate at the time of the March 1 Movement in 1919, and it had to be modified for this movement. As independence fighters expected, a war involving Japan (World War I) broke out in 1914, but Japan emerged victorious from the war in 1918, along with China, Great Britain, France and the United States, contrary to their expectation. This forced them to revise the above strategy for the March 1 Movement.

To understand further the appropriateness of the non-violence approach adopted for the March 1 Movement, we must consider the objective (international and domestic) conditions and the subjective conditions of the time.

The domestic conditions were closely related to the Japanese policy for suppressing the independence movement in the country. Under this policy, Japan had one infantry division at Nanam to control the northern part of the country and another one at Yongsan to control the southern part. In addition, she had a naval base at Chinhae on the southern coast. Moreover, some 15,000 military policemen were stationed at 457 points across the country. And there was a tight administrative network of the Japanese colonial government, called the Government-General of Korea, to rule the Korean people by force. In Japan were five army divisions which were ready for movement to Korea, Manchuria and the Maritime Provinces at any time.

As for the subjective conditions of the independence movement in the country in those days, the Japanese suppressive policy by force did not allow a Korean to have any weapon. Thus, Korean independence fighters in the country were not able to arm themselves. Furthermore, the Japanese did not approve of any association or assembly of Koreans, except schools and religious meetings, and even religious meetings were subject to prior approval of the Japanese authorities concerned.

Between 1911 and 1912, the Japanese colonial government fabricated the so-called assassination attempt at Governor-General Terauchi in an attempt to suppress all independence movements in the country. Some 700 members of the New People's Society were arrested and many underground cells of the society were raided. Of the 700 New People's Society members arrested, 105 were sentenced to prison terms. In addition, some 90,000 people were included in the Japanese black list of possible insurgents for police surveillance.

Under the circumstances, most underground organizations

in the country were cracked down on by the Japanese police, and the independence movement in the country was greatly shrunk. Stricken by the fear of arrest, the independence fighters trained in the enlightenment movement of the late 19th century could not organize themselves into an effective group fighting the Japanese, and some of them, such as Yi Sŭng-hun, Kwŏn Tong-jin and O Se-ch'ang, found a retreat in religions, including Christianity and Ch'ŏndo-gyo, the Korean religion believing in the Heavenly Way. But they clandestinely inspired the young people coming to their churches with nationalism. On the other hand, the more suppressive the Japanese policy was, the stronger the aspiration of the masses for independence, though they could not launch an organized independence movement under the Japanese suppressive policy.

On the other hand, the movement for organizing the independence army abroad was not as smooth as expected in the early years. Leaders of the New People's Society who went into exile in Manchuria established three military schools in Manchuria, Sinhŭng, Taechŏn and Milsan. Small in scale, these schools could not fully function as the trainer or independence army soldiers because of the financial problem and the suppression of the Chinese warlord in Manchuria.

Of the three schools, the largest, Sinhŭng Military School, established in 1911, turned out about 40 officers a year. But there were no enlisted men for these officers to lead and the army these officers organized was a small one with officers only. Then these officers became teachers of Korean children in southern Manchuria and inspired these children with patriotism. But because the children were mostly of poor tenant farmer families, they could not join the independence army. If they joined the army, their parents could not support their families because of labor shortage.

The Korean independence army in Manchuria before the March 1 Movement in1919 was a very small one and therefore not capable of making a war against the Japanese in Korea even if the people at home rose for independence. In the face of this condition, which approach should the leaders of the March 1 Movement adopt, violence or non-violence?

I am of the opinion that the movement leaders had no choice but the non-violence approach. Among the leaders were some men who had knowledge and experience of the violence approach. For example, Son Byŏng-hŭi was commander of the northern force in the 1894 agrarian revolution and Yi Sŭng-hun was head of the North P'yŏngan Province Chapter of the New People's Society who attended the meeting in which the society's strategy for independence was adopted. So they well knew that they must have arms to use violence in the March 1 Movement. When the people were not allowed to have even a pistol how could the leaders tell the people to fight the fully-armed Japanese forces with farm implements and bamboo spears? If they had done so, would the people have risen against Japan?

In view of the above objective and subjective conditions of the time, it is unrealistic to criticize the March 1 Movement leaders for not using violence in the movement. Moreover, the view of attributing the failure of the movement to its non-violence approach is not based on the realities of the country in those days.

In view of the historical facts of the time, it may well be said that if the March 1 Movement had used violence, the movement would have become a small-scale riot which could easily be controlled by a company of a battalion of Japanese troops, instead of a mass uprising which involved some two million of the 15 million people in the country at the time. When the masses know a big gap in arms with their enemy, they do not approve of the use of violence against the enemy. The people are basically empirical and see the fact of life as it is.

As for the objective international conditions of the time, the chance of a decisive independence movement which Koreans so longed for came not in a war that would defeat Japan but in the Paris peace conference in which Japan took part as a victorious power after the First World War. This war, which broke out in 1914, did not provide such a chance for the independence movement of Korea because Japan joined the war as an Allied Power. When the peace conference was held in Paris on January 18, 1919 in which the Wilson doctrine of self-determination was adopted as a means of settling the colonial problems of the defeated powers, including Germany, this peace conference was made use of a chance to advance the independence movement. Because of this chance provided by change in the international situation at the time, a non-violent demonstration could be an effective approach.

In short, the non-violent approach is considered an inevitable and wise choice for the March 1 Movement in 1919, in view of the objective and subjective conditions of the time.

What I want to stress in particular here is that the demonstration march in the March 1 Movement was a unique non-violent effort in the independence movement in Korea. When the non-violent approach was introduced to India, the Indians staged sit-in demonstrations. In Korea, the first non-violent demonstration march was organized by the United People's Association for its anti-Japanese movement in 1898, and this demonstration march had since been used as a non-violent approach to the independence movement until 1945.

In spite of this non-violent approach in the March 1 Movement in 1919, the Japanese killed 7,509 Koreans, wounded 15,961 others and destroyed 715 houses and 47 churches. Japanese soldiers and policemen mercilessly fired at the unarmed people marching in demonstration in the streets. While students, workers and city people were non-violent in the movement, many peasants used violence to lead the movement in a violent manner. Why the peasants used violence is a major subject of study of the March 1 Movement in the future.

Although the March 1 Movement started with a non-violent demonstration, it developed into a half-violent and half-peaceful movement. This can be said to be the natural and unavoidable course because the movement was basically a struggle for independence.

33 Leaders and the Masses

The third wrong view of the March 1 Movement I want to point out in this paper is that the 33 national leaders who signed the Declaration of Independence should be separately treated from the masses who joined the movement. Some people see the movement as an exclusive one of the 33 national leaders only, while other people see it as movement of the masses, disregarding the role of the 33 leaders. These two opposite views have long been hotly discussed.

I think that the two opposite views are due to a failure to see the whole course of the movement. To understand the whole picture of the movement, we must divide it into two stages; the early organization stage and the later mass movement stage. It was in the organization stage that the 33 leaders played a major role, and the masses played the leading role in the later stage of mass movement.

What should be noted here is that the scope of organization made by the 33 leaders in the early stage was quite limited. In other words, it can be said that the organization by the 33 leaders was limited to the areas where copies of the Declaration of Independence were delivered. According to my study,[4] the areas which got copies of the Declaration of Independence were Seoul, Sŏnchŏn, P'yŏngyang, Wŏnsan, Yŏnghŭng, P'yŏnggang, Kimhwa, Haeju, Sariwŏn, Sŏhŭng, Suan, Koksan, Kaesŏng, Ch'ŏngju, Taegu, Masan, Tongnae, Kunsan, Chŏnju and Imsil. But the movement actually spread across the country, from the northernmost part of the country in North Hamgyŏng Province to the southernmost part of the country on Cheju Island. There was no city, country and town of the country where the people did not rise against Japan in March 1919. In fact, in the later stage of the mass movement, the masses voluntarily organized and launched local independence movement.

So it should be made clear that the 33 leaders planned and organized the movement in the early stage. In other words, they were the igniter of the later stage of mass movement across the country. There is no doubt that they were all ready to lay down their lives for national independence when they signed the Declaration of Independence, though some of them turned round later. But their role in the later stage of mass movement was quite limited and indirect. In this stage, the masses voluntarily planned and organized local movements, without the central leadership, and developed them into a nationwide movement against Japanese rule.

The masses were more active in the March 1 Movement and suffered more from the Japanese oppression during and after the movement than the 33 leaders. During the movement, 7,509 people were killed and 15,961 others were wounded by the Japanese soldiers and policemen. Included in the killed were the activists who were sentenced to death.

The Japanese authorities first planned to mete out capital punishment to the 33 leaders, but seeing the movement spreading to every corner and nook of the country, they mitigated this plan to deliver a maximum term of three years in prison to the 33 leaders. This appeasement policy was apparently due to the pressure of the masses who rose in a nationwide uprising.

The March 1 Movement in 1919 was launched in two stages, and it was basically of the nature of a mass movement. Without the early organization stage, it would have been different from what it really was in March 1919. Without the mass movement stage, it would not have become an event whose historical meaning we highly appreciate today.

Today, we highly appreciate the historical meaning of this movement because it developed into a mass movement in the later stage. If we overlook this and emphasize too much the role played by the 33 leaders, we would misunderstand the movement more than we would do by overlooking the 33 leaders' role and emphasizing too much the activities of the masses. The 33 leaders were the igniter and the masses were the bomb ignited by these leaders.

Evaluation of March 1 Movement

The last wrong view of the March 1 Movement I want to correct here is that the movement was a failure from the start.

But the movement achieved more than the objective of the 33 leaders who planned and organized it, unlike similar movements before and after it. But it failed to achieve the goal of immediate independence. So I propose that the historical evaluation of the movement be made by two criteria.

The first criterion is the objective set by the 33 leaders in the early stage of organization. By this criterion, the movement was far more successful than any of the leaders expected in the organization stage. Thus the movement is not comparable to the 1894 agrarian revolution which ended in total failure.

None of the early organizers of the movement expected that the movement would immediately result in independence of the country. For example, the Japanese investigation report on Kwŏn Tong-jin, one of the 33 leaders, includes the following statement:[5]

Question (Japanese prosecutor): Are you going to participate in the independence movement in the future?

Answer (Kwŏn Tong-jin): Yes. I will continue this movement at any cost until we win indepehdence. I know that we cannot win independence now, but I firmly believe that if we sow the seed with our present will to achieve independence we will certainly see the fruit.

Thus Kwŏn saw the movement as a course of action to win independence and as sowing the seed of independence which would certainly grow to be a tree bearing the fruit of independence.

This opinion was also shared by O Se-ch'ang, another of the 33 leaders.[6]

> Question (Japanese prosecutor): Do you know about U.S. President Wilson's doctrine of self-determination which has been reported in newspapers?
>
> Answer (O Se-ch'ang): Yes, I do.
>
> Question: What do you think of this doctrine?
>
> Answer: I don't think that Korea can be independent because we have submitted a petition for independence on the basis of this doctrine.
>
> Question: Do you think that the doctrine is applicable to the annexed and defeated countries or all the countries which were directly involved in the war?
>
> Answer: I think that the doctrine is applicable to the countries involved in the war and not to the other countries.
>
> Question: Then why did you decide to issue the Declaration of Independence on the basis of this doctrine and start an independence movement in the meeting held at the home of Son Byŏng-hūi?
>
> Answer: In view of the rapid development of the world today, we felt the need to announce before the world that the Korean people have the will to determine their own fate and to record this will in history, though such an announcement will not bring about independence. We also thought this better than doing nothing about our country which is being left behind, while other countries are rapidly developing.
>
> Question: Then do you want the independence of Korea now?
>
> Answer: Yes, I want Korea to be independent as soon as possible.

As seen in the above, O Se-ch'ang knew that the Wilson doctrine of self-determination was not applicable to Korea, but he and 32 others signed the Declaration of Independence in order to tell the world that the Korean people had the will of self-determination, availing themselves of the Wilson doctrine, though they knew that such a declaration would not bring about the immediate independence of the country. Other national leaders also had such an opinion. Son Byŏng-ħui said, just before the March 1 Movement, as follows:

> If we declare independence, the country will not be independent immediately. But we must declare independence in order to infuse the people with the spirit of independence.[7]

None of the 33 leaders expected and imagined that the movement they planned and organized would develop into a nationwide uprising against Japan. But it actually became a great mass movement in which some two million people took part. Such a successful development of the movement is attributed to the masses, especially to their voluntary participation, not to the 33 leaders. So to understand the successful aspect of the movement, we must analyze the cause for the voluntary participation of the masses, and this, I think, is an important subject in the future study of the March 1 Movement.

If we consider the independence movement as a prolonged war against Japan, the March 1 Movement in 1919 was certainly a successful campaign of this war. Although it took the lives of 7,509 people, along with 15,961 wounded and 46,948 arrested, its achievements can be said to be far greater than these sacrifices, as discussed later in this paper.

The second criterion is the goal of a immediate independence of the country. By this criterion, the March 1 Movement was a failure. Why Korea failed to win independence immediately after the movement is, I think, a subject that requires a scientific analysis and criticism in the future study of the movement.

First of all, it can be pointed out that the power of independence fighters was much weaker than the power of the Japanese militarist forces. In addition, there was a weak central leadership incapable of organizing the voluntary local movements across the country into a decisive one.

Japan annexed Korea in 1910, and I think that there should have been a government in exile in Shanghai, Manchuria or in the Maritime Province of Siberia to organize and lead centrally all the independence movements. If that had been the case, the March 1 Movement would have been led by such a government in exile, not by the 33 religious and intellectual leaders. But this is simply my wishful assumption, and this problem should be studied in depth by many scholars.

Historical Meaning of March 1 Movement

The March 1 Movement in 1919 was a very significant event not only of Korean history but also of world history. Its historical meaning to Korea can be summarized as follows:

First, the movement fundamentally frustrated the rule by force and the eradication policy against Koreans as a people, which Japan imposed on Korea for 10 years between 1910 and 1919. While executing the iron-fisted colonial policy to eradicate Koreans and exploit their economy internally, the Japanese externally made false propaganda that Koreans were happy under their rule. Because of the March 1 Movement, the militarist Japanese colonial rule in Korea was almost broken and their inhuman treatment of Koreans was brought to light before the world.

Second, the movement strengthened the indestructible power of the Korean people to achieve independence, thus providing the driving force for the independence movement thereafter. Under the unprecedented oppressive policy of Japan, many independence movement organizations in the country were dissolved around 1917. But the March 1 Movement in 1919 encouraged such organizations to emerge again and saved the independence movement from extinction. This is attested to by the far more active independence movements after 1919 than before. The movement provided an opportunity for the Korean people to build the subjective power to win independence, while presenting the possibility of winning independence sooner or later.

Third, the movement resulted in the establishment of a provisional government of the Republic of Korea' in Shanghai, thereby introducing a republic system to the country for the first time in its history. In its early days, the provisional government was represented by all independence movement organizations and all social and political groups of the country, and it led and controlled all independence movements in and out of the country. But in 1923, it was split and thus weakened as a government, which is not the subject to be dealt with in this paper.

Fourth, the movement also resulted in strengthened armed independence movements in Manchuria, and some Independence Army units crossed the border to operate in the country. It must be noted that the strengthened armed struggles of the Independence Army in Manchuria and the Maritime Province were entirely due to the March 1 Movement. Many youths who took part in the movement went to Manchuria and the Maritime Provinces to join the Independence Army units there, along with the Korean youths living in Manchuria. For instance, Sinhŭng Military School, which turned out only 40 officers a year before 1919, had to move to a larger building and even establish a branch school to accommodate the increasing applicants after the March 1 Movement. It turned out some 600 officers and enlisted men a year. In 1920, the Northern Independence Army killed and wounded 3,300 Japanese troops on the battleground in Ch'ŏngsan-ni, and the officers of this army were mostly graduates of Sinhŭng Military School, while its enlisted men were Korean youths who were trained for six months in the same school. It is noteworthy that the March 1 Movement caused the Independence Army to grow strong enough to win battles with regular Japanese Imperial Army divisions in Manchuria.

Fifth, as a result of the movement, the Japanese had to grant the limited freedom of the press, association and assembly to the Korean people, and this limited freedom enabled the people to start cultural, agrarian and labor movements for the building of national power. The so-called cultural colonial policy of Japan in Korea after the movement was aimed at appeasing Koreans, especially nationalists, so as to split the nationalist force of the country. But it must be noted that this shift in the Japanese colonial policy in Korea was entirely due to the March 1 Movement, and therefore it can be considered the achievement of the movement.

Sixth, because of the movement, the Korean people was internationally assured of the independence of their country in due course of time. Because they declared the independence of their country in this nationwide uprising against Japan, the world came to recognize their independence when Japan would be a defeated power in a world war, though in those days the world was not in a position to give such recognition to the Koreans because Japan was a victorious power of World War I. During World War II, the independence of Korea was treated as a foregone conclusion in various meetings of the Allied Powers even though Korea was not represented in such meetings, and this was basically due to the March 1 Movement in 1919.

In addition, the historical meaning of the March 1 Movement is not limited to Korea; it is also a historical event of the world. It provided an opportunity of independence movement for colonial peoples of the victorious powers of World War I. During and after the war, colonial peoples of Germany, Turkey, Italy and Austria launched active independence movements because they knew that these powers would lose the war. But colonial peoples of Great Britain, France, the

United States and Japan could not consider their independence until the March 1 Movement of 1919 in Korea because these powers won the war. Under the circumstances, they were greatly encouraged and influenced by the independence movement of Korea in 1919.

First, the May 4 Movement of China was inspired and influenced by the March 1 Movement of Korea. This Chinese movement which marked an epoch in modern history of China was externally influenced by the March 1 Movement of Korea. Chinese nationalists of the time greatly praised the Korean people for their March 1 Movement and called on the Chinese people to learn from Korea's March 1 Movement. Leaders of this Chinese Nationalist Movement left many records telling that the May 4 Movement was inspired and influenced by the March 1 Movement of Korea.

For example, Ch'en Tu-hsiu, who led the May 4 Movement as a liberal nationalist but later became a communist to organize the Chinese Communist Party, said in his article on the independence movement of Korea published in a weekly dated March 23, 1919, that the March 1 Movement of Korea marked an epoch in the world history of revolutions and added:

> The recent independence movement of Korea was based on a great, sincere, courageous, clear and just thought. It wrote a new chapter in the history of revolutions in the world because it was a revolution based on the people's will, without violence. (....) In the face of this glorious movement of the Korean people, the Chinese people should be ashamed for their inactivity.

Nationalist Pu Ssu-nien in an article, The Lesson from Korea's Independence Movements, published in the April 1919 issue of *Hsinchao* (New Tide) and Anarchist Chen Mei-chiu in his paper on the situation of Korea praised the March 1 Movement of Korea. In short, the March 1 Movement had great influence on the May 4 Movement of China.

Second, in India, the independence movement of the National Congress Party rapidly grew under the influence of the March 1 Movement of Korea. Making use of the British indirect colonial rule, the Indian people introduced the non-violence approach of Korea's March 1 Movement and rapidly developed their independence movement to the extent that they won independence by themselves. The Gandhi-led independence movement in April 1919 was under the influence of the March 1 Movement of Korea. Indian nationalists, including Nehru, highly appreciated the March 1 Movement.

In *Glimpses of World History* which Nehru wrote for his daughter Indira, he described Korea's March 1 Movement of 1919 on December 30, 1932 as follows:

> Korea was given its old name again—Chosŏn, the land of the morning calm.... For many years the struggle for independence continued and there were many outbreaks, the most important one being in 1919. The people of Korea, and especially young men and women, struggled gallantly against tremendous odds. On one occasion, when a Korean organization fighting for freedom formally declared independence, and thus defied the Japanese, the story goes that they immediately telephoned to the police and informed them of what they had done! Thus deliberately they sacrificed themselves for their ideal. The suppression of the Koreans by the Japanese is a very sad and dark chapter in history. You will be interested to know that young Korean girls, many of them fresh from college, played a prominent part in the struggle.

Third, the influence of the March 1 Movement in Korea was felt in Indochina, the Philippines and some Arab countries. The world history of the 19th and early 20th centuries was written by the Big Powers, disregarding the peoples suffering from colonial or semi-colonial rule of these powers though they accounted for three fourths of the world population. Because the independence movements of the oppressed peoples of this period carry weight in the world history, the future world history must be written objectively by all the peoples of the world, including the peoples of minor countries. In that case, the March 1 Movement of Korea will be treated in a new chapter as the first signal light for the oppressed peoples to rise against the Big Powers emerged victorious from World War 1 to win independence.

When Nobel literature laureate Tagore, who was also a leader of the Indian independence movement, visited Tokyo in 1929, the 10th anniversary of the March 1 Movement of Korea, Korean students in the Japanese capital city visited him. He told them about his impression of the March 1 Movement and wrote an impromptu poem on Korea at the request of the Korean students. His poem follows:

> *In the golden age of Asia*
> *Korea was one of its lamp bearers,*
> *And that lamp is waiting to be lighted once again*
> *For the illumination in the East.*

This poem of Tagore gives a new impression of the March 1 Movement to us today just 60 years after the movement took place.

REFERENCES

1. Association of Patriotic Comrades (ed.), *History of Korean Independence Movement*, pp. 95-96.
2. Shin Yong-ha, ''The Subjectivity and the National Self-determinism in

the Samil Independence Movement," *Hanguksasang*, Vol. 15.

3. Shin Yong-ha, "The Initial-founding of Sinmin-hoe and her Retrieval Movement of Sovereignty," *Hangukhakpo*, Vol. 8, 9.
4. Yun Byŏng-sŏk, etc. (ed.), *Essays on Korean Modern History* II, p. 182.
5. Yi Pyŏng-hŏn (ed.), *History of the March 1 Movement*, p. 182.
6. *ibid.*, pp. 514-515, 517. *Biography of Son Byŏng-hŭi*, p. 342.

Contributors in This Volume

Pak Chong-hong   Dr. Pak, deceased, was Dean of the Graduate School of Seoul National University. His field was philosophy.

Yi Ki-yŏng   Professor Yi received his doctorate in Philosophy at Louvain University in Belgium and also studied in France. He is currently teaching at Dongguk University in Seoul.

Yi Ki-baek   Yi Ki-baek is a professor of Korean History at Sogang University in Seoul.

U Chŏng-sang   Professor U formerly was on the faculty of Dongguk University in the Buddhist Studies Department.

Chŏng Chong-bok   Dr. Chŏng has a doctorate in Oriental Philosophy and is on the faculty of Ch'ŏngju Teachers' College in Ch'ungnam Province. He is also the director of the Central Library of Ch'ŏngju Teachers' College.

Yi Sang-ŭn   Professor Yi, deceased, taught in the Philosophy Department of Korea

University in Seoul where he was also the director of the Asiatic Research Center.

Yi U-sŏng

Dr. Yi earned his doctorate from Sungkyunkwan University where he was a professor and the director of the Institute of Korean Studies.

Hong I-sŏp

Professor Hong, deceased, was a dean and also a professor of Korean History at Yonsei University in Seoul.

Kim Yong-dŏk

Professor Kim teaches in the History Department of Chungang University in Seoul from which he received a doctorate in literature.

Han Yŏng-u

Dr. Han has a doctorate in literature from Seoul National University where he is presently on the faculty.

Susan S. Shin

Dr. Shin received her doctorate in History and East Asian Civilization from Harvard University in the United States.

Shin Yong-ha

Professor Shin teaches Sociology at Seoul National University.

An Pyŏng-uk

Professor An is on the faculty of Soong Jun University in Seoul.